Escape
from
Slavery

Freedom-Seeker narratives
as told to William Still

Recorded by William Still
Compiled and Edited by C. Edward Wall

Copyright© 2021, Pierian Press
All Rights Reserved
ISBN: 978-0-87650-404-8

Publisher

Pierian Press, Inc.
3196 Maple Dr.
Ypsilanti, MI 48197

This book is printed on demand by an Amazon subsidiary.
Order copies from Amazon, participating distributors
such as Ingram and Baker and Taylor, or the bookstores they serve.

Dedication

This book is dedicated to those who still seek freedom
from poverty, discrimination, denigration, and fear.

Cover

Composite of elements from Arthur Secunda's
1980 intaglio print "Black and Tan Fantasy"
and his 1968 silkscreen print, "Independence Day".
The design is by Natasha Dierwechter.

Introduction
By C. Edward Wall

William Still was an African-American abolitionist in Philadelphia, Underground Railroad conductor, prominent businessman, and historian.

William Still was born 7 October 1821, in Burlington County, New Jersey, to Levin and Charity Still. Both his parents had been born into slavery in Maryland. His father purchased his freedom and relocated to New Jersey. His mother subsequently escaped to New Jersey with their then four children, two girls and two boys. His mother was recaptured and returned to slavery along with the four children. She escaped again, but this time was able to bring only their two young daughters. In New Jersey, his parents had 14 more children, William being the youngest. Though born on "free soil," because their mother was a fugitive slave, Maryland law defined the children as slaves.

William Still learned of the horrors of slavery through his parents, who instilled in him a strong work ethic and appreciation for education and self-determination. He knew that the keys to his future were the ability to communicate in a white world, and at a time when education was denied most blacks, he taught himself spelling, grammar, and mathematics.

At the age of 23, William Still moved to Philadelphia, and three years later (1847), married Letitia George, with whom he had four children.

In 1847, the Pennsylvania Society for the Abolition of Slavery recognized his writing skills and hired him as clerk. With the passage of the Fugitive Slave Act of 1850, he became Chairman of the Philadelphia Vigilance Committee, which supported and aided fugitives from slavery.

In August 1850, while listening to the account of a freedom-seeker who called himself "Peter Freedman," William Still suddenly realized, based upon stories his mother previously had told him, that this was one of his long-lost brothers. This experience made William Still realize the importance of recording slave narratives in order to help reunite families.

Between 1850 and the onset of the Civil War, William Still, sometimes with help, interviewed approximately 800 fugitive slaves who were passing through Philadelphia. For those who assisted with the interviews, William Still prepared a list of core questions that were to be asked each freedom-seeker, as illustrated in Chapter 19 and several others in this book. In 1872, he self-published a significant book, **The Underground Railroad Records**, which contained these narratives and much additional materials about the Underground Railroad.

Many of the slave narratives in William Still's book are quite brief. The longer narratives from his book are reproduced in this publication, *Escape from Slavery*. These longer accounts document the experiences of about 150 freedom-seekers. In this publication, the slave narratives also are indexed by location of escape, escape method, and escape destination.

Most of the fugitive slaves that escaped with the help of the Philadelphia Vigilance Committee came from the District of Columbia and slave-holding coastal states, including Delaware, Maryland, North and South Carolina, and Virginia, but the book also includes accounts of escapes from Mississippi and Missouri.

Since most of these escapes came from coastal states, many fugitives reached Philadelphia hidden away on cargo ships. But numerous other escape methods were employed, including small boats, horses and carriages, impersonation, official documents, shipping containers (hidden in boxes and chests), trains, and by walking.

Escape destinations included various locations in Canada, England, Massachusetts, Michigan, New Jersey, New York and Pennsylvania.

Also included are accounts of slave catchers, and efforts, sometimes unsuccessful, to prevent both free blacks and fugitive slaves from being kidnapped and taken into bondage.

These personal narratives describe life under slavery, occasionally benign but more often unspeakably cruel, and the often desperate attempts to secure freedom.

Table of Contents

CHAPTER 1. . . . . *1*
William Peel, a.k.a. William Box Peel Jones — Arrived by Steamer, Wrapped in Straw and Boxed Up, April 1859.

CHAPTER 2. . . . . *4*
Wesley Harris, alias Robert Jackson, and the Matterson Brothers — Betrayed While Hiding in a Barn.

CHAPTER 3. . . . . *9*
Abram Harris and the Death of His Friend and Traveling Companion, Romulus Hall.

CHAPTER 4. . . . . *13*
James Mercer, William H. Gilliam, and John Clayton — Stowaways in a Hot Berth.

CHAPTER 5. . . . . *17*
Clarissa Davis — Escaped Dressed in Male Attire.

CHAPTER 6. . . . . *20*
Anthony Blow, alias Henry Levison —
Ten Months Concealed on Land and Eight Days on a Steamer.

CHAPTER 7. . . . . *23*
Sheridan Ford — Hid in the Woods and Escaped on a Steamer.

CHAPTER 8. . . . . *25*
James Hambleton Christian, Former Slave of Ex-President Tyler and a Member of the `Patriarchal Institution,' Flees from Slavery.

CHAPTER 9. . . . . *27*
Mary Epps, alias Emma Brown, and Joseph and Robert Robinson Arrive on a Schooner.

CHAPTER 10. . . . . *33*
George Solomon, Daniel Neall, Benjamin R. Fletcher, and Maria Dorsey Arrive from Washington, D.C.

CHAPTER 11. . . . . *36*
Henry Box Brown Arrives in a Box by Adams' Express.

CHAPTER 12 .... *43*
    Cordelia Loney Flees Her Mistress While Visiting Philadelphia.

CHAPTER 13 .... *49*
    Robert Brown, alias Thomas Jones, Flees Slavery by Crossing a River on Horseback in the Night.

CHAPTER 14 .... *51*
    Barnaby Grigby, alias John Boyer, and Mary Elizabeth, His Wife; Frank Wanzer, alias Robert Scott; and Emily Foster, alias Ann Wood, Arrive by Horse and Carriage.

CHAPTER 15 .... *58*
    William Jordon, alias William Price, Escapes from North Carolina Governor Badger and Spends Ten Months in the Swamps before Finding His Way to the Underground Railroad.

CHAPTER 16 .... *61*
    Joseph Grant and John Speak, Who Arrived in Philadelphia from Mississippi via Liverpool.

CHAPTER 17 .... *64*
    William Taylor Escapes from Richmond City

CHAPTER 18 .... *66*
    Jeremiah W. Smith and His Wife Julia Arrive from Richmond.

CHAPTER 19 .... *68*
    Charles Thompson, Carrier of the ***National American***, Arrives with a Pass.

CHAPTER 20 .... *74*
    Abram Galloway and Richard Eden Arrive on a Vessel Loaded with Turpentine.

CHAPTER 21 .... *78*
    John Pettifoot Escapes on a Steamer, Hidden Among Pots and Pans.

CHAPTER 22 .... *79*
    Emanuel T. White Escapes on a Steamer.

CHAPTER 23 .... *81*
    Emeline Chapman, a Young Slave Mother, Flees Slavery, Leaving Her Young Children Behind — A Case Intertwined with that of Arrah Weems.

CHAPTER 24 . . . . *86*
   Samuel W. Johnson: Arrival from the **Dispatch** Office.

CHAPTER 25 . . . . *89*
   The Amos, alias Johnson, Family Escape from Baltimore.

CHAPTER 26 . . . . *90*
   Elijah Hilton Uses a Pass to Escape from Richmond.

CHAPTER 27 . . . . *92*
   Captain F. Transports 21 Passengers to Freedom on His Boat.

CHAPTER 28 . . . . *102*
   John Henry Hill Makes a Desperate Resistance at a Slave Auction and Escapes after Hiding for Nine Months.

CHAPTER 29 . . . . *115*
   Hezekiah Hill — Uncle of John Henry Hill — Escapes on a Steamer after 13 Months in the Wilderness.

CHAPTER 30. . . . . *117*
   James Hill Escapes on a Boat after Hiding on Land for Three Years.

CHAPTER 31 . . . . *119*
   William B. White, Susan Brooks, alias Susan Cooke, and William Henry Atkins Stowed Away Aboard the City of Richmond.

CHAPTER 32 . . . . *123*
   Four Arrivals, 31 May 1856.

CHAPTER 33 . . . . *135*
   Charles Gilbert Flees Slavery by Hiding up a Tree, under a Floor, and in a Thicket, Disguising Himself as a Woman, and Stowing Away on a Steamer.

CHAPTER 34 . . . . *140*
   Jim Bowlegs, alias Bill Paul, Arrives after `Five or Six Years' of Failed Attempts in the South.

CHAPTER 35 . . . . *142*
   Edward Davis, the Saltwater Fugitive.

CHAPTER 36 . . . . *147*
   Samuel Green, alias Wesley Kinnard, Receives Ten Years in the Penitentiary for Having a Copy of **Uncle Tom's Cabin**.

CHAPTER 37 .... *152*
    Sam Nixon, alias Dr. Thomas Bayne, Arrives on a Schooner.

CHAPTER 38 .... *160*
    Robert McCoy, alias William Donar, and Elizabeth Frances, alias Ellen Saunders, Arrive on a Steamer.

CHAPTER 39 .... *165*
    Lear Green Escapes in a Chest.

CHAPTER 40 .... *167*
    Isaac Williams, Henry Banks, and Kit Nickless.

CHAPTER 41 .... *169*
    Pete Matthews, alias Samuel Sparrows, Arrives from Virginia.

CHAPTER 42 .... *171*
    John Atkinson Escapes on a Ship from a `Worthless Sot'.

CHAPTER 43 .... *174*
    Harriet Shephard, Her Five Children, and Others Escape with Their Master's Horses and Carriages.

CHAPTER 44 .... *175*
    Washington Somlor, alias James Moore, Arrives on a Steamer.

CHAPTER 45 .... *177*
    James Griffin, alias Thomas Brown, Arrives from Baltimore.

CHAPTER 46 .... *178*
    Owen, Otho, and Benjamin Taylor and Their Families Flee on Horseback.

CHAPTER 47 .... *184*
    Woman Arrives in a Box, Speechless.

CHAPTER 48 .... *186*
    William and Ellen Craft Arrive from Georgia — She Dressed as a Man, He as the Man's Servant.

CHAPTER 49 .... *196*
    Lewis Cobb and Nancy Brister Arrive from Richmond, Virginia, by Boat.

CHAPTER 50 .... *199*
    Old Jane Davis Arrives from Maryland to Flee the Auction Block.

CHAPTER 51 . . . . *201*
   Oscar D. Ball and Montgomery Graham Arrive from Alexandria, Virginia in 1857.

CHAPTER 52 . . . . *203*
   James Conner Arrives from New Orleans, 1857.

CHAPTER 53 . . . . *208*
   Harrison Cary Arrives from Washington, D.C.

CHAPTER 54 . . . . *210*
   Harry Grimes Arrives from North Carolina after Having His Feet Slit and Being Flogged and Stabbed.

CHAPTER 55 . . . . *214*
   William Carney and Andrew Allen Arrive from Norfolk, Virginia.

CHAPTER 56 . . . . *216*
   Alfred S. Thornton Arrives from Virginia.

CHAPTER 57 . . . . *218*
   Nancy Grantham Arrives from Virginia.

CHAPTER 58 . . . . *219*
   George Laws and Comrade Arrive from Delaware.

CHAPTER 59 . . . . *221*
   William Thomas Cope, John Boice Grey, Henry Boice and Isaac White Cross the Bay in a Skiff.

CHAPTER 60 . . . . *224*
   Jenny Buchanan Arrives from Virginia.

CHAPTER 61 . . . . *227*
   Thomas Sipple; His Wife, Mary Ann; Henry Burkett; His Wife, Elizabeth; John Purnell; and Hale Burton Cross the Delaware Bay in a Batteau.

CHAPTER 62 . . . . *230*
   On Her Last 'Trip' to Maryland, Harriet Tubman Brings Back Stephen Ennets and His Family of Five from Dorcester County.

CHAPTER 63 . . . . *232*
   A Member of the Vigilance Committee Impersonates Slave Hunter George F. Alberti.

CHAPTER 64 . . . . *235*
Henry Langhord, alias William Scott, Arrives from Richmond, Virginia.

CHAPTER 65 . . . . *239*
Miles Robinson Arrives from Richmond, Virginia.

CHAPTER 66 . . . . *242*
John William Dungy Arrives from Richmond, Virginia, on a Pass from Ex-Governor Gregory.

CHAPTER 67 . . . . *247*
Aunt Hannah Moore Arrives from Missouri.

CHAPTER 68 . . . . *252*
The Kidnapping of Rachel and Elizabeth Parker, and the Murder of Joseph C. Miller.

CHAPTER 69 . . . . *258*
Mary Millburn, alias Louisa F. Jones, Arrives from Norfolk, Virginia, Dressed in Male Attire.

CHAPTER 70 . . . . *260*
Fifteen from Norfolk, Virginia Arrive on a Schooner.

CHAPTER 71 . . . . *263*
Euphemia Williams, Part 1 — Arrested as a Fugitive Slave Under the Fugitive Slave Law after Having Lived in Pennsylvania for More than 20 Years.

CHAPTER 72 . . . . *264*
Euphemia Williams, Part 2 — The Prosecution at Her Trial.

CHAPTER 73 . . . . *272*
Euphemia Williams, Part 3 — The Defense, Judgment, and Aftermath of the Trial.

CHAPTER 74 . . . . *281*
Fugitive Slave Law Kidnappings in Pennsylvania — a Letter from James Miller McKim.

CHAPTER 75 . . . . *286*
Fugitive Slave Law Kidnappings in Pennsylvania — a Letter from Mary B. Thomas.

INDEX 288
    Location of Escape 288
    Method of Escape 289
    Freedom Seeker Destinations 290
    Freedom Seekers: By Name 291

CHAPTER 1

William Peel, a.k.a. William Box Peel Jones — Arrived by Steamer, Wrapped in Straw and Boxed Up, April 1859.

William is 25 years old, unmistakably colored, good-looking, slightly smaller than medium size, and has pleasing manners. William had himself boxed up by a close relative and forwarded by the Ericson line of steamers. He gave the slip to his owner, a grocer and commission merchant named Robert H. Carr, for the following reason: For some time his master had been selling off his slaves every now and then, the same as other groceries, and this indicated to William that he was liable to be in the market any day; consequently, he preferred the box to the auction block.

He did not complain of having been treated badly by Carr, but felt that no man was safe while owned by another. In fact, he "hated the very name of slaveholder." The box in which he shipped himself was so small that he could not straighten himself. While in transit, he developed a cramp and suffered indescribable misery. His faith was taxed to the utmost — indeed he was brought to the very verge of "screaming aloud" before relief came. However, he controlled himself, though only for a short time, for shortly thereafter he became very faint. He thought he was going to die, but his time had not yet come.

After a severe struggle he revived, but only to encounter a third ordeal no less painful than the one through which he had just passed. Next a very "cold chill" came over him, which seemed almost to freeze the very blood in his veins and gave him intense agony, from which he only found relief on awakening, having actually fallen asleep in that condition.

Finally, however, he arrived at Philadelphia via a steamer on a Sunday morning. A devoted friend of his, expecting him, hired a carriage and went to the wharf for the box. He had the bill of lading and the receipt with him, and likewise knew where the box was located on the boat. Although he knew freight was not usually delivered on Sunday, still his deep concern for the safety of his friend caused him to do all that lay in his power to rescue him from his perilous situation. Handing his bill of lading to the proper officer of the boat, he asked if he could get the freight that it called for. The officer looked at the bill and said, "No, we do not deliver freight on Sunday," but, noticing the anxiety of the man, he asked him if he would know the shipping container if he saw it. Slowly — fearing that too much interest might cause suspicion — he replied: "I think I could identify it." Deliberately looking around among all the "freight," he discovered the box, and said, "I think that is it there." The officer stepped to it, looked at the directions on it, then at the bill of lading, and said, "That is right, take it along."

Great relief and joy were experienced by both the recipient of the box and its contents. But another problem quickly presented itself. The size of the box was too large for the carriage, and the driver refused to take it. Nearly an hour and a half elapsed while the friend looked for a furniture hauler.

Finally one was found, and again the box was laid hold of by the occupant's particular friend, when, to his friend's alarm, the poor fellow in the box suddenly coughed. At this startling circumstance he dropped the box. Equally as quickly, although dreadfully frightened, he began singing, "Hush, my babe, lie still and slumber," with the most apparent indifference, at the same time slowly making his way from the box.

Soon his fears subsided, and he concluded that no one was any the wiser on account of the accident, or coughing. Thus, he again laid hold of the box a third time, and finally got it loaded. The furniture mover, totally ignorant of the contents of the box, drove to the address to which he was directed to take the box, left it, and went about his business.

The moment of great anticipation had arrived. The box was opened, the straw removed, and the poor fellow was let out. He rejoiced, as only a person who has been in mortal danger, and survived, can rejoice. This particular friend was scarcely less overjoyed, however, and their joy did not subside for several hours; nor was it confined to themselves, for two invited members of the Vigilance Committee of Philadelphia were also there.

This box man was named William Box Jones. He was boxed up in Baltimore by the friend who picked him up at the wharf in Philadelphia, who did not come in the boat with him, but came by different conveyance and met him at the wharf. The trial in the box lasted just 17 hours before victory was achieved. Jones was well cared for by the Vigilance Committee and sent on his way rejoicing, feeling that resolution, the Underground Railroad, and liberty were invaluable.

On his way to Canada, he stopped at Albany, New York, from which the following letter was mailed:

First Letter

"Mr. Still: — I take this opportunity of writing a few lines to you hoping that they may find you in good health. I am doing well at present and am now in a store and getting $16 a month at present. I feel very much obliged to you and your family for your kindness to me while I was with you. I have gotten along without any trouble at all. I am now in Albany City. Give my love to Mrs. and Mr. Miller and tell them I am very much obliged to them for their kindness. Give my love to my brother....Tell him I should like to hear from him very much and urge him to write. Tell him to give my love to all of my particular friends and tell them I should like to see them very much. Tell him that he must come to see me for I want to see him for some very specific reasons. Please answer this letter as soon as possible and excuse me for not writing sooner as I don't write myself. No more at the present.

"*William Jones.*

"Direct to one hundred 125 Lydus Street."

His good friend returned to Baltimore the same day the box man started for the North, and immediately sent through the mail the following brief letter, worded in Underground Railroad parables:

Second Letter

"Baltimore, 16 April 1859

"W. Still: — Dear brother,

"I have taken the opportunity of writing you these few lines to inform you that I am well and hoping these few lines may find you enjoying the same good blessing. Please write to me word at what time was it when Israel went to Jericho. I am very anxious to hear for there is a mighty host that will pass over and you and I, my brother, will sing hallelujah. I shall notify you when the great catastrophe shall take place. No more at the present but remain your brother.

"*N.L.J.*"

CHAPTER 2

Wesley Harris, alias Robert Jackson, and the Matterson Brothers — Betrayed While Hiding in a Barn.

In setting out for freedom, Wesley was the leader of this party. After two nights of exhausting travel to a distance of about 60 miles from home, the young seekers of liberty were betrayed, and in an attempt to capture them a most bloody conflict occurred. Both fugitives and pursuers were the recipients of severe wounds from gun shots and from other weapons used in the battle.

Wesley bravely used his firearms until almost fatally wounded by one of the pursuers, who with a heavily loaded gun discharged the contents with deadly aim in Wesley's left arm, raking the flesh from the bone for a space of about six inches in length. One of Wesley's companions also fought heroically and only yielded when badly wounded and quite overpowered. The two younger brothers of C. Matterson apparently made no resistance.

In order to recall the adventures of this struggle, and the success of Wesley Harris, it is only necessary to look at the written report as told by this young hero while on the Underground Railroad, even then very critically wounded. Most fearful indeed was his condition when he was brought to the Vigilance Committee of Philadelphia.

Underground Railroad Record

2 November 1853, Arrived: Robert Jackson (shot man), alias Wesley Harris; age 22 years; dark color; medium height; and of slender stature.

Robert was born in Martinsburg, Virginia, and was owned by Philip Pendleton. From the time of his boyhood, he had always been hired out. At the first of this year he commenced services with Mrs. Carroll, proprietress of the United States Hotel at Harpers Ferry. Of Mrs. Carroll he speaks in very grateful terms, saying that she was kind to him and all the servants and promised them their freedom at her death. She excused herself for not giving them their freedom earlier on the ground that her husband died insolvent, leaving her the responsibility of settling his debts.

But while Mrs. Carroll was very kind to her servants, her manager was equally as cruel. About a month before Wesley left, the overseer, for some insignificant cause, attempted to flog him, but Wesley resisted, and instead the overseer was flogged. The overseer regarded the slave's resistance as an unpardonable offense; consequently he told his owner of the act, and was instructed that if he should ever again attempt to correct Wesley and the slave should resist, the overseer was to put him in prison and sell him. Whether he offended again or not, the following Christmas he was to be sold anyway.

Wesley's mistress was kind enough to warn him of the intentions of his owner and the overseer, and told him that if he could help himself he had better do so. So from that time Wesley began to contemplate how he should escape the doom which had been planned for him.

"A friend," says he, "by the name of C. Matterson told me that he was going off. Then I told him of my master's writing to Mrs. Carroll concerning selling ... and that I was going off, too. We then concluded to go together. There were two others, brothers of Matterson, who were told of our plan to escape and readily joined with us in the undertaking. So one Saturday night, at twelve o'clock, we set out for the North. After traveling upwards of two days and over 60 miles, we found ourselves unexpectedly in Terrytown, Maryland. There we were informed by a friendly colored man of the danger we were in and of the bad character of the place towards colored people, especially those who were escaping to freedom, and he advised us to hide as quickly as we could. We at once went to the woods and hid.

"Soon after we had hidden ourselves a man came nearby and started to split wood, which alarmed us. We then moved to another hiding place in a thicket near a farmer's barn, where we were approached by a barking dog. The attention of the owner of the dog was drawn to his barking and to where we were. The owner of the dog was a farmer. He asked us where we were going. We replied to Gettysburg — to visit some relatives, etc. He told us that we were running off. He then offered friendly advice, talked like a Quaker, and urged us to go with him to his barn for protection. After much persuasion, we consented to go with him.

"Soon after putting us in his barn, himself and his daughter prepared us a nice breakfast, which cheered our spirits, as we were hungry. For this kindness we paid him one dollar. He next told us to hide in the mow until evening, when he would safely direct us on our road to Gettysburg. Everyone, very much exhausted from traveling, fell asleep, except myself; I could not sleep [because] felt as if all was not right.

"About noon, men were heard talking around the barn. I woke my companions up and told them that the man had betrayed us. At first they did not believe me. In a moment afterwards the barn door was opened, and in came the men, eight in number. One of the men asked the owner of the barn if he had any long straw.

'Yes,' was the answer. So up in the mow came three of the men, when, to their great surprise, as they pretended, we were discovered. The question was then asked of the owner of the barn by one of the men, if he harbored runaway negroes in his barn. He answered, 'No,' and pretended to be entirely ignorant that runaway slaves were in the barn. One of the men replied that four negroes were in the mow, and he knew of it. The men then asked us where we were going. We told them to Gettysburg, that we had aunts and a mother there. Also we spoke of a Mr. Houghman, a gentleman we happened to have some knowledge of, having seen him in Virginia.

"We were next asked for our passes. We told them that we hadn't any [because] we had not been required to carry them where we came from. They then said that we would have to go before a magistrate, and if he allowed us to go on, well and good. The men, all being armed and furnished with ropes, were ordered to tie the slaves up. I told them if they took me they would have to take me dead or crippled. At that instant one of my friends cried out, 'Where is the man that betrayed us?' Spying him at the same moment, he shot him (badly wounding him).

"Then the conflict fairly began. The constable seized me by the collar, or rather behind my shoulder. I at once shot him with my pistol, but in consequence of his throwing up his arm, which hit mine as I fired, the effect of the load of my pistol was much turned aside; his face, however, was badly burned, besides his shoulder being wounded. I again fired on the pursuers, but do not know whether I hit anybody or not. I then drew a sword [that] I had brought with me, and was about cutting my way to the door, when I was shot by one of the men, receiving the entire contents of one load of a double-barreled gun in my left arm, that being the arm with which I was defending myself. The load brought me to the ground, and I was unable to make further struggle for myself. I was then badly beaten with guns, etc.

"In the meantime, my friend Craven, who was defending himself, was shot badly in the face, and most violently beaten until he was conquered and tied. The two young brothers of Craven stood still, without making the least resistance. After we were fairly captured, we were taken to Terrytown, which was in sight of where we were betrayed.

"By this time I had lost so much blood from my wounds that they concluded my situation was too dangerous to take me any further; so I was made a prisoner at a tavern kept by a man named Fisher. There my wounds were dressed and shot was taken from my arm. For three days I was crazy and they thought I would die. During the first two weeks, while I was a prisoner at the tavern, I lost a great deal of blood, and was considered in a very dangerous condition, so much so that persons desiring to see me were not permitted.

"Afterwards I began to get better, and was then kept very privately, and was strictly watched day and night. Occasionally, however, the cook, a colored woman (Mrs. Smith), would manage to get to see me. Also James Matthews succeeded in getting to see me; consequently, as my wounds healed, and my senses came to me, I began to plan how to make another effort to escape. I asked one of the friends, alluded to above, to get me a rope. He got it. I kept it about me four days in my pocket; in the meantime I [obtained] three nails.

"On Friday night, 14 October, I fastened my nails in under the window sill, tied my rope to the nails, threw my shoes out of the window, put the rope in my mouth, then took hold of it with my well hand, climbed into the window, very weak, but I managed to let myself down to the ground. I was so weak that I could scarcely walk, but I managed to hobble off to a place three-quarters of a mile from the tavern, where a friend had fixed upon for me to go, if I succeeded in making my escape.

"There I was found by my friend, who kept me secure until Saturday evening, when a swift horse was furnished by James Rogers, and a colored man was found to conduct me to Gettysburg. Instead of going direct to Gettysburg, we took a different road, in order to avoid our pursuers, as the news of my escape had created general excitement. My three other companions, who were captured, were sent to Westminster Jail, where they were kept for three weeks, and were afterwards sent to Baltimore and sold for $1200 apiece, as I was informed while at the tavern in Terrytown."

The Vigilance Committee of Philadelphia obtained good medical attention and provided the fugitive time for recuperation, furnished him with clothing and a free ticket, and sent him on his way greatly improved in health, and strong in the faith that "He who would be free, himself must strike the blow." His safe arrival in Canada, with his thanks, were duly announced. And some time after becoming naturalized as a Canadian citizen, in one of his letters, he wrote that he was a brakeman on the Great Western R.R. (in Canada — promoted from the U.G.R.R.), the benefit of being under the protection of the British Lion.

CHAPTER 3

Abram Harris and the Death of His Friend and Traveling Companion, Romulus Hall.

In March 1857, Abram Harris fled from John Henry Suthern, who lived near Benedict, Charles County, Maryland, where he was engaged in the farming business and was the owner of about 70 head of slaves. Suthern kept an overseer, who usually had flogging administered daily on male and female, old and young alike. Becoming very sick of this treatment, Abram resolved, about the first of March, to seek out the Underground Railroad. If it had not been for his strong attachment to his wife (who was owned by Samuel Adam, but was "pretty well treated"), he never would have consented to "suffer" as much and as long as he did. Here no hope of comfort for the future seemed to remain. So Abram consulted with a fellow servant by the name of Romulus Hall, alias George Weems, and being very close friends, concluded to start together. Both had wives to "tear themselves from," and each was equally ignorant of the distance they had to travel, as well as the dangers and sufferings to be endured. But they "trusted in God" and kept the North Star in view.

For nine days and nights, without a guide, they traveled at a very exhausting rate, especially as they had to go fasting for three days, and to endure very cold weather. Abram's companion, being about 50 years of age, could not handle the hunger and the cold, and had to be left on the way. Abram was a man of medium size, tall, and dark chestnut color. He could read and write a little and was quite intelligent, "was a member of the Mount Zion Church," occasionally officiated as an "exhorter," and really appeared to be a man of genuine faith in the Almighty, and equally as much in freedom.

In substance, Abram gave the following information concerning his knowledge of affairs on the farm under his master:

"Master and Mistress very frequently visited the Protestant church, but were not members. Mistress was very bad. About three weeks before I left, the overseer, in a violent fit of bad temper, shot and badly wounded a young slave man by the name of Henry Waters, but no sooner than he got well enough he escaped, and had not been heard of up to the time Abram left. About three years before this happened, an overseer of my master was found shot dead on the road. At once some of the slaves were suspected, and were all taken to the Courthouse at Serentown, St. Mary's County, but all came off clear.

"After this occurrence a new overseer, by the name of John Decket, was employed. Although his predecessor had been dead three years, Decket nevertheless concluded that it was not too late to flog the secret out of some of the slaves. Accordingly, he selected a young slave man for his victim, and flogged him so cruelly that he could scarcely walk or stand, and to keep from being actually killed, the boy told an untruth, and confessed that he and his Uncle Henry killed Webster, the overseer, whereupon the poor fellow was sent to jail to be tried for his life."

But Abram did not wait to hear the verdict. He reached the Vigilance Committee of Philadelphia, was furnished with a free ticket and other needed assistance, and was sent on his way rejoicing. After reaching his destination, he wrote back to learn how his friend and companion (George) was getting along, but in less than three weeks after he had passed, the following brief story reveals the sad fate of poor Romulus Hall, who had journeyed with Abram until exhausted from hunger and badly frostbitten.

A few days after his younger companion had passed on to the North, Romulus was brought by a pitying stranger to the Committee, in a most shocking condition. The frost had greatly affected his feet and legs, so much so that all sense of feeling had departed from them.

How he ever reached this city is a marvel. On his arrival medical attention and other necessary comforts were provided by the Committee, who hoped with himself that he would be restored to health with the loss of his toes alone. For one week he seemed to be improving; at the end of this time, however, his symptoms changed, indicating not only the end of his bondage, but also the end of all his earthly troubles.

Lockjaw set in in the most malignant form, and for nearly 36 hours the unfortunate victim suffered in extreme agony, though he never complained for having brought upon himself in seeking his liberty this painful infliction and death. It was wonderful to see how resignedly he endured his fate.

Being anxious to get his testimony relative to his escape, etc., the Chairman of the Committee took his pencil and expressed to him his wishes in the matter. Among other questions, he was asked:

"Do you regret having attempted to escape from slavery?"

After a severe spasm, Weems said, as his friend was about to turn to leave the room, resigned to not receiving an answer:

"Don't go! I have not answered your question. I am glad I escaped from slavery!"

He then gave his name, and tried to tell the name of his master, but was so weak he could not be understood.

At his bedside, day and night, slavery looked more evil than it ever had before. Only think how this poor man, in an enlightened Christian land, for the bare hope of freedom, in a strange land among strangers, was obliged to bear not only the sacrifice of his wife and kindred, but also of his own life.

Nothing ever appeared more sad than seeing him in a dying posture, and instead of reaching his much coveted destination in Canada, going to that "whence no traveler returns." Of course, it was expedient, even after his death, that only a few friends should attend his funeral. Nevertheless, he was decently buried in the beautiful Lebanon Cemetery.

In his purse was found one single five-cent piece.

This was the first instance of death on the Underground Railroad in this region.

The Committee was indebted to the medical services of the well-known friends of the fugitive, Drs. J.L. Griscom and H.T. Childs, whose faithful services were freely given, and likewise to Mrs. H.S. Duterte and Mrs. Williams, who generously performed the offices of charity and friendship at his burial.

From his companion, who passed on to Canada without delay, we received a letter, from which, as an item of interest, we make the following extract:

First Letter.

"I am enjoying good health, and hope when this reaches you, you may be enjoying the same blessing. Give my love to Mr. and family, and tell them I am in a land of liberty! I am a man among men!" (The above was addressed to the deceased.)

The letter below, from Rev. L.D. Mansfield, expressed on behalf of Romulus' companion, his sad feelings on hearing of his friend's death. And here it may not be inappropriate to add that clearly enough is it to be seen that Rev. Mansfield was one of the rare order of ministers who believed it right "to do unto others as one would be done by" in practice, not in theory alone, and who felt that they could no more be excused for "falling down," in obedience to the Fugitive Slave Law under President Fillmore, than could Daniel for worshiping the "golden image" under Nebuchadnezzar.

Second Letter.

"Auburn, New York, 4 May 1857 "Dear Mr. Still:

"Henry Lemmon wishes me to write to you in reply to your kind letter, conveying news of the death of your fugitive guest, George Weems. He was deeply affected by the news, for he was most devotedly attached to him and had been for many years. Mr. Lemmon now expects his sister to come on, and wishes you to aid her in any way in your power — as he knows you will.

"He wishes you to send the coat and cap of Weems by his sister when she comes, and when you write out the history of Weems' escape, and it is published, that you would send him a copy of the papers. He has not been very successful in getting work yet.

"Mr. and Mrs. Harris left for Canada last week. The friends made them a purse of $15 or $20, and we hope they will do well.

"Mr. Lemmon sends his respects to you and Mrs. Still. Give my kind regards to her and accept also yourself.

"Yours very truly, "*L.D. Mansfield.*"

CHAPTER 4

James Mercer, William H. Gilliam, and John Clayton — Stowaways in a Hot Berth.

This arrival came by steamer. But they neither came in the stateroom nor as cabin, steerage, or deck passengers. They hid in a certain space, not far from the boiler, where the heat and coal dust were almost intolerable. In response for a safe place to hide, the colored steward on the boat could point to no other place for concealment but this. Nor was he at all certain that they could endure the intense heat of that place. It allowed no other posture than lying flat down, entirely shut out from the light, and nearly in the same situation with regard to the air. Here, however, was a chance of escaping slavery, even if it cost them their lives. They considered and decided to try it, despite the risk.

Henry Box Brown's sufferings were nothing compared to what these men submitted to during their entire journey. They reached the house of one of the members of the Vigilance Committee of Philadelphia about 3:00 A.M. All the way from the wharf the cold rain poured down in torrents and they got completely drenched, but their hearts were swelling with joy and indescribable gladness. From the thick coating of coal dust, and the effect of the rain added to the dust, all traces of natural appearance were entirely obliterated, and they looked frightful in the extreme. But they had placed their lives in mortal peril for freedom — and won.

Every step of their critical journey was reviewed and commented on, with matchless natural eloquence, how, when almost on the eve of suffocating in their warm berths, in order to catch a breath of air, they were compelled to crawl, one at a time, to a small aperture; but scarcely would one poor fellow pass three minutes being thus refreshed, before the others would insist that he should "go back to his hole." Air was precious, but for the time being they valued their liberty at still greater price.

After they had talked to their hearts' content, and after they had been thoroughly cleansed and changed in apparel, their physical appearance could be easily discerned, which made it less a wonder when such outbursts of eloquence had emanated. They bore every mark of determined manhood.

The date of this arrival was 26 February 1854, and the following description was then recorded:

Arrived, by Steamer Pennsylvania: James Mercer, William H. Gilliam, and John Clayton, from Richmond.

James was owned by the widow, Mrs. T.E. White. He was 32 years of age, of dark complexion, well-made, good-looking, was able to read and write, was very fluent in speech, and was remarkably intelligent. From boyhood, he had been hired out. The last place he had the honor to fill before escaping was with Messrs. Williams and Brother, wholesale commission merchants. For his services in this store the widow had been drawing $125 per year, clear of all expenses.

He did not complain of bad treatment from his mistress; indeed, he spoke rather favorably of her. But he could not close his eyes to the fact that at one time Mrs. White had been in possession of 30 slaves, although at the time he was counting the cost of escaping, only 2 slaves remained — himself and William (save a little boy), and on himself a mortgage for $750 dollars was then resting. He could, therefore, with his remarkably quick intellect, estimate how long it would take before he reached the auction block.

James had a wife but no child. She was owned by Mr. Henry W. Quarles. So out of that Sodom he felt he would have to escape, even at the cost of leaving his wife behind. Of course he felt hopeful that the way would open by which she could escape at a future time, and so it did, as will appear by and by. His aged mother he also had to leave.

William Henry Gilliam likewise belonged to the widow White, and he had been hired to Messrs. White and Brother to drive their bread wagon. William was a baker by trade. For his services his mistress had received $135 per year. He thought his mistress quite as good, if not a little better than most slaveholders. But he had never felt persuaded to believe that she was good enough for him to remain a slave for her support.

Indeed, he had made several unsuccessful attempts before this time to escape from slavery and its horrors. He was fully posted from A to Z, but in his own person he had been smart enough to escape most of the more brutal outrages. He knew how to read and write, and in readiness of speech and general natural ability was far above the average slaves.

He was 25 years of age, well-made, of light complexion, and might be put down as a valuable piece of property.

The loss of these slaves fell with crushing weight upon the kindhearted mistress, as will be seen in a letter, which she wrote to the unfaithful William some time after he had fled.

Letter from Mrs. L.E. White

"Richmond, 16th, 1854 "Dear Henry:

"Your mother and myself received your letter; she is much distressed at your conduct; she is remaining just as you left her, she says, and she will never be reconciled to your conduct.

"I think, Henry, you have acted most dishonorably; had you made a confidant of me I would have been better off; and you as you are. I am badly situated, living with Mrs. Palmer, and having to put up with everything, your mother is also dissatisfied, I am miserably poor, and do not get a cent of your hire or James's, besides losing you both, but if you can reconcile so do. By renting a cheap house, I might have lived, now it seems starvation is before me. Martha and the doctor are living in Portsmouth; it is not in her power to do much for me. I know you will repent it. I heard six weeks before you went that you were trying to persuade him off, but we all liked you, and I was unwilling to believe it; however, I leave it in God's hands, He will know what to do. Your mother says that I must tell you [that] servant Jones is dead and old Mrs. Galt. Kit is well, but we are very uneasy, losing your and James's hire, and I fear poor little fellow, that he will be obliged to go, as I am compelled to live, and it will be your fault. I am quite unwell, but of course, you don't care.

"Yours, "*L.E. White.*

"If you choose to come back you could. I would do a very good part by you, Toler and Cook has none."

This touching letter was given by the disobedient William to a member of the Vigilance Committee, when on a visit to Canada in 1855, and it was thought to be of too much value to be lost. It was put away with other valuable U.G.R.R. documents for future reference. Touching the "rascality" of William and James and the unfortunate predicament in which it placed the kindhearted widow, Mrs. Louisa White, the following editorial clipped from the documents as conclusive testimony to the successful working of the U.G.R.R. in the Old Dominion. It reads thus:

"Rascality Somewhere —

"We called attention yesterday to the advertisement of two negroes belonging to Mrs. Louisa White, by Toler & Cook, and in the call we expressed the opinion that they were still lurking about the city, preparatory to going off. Mr. Toler, we find, is of a different opinion. He believes that they have already cleared themselves, have escaped to a Free State, and we think it extremely probable that he is in the right. They were both of them uncommonly intelligent negroes. One of them, the one hired to Mr. White, was a tip-top baker. He had been all about the country, and had been in the habit of supplying the U.S. Pennsylvania with bread; Mr. W. having the contract. In his visits for this purpose, of course, he formed acquaintances with all sorts of seafaring characters; and there is every reason to believe that he has been assisted to get off in that way, along with the other boy, hired to the Messrs. Williams. That the two acted in concert, can admit of no doubt. The question is now to find out how they got off. They must undoubtedly have had white men in the secret. Have we then a nest of abolition scoundrels among us? There ought to be a law to put a police officer on board every vessel as soon as [it] lands at the wharf. There is one, we believe, for inspecting vessels before they leave. If there is not, there ought to be one.

"These negroes belong to a widow lady and constitute all the property she has on earth. They have both been raised with the greatest indulgence. Had it been otherwise, they would never have had an opportunity to escape, as they have done. Their flight has left her penniless. Either of them would readily have sold for $1200; and Mr. Toler advised their owner to sell them at the commencement of the year, probably anticipating the very thing that has happened. She refused to do so, because she felt too much attachment to them. They have made a fine return, truly."

No comment is necessary on the above editorial except simply to express the hope that the editor and his friends who seemed to be utterly befogged as to how these "uncommonly intelligent negroes" made their escape, will find the problem satisfactorily solved here.

CHAPTER 5

Clarissa Davis — Escaped Dressed in Male Attire.

Clarissa Davis fled from Portsmouth, Virginia in May 1854 with two of her brothers. Two and a half months before she succeeded in getting off, Clarissa had made a desperate effort, but failed. The brothers succeeded, but she was left. She had not given up all hope of escape, however, and therefore sought "a safe hiding place until an opportunity might offer," by which she could follow her brothers on the Underground Railroad. Clarissa was owned by Mrs. Brown and Mrs. Burkley, of Portsmouth, under whom she had always served.

Of them she spoke favorably, saying that she "had not been used as hard as many others were." At this period, Clarissa was about 22 years old, of a bright brown complexion, with handsome features, exceedingly respectful and modest, and possessed all the characteristics of a well-bred young lady. For one so little acquainted with books as she was, the correctness of her speech was perfectly astonishing.

For Clarissa and her two brothers a "reward of one thousand dollars" was kept standing in the papers for a length of time, as these ("articles", slaves) were considered very rare and valuable, "the best" that could be produced in Virginia.

In the meanwhile the brothers had passed safely on to New Bedford, but Clarissa remained secluded, "waiting for the storm to subside." Keeping up courage day-by-day, for 75 days, with constant fear of being detected and severely punished, and then sold, after all her hopes and struggles, required the faith of a martyr. Time after time, when she hoped to succeed in making her escape, ill luck seemed to disappoint her, and nothing but intense suffering appeared to be in store for her.

Like many others under the crushing weight of oppression, she thought she "should have to die" before she tasted liberty. In this state of mind, one day word was conveyed to her that the steamship City of Richmond had arrived from Philadelphia, and that the steward on board (with whom she was acquainted), had consented to stow her away on the return trip, if she could manage to safely reach the ship. The ship was scheduled to leave the next day.

This news was both cheering and painful. Clarissa had been "praying all the time while waiting," but now she felt "that if it would only rain right hard the next morning about three o'clock, to drive the police officers off the street, then she could safely make her way to the boat." Therefore she prayed anxiously all that day that it would rain, "but no sign of rain appeared till towards midnight." The prospect looked horribly discouraging, but she prayed on, and at the appointed hour (3:00 A.M.), the rain descended in torrents.

Dressed in male attire, Clarissa left the miserable coop where she had been almost without light or air for two and a half months, and, unchallenged, reached the boat safely. There she was hidden in a box by William Bagnal, a clever young man who sincerely sympathized with the slave, having a wife in slavery himself. By these means Clarissa was safely delivered into the hands of the Vigilance Committee of Philadelphia.

In Philadelphia, on the advice of the Vigilance Committee, Clarissa Davis dropped her old name and was straightaway christened "Mary D. Armstead." Desiring to join her brothers and sister in New Bedford, she was duly furnished with her U.G.R.R. passport and directed to that destination.

Her father, who was left behind when she made her escape, soon made his way to the North and joined his children. He was too old and infirm to be financially very valuable, and had been allowed to go free, or to purchase himself for a mere nominal sum. Slaveholders would, on some such occasions, show wonderful liberality in letting their old slaves go free when they could work no more.

After reaching New Bedford, Clarissa showed her gratitude in writing to her friends in Philadelphia repeatedly, and took a very lively interest in the U.G.R.R. The following letter indicates her sincere feelings of gratitude and deep interest in the cause:

"New Bedford, 26 August 1855 "Mr. Still:

"I avail myself to write you these few lines hoping they may find you and your family well, as they leave me very well and all the family well, except for my father. He seems to be improving with his shoulder and he has been able to work a little. I received the papers. I was highly delighted to receive them and I was very glad to hear from you in the Wheeler case. I was very glad to hear that the persons were safe, but I was very sorry to hear that Mr. Williamson was put in prison. But I know if the praying part of the people will pray for him and if he will put his trust in the Lord, he will...conquer.

Please remember my dear old father and sisters and brothers to your family. Kiss the children for me. I hear that the yellow fever is very bad down south now. If the Underground Railroad could have free course, the immigrant would cross the river of Jordan rapidly. I hope it may continue to run and I hope the wheels of the car may be greased with more substantial grease, so they may run swiftly. I would have written before, but circumstances would not permit me. Miss Sanders and all the friends desired to be remembered to you and your family. I shall be pleased to hear from the Underground Railroad often.

"Yours respectfully, "*Mary D.*"

CHAPTER 6

Anthony Blow, alias Henry Levison — Ten Months Concealed on Land and Eight Days on a Steamer.

Anthony Blow arrived from Norfolk, Virginia about 1 November 1854. Ten months before starting, Anthony had been closely concealed. He belonged to the estate of Mrs. Peters, a widow who had been dead about one year before his concealment. On the settlement of his old mistress' estate, which was to take place one year after her death, Anthony was to be transferred to Mrs. Lewis, a daughter of Mrs. Peters (the wife of James Lewis, Esq.).

Anthony had no wish to please the "tyrannical whims" of his anticipated master, young Lewis, and he hated the idea of having to come under his yoke. What made the prospects still more unpleasant for Anthony was that Mr. Lewis would frequently remind him that it was his intention to "sell him as soon as he got possession, the first day of January."

"I can get $1500 for you easily, and I will do it." This contemptuous threat had caused Anthony's blood to boil time and again. But Anthony had to take the matter as calmly as possible, which, however, he was not always able to do.

At any rate, Anthony concluded that his "young master had counted the chickens before they were hatched." Indeed, Anthony became a deep thinker. He thought, for instance, that he had already been shot three times, at the instance of slaveholders. The first time he was shot was for refusing a flogging when he was 18 years of age.

The second time he was shot in the head with squirrel shot by the sheriff, who was attempting to arrest him for having resisted three "young white ruffians," who wished to have the pleasure of beating him, but got beaten themselves. And in addition to being shot this time, Anthony was still further "broke in" by a terrible flogging from the sheriff.

The third time Anthony was shot he was about 21 years old. This time his injury from being shot was light, compared with the two preceding attacks. But, in connection with these murderous conflicts, Anthony could not forget that he also had been sold on the auction block.

Anthony had still deeper thinking to do. He determined that his young master should never get "$1500 for him on the 1st of January," unless he got them while he (Anthony) was running. For Anthony had fully made up his mind that when the last day of December ended, his bondage should end also, even if he should have to accept death as a substitute. He then began to think about the Underground Railroad and of Canada. However, Anthony did not know who the agents were, or how to find the "depot." His time was getting short and he had to act quickly. In this frame of mind he found a man who claimed to know something about the Underground Railroad, and for $30 promised to aid him in his escape.

The $30 were raised by the hardest effort and passed over to the pretended friend, with the expectation that it would result in a way out of his emergency. But Anthony found himself cheated out of the $30, as nothing was done for him. Nevertheless, when the 1st day of January arrived, Anthony was not to be found to answer to his name at roll call. He had taken off very early in the morning. Daily he prayed in his place of concealment for a way to find the U.G.R.R. Ten months passed away, during which time he almost suffered death, but persuaded himself to believe that even that was better than slavery.

With Anthony, as it had been with thousands of others similarly situated, just as everything was looking the most hopeless, word came to him in his place of concealment that a friend named Minkins, who was employed on the steamship City of Richmond, would undertake to hide him on the boat. That place of concealment was described as the only spot where he would be perfectly safe. This was glorious news to Anthony; but it was well for him that he was ignorant of the situation that awaited him on the boat, or his heart might have failed him. He was willing, however, to risk his life for freedom, and therefore went joyfully. The hiding place was small and he was large. The only way he could possibly occupy it was to sit. He was contented, however. This place was "near the range [stove], directly over the porter," and of course, was very warm. Nevertheless, Anthony felt that he would not murmur, since he already knew what real suffering was, and especially as he took it for granted that he would be free in about a day and a half, the usual time it took the steamer to make her trip.

At the appointed hour the steamer left Norfolk for Philadelphia, with Anthony sitting in his U.G.R.R. berth, thoughtful and hopeful. But before the steamer had made half its distance a storm began tossing the ship fearfully. Headwinds blew terribly, and for a number of days the elements seemed perfectly mad. When the storm subsided, fog took its place and controlled the movement of the ship for several more days. Finally the storm, wind, and fog all disappeared, and on the eighth day of its eventful passage the steamship landed at the wharf of Philadelphia with this giant and hero on board who had suffered for ten months concealed on land and for eight days on the ship.

Anthony was of very powerful physical person, being six feet three inches in height, quite black, very intelligent, and of a temperament that would not submit to slavery. For some years, his master, Col. Cunnagan, had hired him out in Washington, where he was accused of being in the schooner Pearl, with Capt. Drayton's memorable "seventy fugitives on board, bound for Canada." At that time Anthony was a stoker in a machine shop, and was at work on an anchor weighing "ten thousand pounds." In the excitement over the attempted escape in the Pearl by 70 slaves, many were arrested, and the officers with irons visited Anthony at the machine shop to arrest him. Anthony declined to let them put the handcuffs on him, but consented to go with them, if permitted to do so without being shackled. The officers yielded, and Anthony went willingly to the jail.

Anthony left his wife, Ann, and three children, Benjamin, John, and Alfred, all owned by Col. Cunnagan. In this brave-hearted man, the Vigilance Committee of Philadelphia held a deep interest, and offered him its usual hospitality.

CHAPTER 7

Sheridan Ford — Hid in the Woods and Escaped on a Steamer.

About 29 January 1855, Sheridan Ford arrived from the Old Dominion and a life of bondage, and was welcomed cordially by the Vigilance Committee of Philadelphia. Miss Elizabeth Brown of Portsmouth, Virginia claimed Sheridan as her property. He spoke rather kindly of her, and felt that he "had not been used very hard" as a general thing, although he wisely added, "the best usage was bad enough." Sheridan had nearly reached his 28th year, was tall and well-made, and possessed a considerable share of intelligence.

A short time before making up his mind to escape, Sheridan had been "stretched up with a rope by his hands," and "whipped unmercifully." In addition to this he had "got wind of the fact" that he was to be auctioned off. Soon these things brought serious reflections to Sheridan's mind, and among other questions, he began to ponder how he could get a ticket on the Underground Railroad, and exchange this "place of torment" for a place where he might have the benefit of his own labor.

In this state of mind, he took his first daring step about 14 November. He did not go to learned lawyers or able ministers of the Gospel in his distress and trouble, but made his way "directly to the woods," where he felt that he would be safer with the wild animals and reptiles, in solitude, than with the barbarous civilization that existed in Portsmouth.

He passed the first day in the woods in constant prayer and all alone. In this particular place of seclusion he remained four days and nights, suffering severely from hunger, cold, and thirst for two days. However, one who was a friend to him, and knew of his whereabouts, managed to get some food to him along with some consoling words. But at the end of the four days this friend got into some difficulty and Sheridan was left to "wade through deep waters and headwinds" in an almost hopeless state.

He could not stay in the woods and starve to death. Accordingly, he left and found another place of seclusion, with a friend in the town, in exchange for money. A secret passage was obtained for him on one of the steamers running between Philadelphia and Richmond, Virginia.

When he left Virginia, his poor wife, Julia, was then "lying in prison to be sold" on the simple charge of having been suspected of helping her husband escape. As a woman, she had known something of the "barbarism of slavery" from everyday experience, which the large scars about her head indicated, according to Sheridan's testimony. She was the mother of two children, but had never been allowed to have the care of either of them. The husband, utterly powerless to offer her the least sympathy in word or deed, left this dark habitation of cruelty with no hope of ever seeing wife or children again in this world.

The Vigilance Committee provided him the usual aid and comfort, and passed him on to the next station, with his face set towards Boston. He had heard the slaveholders "curse" Boston so much that he concluded it must be a pretty safe place for the fugitive.

CHAPTER 8

James Hambleton Christian, Former Slave
of Ex-President Tyler and a Member
of the 'Patriarchal Institution,' Flees from Slavery.

James Hambleton Christian was a remarkable example of the "well-fed, etc." In talking with him about his life as a slave, he said very promptly, "I have always been treated well; if I only have half as good times in the North as I have had in the South, I shall be perfectly satisfied. Any time I desired spending money, five or ten dollars were no object."

At times, James had borrowed one, two, and three hundred dollars from his master, to loan out to some of his friends. With regard to clothing and jewelry, he had worn the best as everyday adornment. With regard to food, he also had fared as well as the heart could wish, with an abundance of leisure time at his command. His bearing was very refined and gentlemanly. About 50 per cent Anglo-Saxon blood was reflected in his features and his hair, which gave him no considerable claim to sympathy and care.

He had been to William and Mary's College in his younger days to wait on young master James B.C., where, through the kindness of some of the students, he had picked up some book learning. In summary, this man was born the slave of old Major Christian on the Glen Plantation, Charles City County, Virginia. The Christians were wealthy and owned many slaves, and belonged in reality to the First Families of Virginia. On the death of the old major, James fell into the hands of his son, Judge Christian, who was executor to his father's estate. Subsequently he fell into the hands of one of the judge's sisters, Mrs. John Tyler (wife of President Tyler). There he became a member of the president's domestic household and was at the White House, under the president, from 1841 to 1845. Though very young at that time, James was trained in the art, science, and psychology of waiting on others, in which profession pains were taken to prepare him completely for his calling.

After a lapse of time, his mistress died. According to her request, after this event, James and his old mother were handed over to her nephew, William H. Christian, Esq., a merchant in Richmond. From this gentleman, James had the "foolishness" to flee.

When questioned by the Vigilance Committee of Philadelphia, he provided a few additional details related to his remarkable history.

"How did you like Mr. Tyler?" asked an inquisitive member of the Committee. "I didn't like Mr. Tyler much," was the reply.

"Why?" again inquired the member of the Committee.

"Because Tyler was a poor man. I never did like poor people. I didn't like his marrying into our family, who were considered...Tyler's superiors [by far].

"On the plantation," he said, "Tyler was a very cross man, and treated the servants very cruelly; but the house servants were treated much better, owing to their having belonged to his wife, who protected them from persecution, as they had been favorite servants in her father's family."

James estimated that "Tyler got about $35,000 and 29 slaves, young and old, by his wife."

What prompted James to leave such pleasant quarters? It was this: he was in love with a young and respectable free girl in Richmond, with whom he could not be united in marriage solely because he was a slave, and did not own himself. The frequent sad separations of such married couples (where one or the other was a slave) also could not be overlooked; consequently, the poor fellow concluded that he would stand a better chance of gaining his objective in Canada than by remaining in Virginia. Furthermore, he began to feel that he might himself be sold some day, and thus the resolution came home to him very forcibly to make tracks for Canada.

In speaking of the good treatment he had always received, a member of the Committee remarked, "You must be a kin to someone of your master's family?"

To which James replied, "I am Christian's son."

Unquestionably this passenger was one of that "happy class" so commonly referred to by apologists of slavery as the "Patriarchal Institution."

The Committee heartily welcomed him and supported his objective to obtain the hand of his betrothed. All felt assured that the struggles and hardships he had submitted to in escaping, as well as the luxuries he was leaving behind, were nothing compared to the blessings of liberty and a free wife in Canada.

CHAPTER 9

Mary Epps, alias Emma Brown, and Joseph and Robert Robinson Arrive on a Schooner.

Mary Epps fled from Petersburg, and Joseph and Robert Robinson from Richmond. A Fugitive Slave Law-breaking captain by the name of B., who owned a schooner and would bring any kind of freight that would pay the most, was the conductor in this instance. Quite a number of passengers at different times took advantage of his accommodations and thus succeeded in reaching Canada.

His risk was very great. On this account he claimed, as did certain others, that it was no more than fair to charge for his services. Indeed he did not claim to bring persons for nothing, except in rare instances. In this matter the Vigilance Committee of Philadelphia did not feel disposed to interfere directly in any way, other than to suggest that whatever understanding was agreed upon by the parties themselves should be honored.

Many slaves in cities could raise, "by hook or by crook," $50 or $100 to pay for a passage, providing they could find someone who was willing to risk aiding them. Thus, while the Vigilance Committee of Philadelphia neither charged nor accepted anything for their services, it was not to be expected that any of the southern agents could afford to do likewise.

Mary Epps

The husband of Mary for a long time had wanted his own freedom, but did not feel that he could go without his wife; in fact, he resolved to get her off first, then to try and escape himself, if possible. The first essential step towards success, he considered, was to save his money and make it an object for the captain to help him. So when he had managed to save $100, he willingly offered this sum to Captain B., if he would engage to deliver his wife into the hands of the Vigilance Committee of Philadelphia. The captain agreed to the terms and fulfilled his engagement to the letter.

About 1 March 1855, Mary was presented to the Vigilance Committee. She was of agreeable manners, about 45 years of age, dark complexion, round-built, and intelligent. She had been the mother of 15 children, 4 of whom had been sold away from her; 1 still held in slavery in Petersburg; the others all dead.

At the sale of one of her children she was so affected with grief that she was thrown into violent convulsions, which caused the loss of her speech for one entire month. But this little episode was not a matter to excite sympathy among the highly refined and tender-hearted Christian mothers of Petersburg. By the mercy of God, however, Mary's reason and strength returned.

She had formerly belonged to the late Littleton Reeves, whom she represented as having been "kind" to her, much more so than her mistress (Mrs. Reeves). Said Mary, "She, being of a jealous disposition, caused me to be hired out with a hard family, where I was much abused, frequently flogged, and stinted for food," etc.

But the potential rewards of freedom in the care of the Vigilance Committee now delighted her mind, and the hope that her husband would soon follow her to Canada inspired her with expectations that she would one day "sit under her own vine and fig tree where none dared to molest or make her afraid." The Committee provided her with the usual assistance, and in due time, forwarded her on to Queen Victoria's free land in Canada. On her arrival she wrote back as follows:

———

"Toronto, 14 March 1855 "Dear Mr. Still:

"I take this opportunity of addressing you with these few lines to inform you that I arrived here today, and hope that this may find yourself and Mrs. Still well, as this leaves me at the present. I will also say to you that I had no difficulty in getting along. The two young men that were with me left me at Suspension Bridge. They went another way.

"I cannot say much about the place as I have been here but a short time but so far as I have seen I like it very well. You will give my respect to your lady, and Mr. and Mrs. Brown. If you have not written to Petersburg, will you please write as soon as you can. I have nothing more to write at present.

"Respectfully,

"*Emma Brown* (old name Mary Epps)."

Joseph and Robert Robinson

Joseph and Robert were Mary's associate passengers from Richmond. Joseph was of a dark orange color, medium size, very active and intelligent, and doubtless, well understood the art of behaving himself. He was well acquainted with the auction block, having been sold three times, and had had the misfortune to fall into the hands of a cruel master each time.

Under these circumstances Joseph had had few privileges. Sundays and weekdays alike he was kept pretty severely bent down to duty. He had been beaten and knocked around shamefully. He had a wife, and spoke of her in most endearing terms, although on leaving, he did not feel at liberty to tell her of his plans, "fearing that it would not be safe to do so." His four little children, to whom he appeared warmly attached, he left as he did his wife, in slavery. He declared that he "stuck to them as long as he could."

George E. Sadler, the keeper of an oyster house, held the deed for "Joe," and a most heartless person he was in Joe's estimation and description. The truth was, Joe could not stand the burdens and abuses which Sadler was inclined to heap upon him. So he concluded to join his brother and go off on the Underground Railroad.

Robert, his younger brother, was owned by Robert Slater, Esq., a regular negro trader. Eight years this slave's duties had been at the slave prison, and among other daily duties he had to attend to, was to lock up the prison, prepare the slaves for sale, etc. Robert was a very intelligent young man, and from long and daily experience with the customs and usages of the slave prison, he was as familiar with the business as a Pennsylvania farmer with his barnyard stock. His account of things was too harrowing to detail here, except in the briefest manner, and that only with reference to a few particulars.

In order to prepare slaves for the market, it was usual to have them greased and rubbed to make them look bright and shining. The separation of families was not given a second thought. And Robert went on further to state that "females as well as males were not uncommonly stripped naked, lashed flat to a bench, and then held by two men, sometimes four, while the brutal trader would whip them with a broad leather strap." The strap was preferred to the cowhide, as it would not break the skin, and damage the sale. "One hundred lashes would be a common flogging."

While not yet 23 years of age, Robert expressed himself as having become so daily sickened by the brutality and suffering that he had witnessed that he felt he could not possibly stand it any longer, let the cost be what it might. "Often I have been flogged for refusing to flog others," he said. In this state of mind he met with Captain B.

Only one obstacle stood in the way of Robert's freedom: financial means. It occurred to Robert that he had frequent access to the money drawer, and often it contained the proceeds of fresh sales of flesh and blood. He reasoned that if some of that would help him and his brother to freedom, there could be no harm in helping himself, come the first opportunity.

The captain had agreed, provided he could get three passengers at $100 each, to set sail without much other freight. Of course he was too shrewd to take out "sailing papers" for Philadelphia. That would betray him at once. Washington or Baltimore, or even Wilmington, Delaware were names that did not cause suspicion in the eyes of Virginians. Consequently, being able to pack the fugitives away in a very private hole of his boat, and being only bound for a southern port, the captain was willing to risk his share of the danger.

"Very well," said Robert, "today I will please my master so well that [I] will catch him at an unguarded moment, and will ask him for a pass to go to a ball tonight (slaveholders loved to see their slaves fiddling and dancing at night). As I am hurriedly leaving, I will grab some money from the day's sale, and when Slater hears of me again, I will be in Canada."

Consistent with this plan, after having attended to all his disagreeable duties, he made his "grab" and left. He did not know, however, how much he had or if it would be enough. However, that evening, instead of participating with the happy dancers, he was just one degree lower down than the regular bottom of Captain B.'s deck. And he had several hundred dollars in his pocket, after paying the worthy captain $100 each for himself and his brother, besides making the captain an additional present of nearly $100. Wind and tide were now what they prayed for to speed on the U.G.R.R. schooner, until they might reach the depot at Philadelphia.

The **Richmond Dispatch**, an enterprising paper in the interest of slaveholders, which came daily to the Committee, was received in advance of the passengers. There, lo and behold, in turning to the interesting column containing the elegant illustrations of "runaway negroes," it was learned that unfortunate Slater had "lost $1500 in North Carolina money, and also his dark orange-colored, intelligent, and good-looking turnkey, Bob."

"Served him right, it is not stealing for one piece of property to go off with another piece," reasoned a member of the Committee. In a couple of days after the **Dispatch** brought the news, the three U.G.R.R. passengers were safely landed at the usual place, and so accurate were the descriptions in the paper that, on first seeing them, the Committee recognized them instantly, and, without any previous ceremonies, read to them the advertisement relative to the "$1500 in North Carolina money, etc.," and put the question to them direct: "Are you the ones?"

"We are," they answered without hesitation. The Committee did not see a dollar of their money, but believed they had about $900 left, after paying the captain. While Bob said that he had made a "very good grab," he did not admit that the amount advertised was correct. After a reasonable time to recover from being so long in the hole of the vessel, they took their departure for Canada.

From Joseph, the elder brother, a short letter was received, which announced their arrival and condition under the British Lion:

"St. Catharines, 16 April 1855 "Mr. William Still,
"Dear Sir:
"Your letter of 7 April I have just got, and it had been opened before it came to me. I have not received any other letter from you and can get no account of them in the post office in this place. I am well and have got a good situation in this city and intend on staying here. I should be very glad to hear from you as soon as convenient and also from all of my friends near you. My brother is also at work with me and doing well.

"There is nothing here that would interest you in the way of news. There is a Masonic Lodge of our people and two churches and societies here and some other institutions for our benefit. Be kind enough to send a few lines to the lady spoken of for that mocking bird and I'll be much obliged. Write me soon and believe me your obedient servant.

"Love and respects to lady and daughter, *Joseph Robinson.*"

As well as writing to a member of the Committee, Joe and Bob had the assurance to write back to the trader and oyster house keeper. In their letter they stated that they had arrived safely in Canada, and were having good times, in the eating line had an abundance of the best, also had very choice wines and brandies, which they supposed that they (trader and oyster house keeper) would give a great deal to have a "smack" of. Then they gave them a very cordial invitation to make them a visit, and suggested that the quickest way they could come would be by telegraph, which they admitted was slightly dangerous, and without first greasing themselves, and then hanging on very fast, the journey might not prove altogether advantageous to them. This was "wormwood and gall" to the trader and oyster house man.

A most remarkable coincidence was that, about the time this letter was received in Richmond, the captain who brought away the three passengers made it his business for some reason or other, to call at the oyster house kept by the owner of Joe. While there, this letter was read and commented on in torrents of Billingsgate phrases; and the trader told the captain that he would give him "$2000 if he would get them." Finally the former owner told the captain that he would "give every cent they would bring, which would be much over $2000," as they were "so very likely."

CHAPTER 10

George Solomon, Daniel Neall, Benjamin R. Fletcher, and Maria Dorsey Arrive from Washington, D.C.

The above representatives of the unrequited laborers of the South fled directly from Washington, D.C. Nothing unusual was discovered in their stories of slave life; thus, their narratives will be brief.

George Solomon was owned by Daniel Minor, of Moss Grove, Virginia. George was about 33 years of age, of mixed race, intelligent, and of prepossessing appearance. His old master valued George's services very highly, and had often declared to others, as well as to George himself, that without him he should hardly know how to manage.

Frequently George was told by the old master that at his [the old master's] "death he was not to be a slave any longer, as he would have provision made in his will for his freedom." For a long time, George clung pretty hopefully to this prospect, but his "old master hung on too long." Consequently George's patience became exhausted.

Since he had heard a good deal about Canada, the Underground Railroad, and the abolitionists, George concluded that it would do no harm to hint to a reliable friend or two the names of these places and people, to see what impression would be made on their minds, in short, to see if they were ready to second a motion to flee bondage. In thus exposing his thoughts to his friends, he soon found agreement in each of their hearts, and they put their heads together to figure out the costs and to fix a time for leaving Egypt and the host of Pharaoh to do their own "hewing of wood and drawing of water."

Accordingly, George, Daniel, Benjamin, and Maria, all of one heart and mind, resolved one Saturday night that the next Sunday should find them on the Underground Railroad, with their faces turned toward Canada.

Daniel was young, only 23, good-looking, and half white, with a good share of intelligence. As regards his slave life, he acknowledged that he had not had it very rough as a general thing; nevertheless, he was fully persuaded that he had "as good a right to his freedom" as his "master had to his," and that it was his duty to contend for it.

Benjamin was 27 years of age, small of stature, dark-complexioned, of a pleasant countenance, and quite smart. He testified that "ill-treatment from his master," Henry Martin, who would give him "no chance at all," was the cause of his leaving. He left a brother and sister, both belonging to Martin, as well as two other sisters in bondage, Louisa and Letty. But his father and mother were both dead.

Therefore, the land of slave whips and auction blocks had no charm for him. He loved his sisters, but he knew if he could not protect himself, much less could he protect them. So he concluded to say goodbye to them forever in this world.

In turning to Maria, it should be stated here that females in attempting to escape from a life of bondage undertook three times the risk of failure that males were liable to, not to mention the additional trials and struggles they had to contend with. In justice, therefore, to the heroic female who was willing to endure the most extreme suffering and hardship for freedom, double respect is due.

Maria, the heroine of the party, was about 40 years of age, chestnut color, medium size, and possessed a good share of common sense. She was owned by George Parker. As was a common thing with slaveholders, Maria had found her owners hard to please, and quite often, without the slightest reason, they would threaten to "sell her or make a change." These threats only made matters worse, or, rather, they only served to give Maria additional resolve to escape her bondage. The party walked almost the entire distance from Washington to Harrisburg, Pennsylvania.

In the meantime George Parker, the so-called owner of Daniel and Maria, hurriedly rushed their good names to the papers.

"Four Hundred Dollars Reward, Runaway from my house on Saturday night, 30 August, my negro man 'Daniel,' 25 years of age, bright yellow mulatto, thick-set, and stout-made.

"Also, my negro woman, 'Maria,' 40 years of age, bright mulatto. The above reward will be paid if delivered in Washington City.

"*George Parker.*"

While this advertisement was in the Baltimore papers, these noble passengers were enjoying the hospitality of the Vigilance Committee of Philadelphia, and finally a warm reception in Canada. The following letter from Rev. H. Wilson provides some insight into the Canadian destinations of Benjamin and Daniel:

"St. Catharines, C.W., 15 September 1856 "Mr. William Still:
"Dear Sir,
"Two young men arrived here last Friday evening from Washington: Benjamin Fletcher and Daniel Neall. Mr. Neall (or Neale) desires to have his box of clothing forwarded on to him. It is at Washington in the care of John Dade, a colored man, who lives at Doctor W.H. Gilman's, who keeps an apothecary store on the corner of 4 1/2 and Pennsylvania Avenue. Mr. Dade is a slave, but a free dealer. You will please write to John Dade, in the care of Doctor W.H. Gilman, on behalf of Daniel Neale; but make sure to use the name of George Harrison, instead of Neale, and Dade will understand it. Please have John Dade direct the box by express to you in Philadelphia; he has the means of paying the charges on it in advance, as far as Philadelphia; and as soon as it comes will you please forward it on to my care at St. Catharines. Say to John Dade that George Harrison sends his love to his sister and Uncle Allen Sims, and all inquiring friends. Mr. Fletcher and Mr. Neale both send their respects to you, and I add mine.

"Yours truly, "*Hiram Wilson.*

"P.S. Mr. Benjamin R. Fletcher wishes to have Mr. Dade call on his brother James, and communicate to him his affectionate regards, and make known to him that he is safe and cheerful and happy. He desires his friends to know, through Dade, that he found Mrs. Starke here, his brother Alfred's wife's sister; that she is well, and living in St. ss, C.W., near Niagara Falls.

"*H.W.*"

CHAPTER 11

Henry Box Brown Arrives in a Box by Adams' Express.

Although the name of Henry Box Brown has been echoed over the land for a number of years, and the simple facts connected with his marvelous escape from slavery in a box published widely through the medium of antislavery papers, nevertheless it is not unreasonable to summarize them here:

Brown was a man of invention as well as a hero. In point of interest, however, his case is no more remarkable than many others. Indeed, neither before nor after escaping did he suffer half of what many others have experienced.

He was decidedly an unhappy "piece of property" in the city of Richmond, Virginia. He felt that it would be impossible for him to remain in the condition of a slave. He was well aware, however, that it was no easy task to escape the vigilance of Virginia slave hunters; and he knew the wrath he would face from his enraged master for committing the unpardonable sin of attempting to escape to a land of liberty if his attempt failed.

Thus, Brown carefully considered the costs and risks before venturing upon this hazardous undertaking. Ordinary modes of travel he concluded might prove disastrous to his hopes; he, therefore, hit upon a new invention altogether, which was to have himself boxed up and forwarded to Philadelphia direct by express.

Brown determined the size of the box and how it was to be equipped. He made it two feet eight inches deep, two feet wide, and three feet long, and lined with baize [a thick woolen or cotton cloth, which looks like felt and is used on billiard tables]. His resources with regard to food and water consisted of the following: One bladder of water and a few small biscuits. His only tool to insure a supply of fresh air was one large gimlet [a hand tool with a tapered, spiral end, used for boring holes].

Satisfied that it would be far better to imperil his life for freedom in this way than to remain under the yoke of slavery, he entered his box, which was securely nailed up and wrapped with five hickory hoops. The crate was then addressed by his friend, James A. Smith, a shoe dealer, to William H. Johnson, Arch Street, Philadelphia, marked, "This side up with care." In this condition he was sent to Adams' Express office, and then by overland express to Philadelphia.

It took 26 hours from the time he left Richmond until he arrived in the City of Brotherly Love. The notice, "This side up, etc.," had no influence on the different express men, who didn't hesitate to handle the box in their usual rough manner. For a while they actually had the box upside down, and had him on his head for miles.

A few days before he was expected, advance word was conveyed to a member of the Vigilance Committee of Philadelphia that a box should be expected via the three o'clock morning train from the South, which might contain special property. One of the most nervous walks the member ever took, and there had been many to meet and accompany passengers, was this trip to the depot.

The Committee member arrived at the depot at half past two o'clock that morning. He constantly wondered if the slave would be dead. He anxiously watched while the freight was being unloaded from the cars to see if he could recognize a box that might contain a man. Only one had that appearance, and he confessed it really seemed as if there was the scent of death about it. But on inquiry, he soon learned that it was not the box he was looking for, and he experienced a marked sense of relief. The box he was expecting was not on that train.

That same afternoon, however, he received from Richmond a telegram, which read thus, "Your case of goods is shipped and will arrive tomorrow morning."

At this turn of affairs, Mr. McKim, who had been engineering this important undertaking, decided to change the program slightly in order to insure greater safety. Instead of having a member of the Committee go again to the depot for the box, which might excite suspicion, it was decided that it would be best to have the express company bring it directly to the Anti-Slavery Office.

But all apprehension of danger did not now disappear, for there was no room to suppose that Adams' Express office had any sympathy with the abolitionist or the fugitive. Consequently, for Mr. McKim to appear personally at the express office to give directions with reference to the box, which would be arriving from Richmond, posed a risk. An even greater risk would result from directing the box to Arch Street, which was not its real destination, for the Anti-Slavery Office was at 107 North Fifth Street. No great insight was needed to foresee that this plan was dangerous and that a more indirect and covert method would have to be adopted. In this crisis, Mr. McKim, with his usual good judgment and remarkably quick, strategical mind, especially in matters pertaining to the Underground Railroad, hit upon the following plan. He went to his friend, E.M. Davis, who was then extensively engaged in mercantile business, and explained the circumstances. [E.M. Davis was a member of the Executive Committee of the Pennsylvania Anti-Slavery Society and a long-time abolitionist, as well as the son-in-law of James and Lucretia Mott.] Since Davis had daily interaction with the Adams' Express office, and was well acquainted with the firm and some of the drivers, Mr. Davis could, as Mr. McKim thought, talk about "boxes, freight, etc.," from any part of the country without risk. Mr. Davis heard Mr. McKim's plan and instantly agreed to help.

"Dan, an Irishman, one of Adams' Express drivers, is just the fellow to go to the depot after the box," said Davis. "He drinks a little too much whiskey sometimes, but he will do anything I ask him to do, promptly and obligingly. And I trust Dan to do things right."

The problem that had caused Mr. McKim so much anxiety was thus pretty well settled. It was agreed that Dan should go after the box next morning before daylight and bring it directly to the Anti-Slavery Office. And to make sure that Dan would agree to get up out of his warm bed and go on this errand before daylight, it was decided that Dan should be given a five-dollar gold piece as a "tip." Thus, with these plans set, it only remained for Mr. Davis to see Dan and give him his instructions.

Next morning, according to arrangement, the box was at the Anti-Slavery Office in due time. The witnesses present to behold the uncrating were J.M. McKim, Professor C.D. Cleveland, Lewis Thompson, and the writer.

Mr. McKim was deeply concerned about Mr. Brown, but having been long identified with the antislavery cause as one of its oldest and ablest advocates in the darkest days of slavery and mobs, and always found by the side of the fugitive to counsel and assist, he was on this occasion perfectly composed.

Professor Cleveland, however, was greatly moved. His zeal and earnestness in the cause of freedom, especially in rendering aid to passengers, knew no limit. And his emotions were overpowering him.

Mr. Thompson of the firm of Merrihew & Thompson, about the only printers in the city who for many years dared to print such controversial documents as antislavery papers and pamphlets, was composed and prepared to witness the scene.

All was quiet. The door had been safely locked. The proceedings commenced. Mr. McKim rapped quietly on the lid of the box and called out, "All right!" Instantly came the answer from within, "All right, sir!"

The witnesses will never forget that moment. Saw and hatchet quickly had the five hickory hoops cut and the lid off, and the marvelous resurrection of Mr. Brown ensued. Rising up in his box, he reached out his hand, saying, "How do you do, gentlemen?"

The little group hardly knew what to think or do at the moment. Mr. Brown was about as wet as if he had come up out of the Delaware. Very soon he remarked that, before leaving Richmond he had selected for his arrival hymn (if he lived) the Psalm beginning with these words: "I waited patiently for the Lord, and He heard my prayer." And most touchingly, he then sang the Psalm, much to his own relief, as well as to the delight of his small audience.

He was then christened "Henry Box Brown," and soon afterwards was sent to the hospitable residence of James Mott and E.M. Davis, on Ninth Street, where, it is needless to say, he met a most cordial reception from

Mrs. Lucretia Mott and her household. Clothing and other necessities were furnished, and delight and joy filled all hearts in that stronghold of philanthropy.

Since he had been so long doubled up in the box, Henry Brown needed to walk extensively in the fresh air. Thus, James Mott put one of his broad-brim Quaker hats on Brown's head and offered him the use of his yard as well as his house. And while Brown promenaded the yard, flushed with victory, great was the joy of his friends.

After his visit at Mr. Mott's, he spent two days with the writer, and then took his departure for Boston, evidently feeling quite conscious of the wonderful feat he had performed. At the same time it may be safely said that those who witnessed this strange resurrection were not only elated at his success, but were made to sympathize more deeply than ever before with the slave.

Also the noble-hearted Smith who boxed him up rejoiced over Brown's victory, and was thereby encouraged to render similar service to two other young bondmen, who appealed to him for deliverance. But, unfortunately, in this attempt the undertaking proved a failure. Two boxes containing the young fugitives, after having been duly expressed and some distance on the road, were intercepted. Their escape had been betrayed, and through the use of the telegraph, the heroic young fugitives were captured in their boxes and dragged back to hopeless bondage. As a result of this deplorable failure, Samuel A. Smith was arrested, imprisoned, and was called upon to suffer severely, as may be seen from the following correspondence, taken from the *New York Tribune*, which was published soon after Smith's release from the penitentiary.

"The Deliverer of Box Brown, Meeting of the Colored Citizens of Philadelphia "Philadelphia, Saturday, 5 July 1856

"Samuel A. Smith, who boxed up Henry Box Brown in Richmond, Virginia, and forwarded him by overland express to Philadelphia, and who was arrested and convicted eight years ago for boxing up two other slaves, also directed to Philadelphia, having served out his imprisonment in the penitentiary, was released on the 18th and arrived in this city on the 21st.

"Though he lost all his property; though he was refused witnesses at his trial (no officer could be found who would serve a summons on a defense witness); though for five long months, in hot weather, he was kept heavily chained in a cell four by eight feet in dimensions; though he received five dreadful stabs, aimed at his heart, by a bribed assassin; nevertheless he still rejoices in the motives which prompted him to 'undo the heavy burdens, and let the oppressed go free.'

"Having resided nearly all his life in the South, where he had traveled and seen much of the 'peculiar institution,' and had witnessed the most horrid enormities inflicted upon the slave, whose cries were ever ringing in his ears, and for whom he had the warmest sympathy, Mr. Smith could not refrain from believing that the black man, as well as the white, had God-given rights. Consequently, he was not accustomed to shed tears when a poor creature escaped from his 'kind master'; nor was he willing to turn a deaf ear to his appeals and groans when he knew he was thirsting for freedom. From 1828 up to the day he was incarcerated, many had sought his aid and counsel, and they had not sought it in vain. In various places he operated with success.

"In Richmond, however, it seemed expedient to invent a new plan for certain emergencies, hence the box and express plan was devised, at the instance of a few heroic slaves who had shown their willingness to die in a box on the road to liberty, rather than continue longer under the yoke. But these heroes fell into the power of their enemies. Mr. Smith had not been long in the penitentiary before he had fully gained the esteem and confidence of the superintendent and other officers. Finding him to be humane and generous-hearted, showing kindness toward all, especially in buying bread, etc., for the starving prisoners, and by a timely note of warning, which had saved the life of one of the keepers, for whose destruction a bold plot had been arranged — the officers felt disposed to show him such favors as the law would allow. But their good intentions were soon frustrated. The Inquisition (commonly called the Legislature), being in session in Richmond, hearing that the superintendent had been speaking well of Smith and circulating a petition for his pardon, indignantly demanded to know if the rumor was well-founded. Two weeks were spent by the Inquisition, and many witnesses were placed upon oath, to solemnly testify in the matter. One of the keepers swore that his life had been saved by Smith. Col. Morgan, the superintendent, frequently testified in writing and verbally to Smith's good character; acknowledging that he had circulated petitions, etc., and took the position that he sincerely believed that it would be to the interest of the institution to pardon him; calling the attention of the Inquisition, at the same time, to the fact that not infrequently pardons had been granted to criminals, under sentence of death, for the most cold-blooded murder, to say nothing of other gross crimes. The effort for pardon was soon abandoned, for the following reason given by the governor: "I can't, and I won't pardon him!" "In view of the unparalleled injustice which Mr. S. had suffered, as well as on account of the aid he had rendered to the slaves, on his arrival in this city, the colored citizens of Philadelphia felt that he was entitled to sympathy and aid, and straightaway invited him to remain a few days, until arrangements could be made for a mass meeting to receive him. Accordingly, on last Monday evening, a mass meeting convened in the Israel Church, and the Reverend William T. Catto was called to the chair, and William Still was appointed secretary. The chairman briefly stated the object of the meeting. Having lived in the South, he claimed to know something of the workings of the oppressive system of slavery generally, and declared that, notwithstanding the many exposures of the evil which came under his own observation, the most vivid descriptions fell far short of the realities his own eyes had witnessed. He then introduced Mr. Smith, who arose and in a plain manner briefly told his story, assuring the audience that he had always hated slavery, and had taken great pleasure in helping many out of it, and though he had suffered much physically and financially for the cause's sake, he did not complain, but rejoiced in what he had done. After taking his seat, addresses were made by the Rev. S. Smith, Messrs. Kinnard, Brunner, Bradway, and others. The following preamble and resolutions were adopted:

"Whereas, We, the colored citizens of Philadelphia, have among us Samuel Smith, who was incarcerated over seven years in the Richmond Penitentiary, for doing an act that was honorable to his feelings and his sense of justice and humanity, therefore, "Resolved, That we welcome him to this city as a martyr to the cause of Freedom.

"Resolved, That we heartily tender him our gratitude for the good he has done to our suffering race.

"Resolved, That we sympathize with him in his losses and sufferings in the cause of the poor, downtrodden slave.

"W.S." Still

During his stay in Philadelphia, on this occasion, he stopped for about 10 days with the writer, and it was most gratifying to learn from him that he was no new worker on the Underground Railroad, but that he had long hated slavery thoroughly, and although surrounded with perils on every side, he had not failed to help a poor slave whenever the opportunity was presented.

Financial aid, to some extent, was rendered him in this city, for which he was grateful, and after being united in marriage by William H. Furness, D.D., to a lady who had remained faithful to him through all his trials and sufferings, he took his departure for western New York, with a good conscience and an unshaken faith in the belief that in aiding his fellow man to freedom he had but simply obeyed the word of God, who taught man to do unto others as he would be done by them.

CHAPTER 12

Cordelia Loney Flees Her Mistress While Visiting Philadelphia.

Rarely did the peculiar institution present the relations of mistress and maid-servant in a light so apparently favorable as in the case of Mrs. Joseph Cahell (widow of the late Hon. Joseph Cahell, of Virginia), and her slave, Cordelia.

The Vigilance Committee's first knowledge of either of these memorable persons was brought about in the following manner:

About 30 March 1859, a member of the Vigilance Committee of Philadelphia was notified by a colored servant, living at a fashionable boardinghouse on Chestnut Street, that a lady with a slave woman from Fredericksburg, Virginia was boarding at the house, and that the slave woman desired to receive counsel and aid from the Committee, as she was anxious to secure her freedom before her mistress returned to the South.

On further consultation about the matter, a suitable hour was named for the meeting of the Committee and the slave at the boardinghouse. Finding that the woman was thoroughly reliable, the Committee told her "that two modes of deliverance were open before her. One was to take her trunk and all her clothing and quietly slip away." The other was to "sue out a writ of habeas corpus, and bring the mistress before the court, where she would be required, under the laws of Pennsylvania, to show cause why she restrained this woman of her freedom."

Cordelia decided to adopt the first method, provided the Committee would protect her. Without hesitation the Committee answered her that to the extent of their ability, she should have their aid with pleasure, and without delay. Consequently a member of the Committee was directed to be on hand at a given hour that evening, as Cordelia would certainly be ready to leave her mistress to take care of herself. Thus, at the appointed hour, Cordelia, very deliberately, accompanied the Committee away from her "kindhearted old mistress."

In the quiet and security of the Vigilance Committee room, Cordelia related substantially the following brief story about her relationship as a slave to Mrs. Joseph Cahell. In this case, as with thousands and tens of thousands of others, as the old adage fitly expresses it, "All is not gold that glitters." Under this apparently kind and noble-minded lady, it will be seen that Cordelia had known nothing but misery and sorrow.

Mrs. Cahell, having engaged board for a month at a fashionable private boardinghouse on Chestnut Street, took an early opportunity to caution Cordelia against going into the streets, and against having anything to say or do with "free [negroes] in particular." Furthermore, she appeared unusually kind, so much so, that before retiring to bed in the evening, she would call Cordelia to her chamber, and by her side would take her prayer book and

Bible, and go through the forms of devotional service. She stood very high both as a church communicant and a lady in society.

For about 10 days it seemed as though her prayers were to be answered, for Cordelia apparently bore herself as submissively as ever, and Madame received calls and accepted invitations from some of the elite of the city, without suspecting any intention on the part of Cordelia to escape. But Cordelia could not forget how her children had all been sold by her mistress!

Cordelia was about 57 years of age, with about an equal proportion of colored and white blood in her veins. She was very neat, respectful, and possessed good manners.

From her birth to the hour of her escape she had worn the yoke of slavery under Mrs. C., serving as her most efficient and reliable maid-servant. She had been at her mistress' beck and call as seamstress, dressing maid, nurse in the sickroom, etc., under circumstances that might appear to the casual observer uncommonly favorable for a slave. Indeed, on his first interview with her, the Committee representative was so forcibly impressed with the belief that her condition in Virginia had been favorable that he hesitated to ask her if she really wanted her liberty. A few moments' conversation with her, however, convinced him of her good sense and decision of purpose with regard to this matter.

In answer to the first question he put to her, she answered that "As many creature comforts and religious privileges as she had been the recipient of under her 'kind mistress,' still she 'wanted to be free' and 'was bound to leave.' In reality, she said, although she may have had physical comfort, she had suffered great mental pain; she had been 'treated very cruelly, her children had all been sold away' from her, and she had been threatened with sale herself 'on the first insult.'" She was willing to take the entire responsibility of taking care of herself. On the suggestion of a friend, before leaving her mistress, she was disposed to sue for her freedom, but upon a reconsideration of the matter, she chose rather to accept the hospitality of the Underground Railroad, and leave in a quiet way and go to Canada, where she would be free indeed. Accordingly she left her mistress and was soon a free woman.

The following sad experience she related calmly, in the presence of several friends, an evening or two after she left her mistress:

Two sons and two daughters had been sold from her by her mistress, within the last three years, since the death of her master. Three of her children had been sold to the Richmond market and the other in Nelson County.

Paulina was the first sold, two years ago last May. Nat was the next; he was sold to Abram Warrick, of Richmond. Paulina was sold before Cordelia had been told that it had entered her mistress's mind to dispose of the child. Nancy, from infancy, had been in poor health. Nevertheless, she had been obliged to take her place in the field with the rest of the slaves, of more rugged constitution, until she had passed her 20th year, and had become a mother. Under these circumstances, the overseer and his wife complained to the mistress that her health was really too bad for a field hand and begged that she might be taken where her duties would be less oppressive. Accordingly, she was withdrawn from the field, and was set to spinning and weaving. When too sick to work, her mistress invariably took the ground that "nothing was the matter," notwithstanding the fact that her family physician, Dr. Ellsom, had pronounced her "quite weakly and sick."

In an angry mood one day, Mrs. Cahell declared she would cure her and again sent her to the field "with orders to the overseer to whip her every day, and make her work or kill her." Again the overseer said it was "no use to try, for her health would not stand it," and she was forthwith returned. The mistress then concluded to sell her.

One Sunday evening a nephew of hers, who resided in New Orleans, happened to be on a visit to his aunt, when it occurred to her that she had "better get Nancy off if possible." Accordingly, Nancy was called in for examination. Being dressed in her "Sunday best" and "before a poor candlelight," she appeared to good advantage; and the nephew concluded to start with her on the following Tuesday morning. However, the next morning, he happened to see her by the light of the sun, and in her working garments, which satisfied him that he had been grossly deceived, that she would barely live to reach New Orleans. He positively refused to carry out the previous evening's contract, thus leaving her in the hands of her mistress, with the advice that she should "doctor her up."

The mistress, not to be defeated, got around the problem by selecting a little boy, made a lot of the two, and thus made it an inducement to a purchaser to buy the sick woman. Together, the boy and the woman brought $700.

In the sale of her children, Cordelia was as little regarded as if she had been a cow.

"I felt wretched," she said, with emphasis, "when I heard that Nancy had been sold," which was not until after she had been removed. "But," she continued, "I was not at liberty to make my grief known to a single white soul. I wept and couldn't help it." But remembering that she was liable, "on the first insult," to be sold herself, she sought no sympathy from her mistress, whom she described as "a woman who shows as little kindness towards her servants as any woman in the states of America. She neither likes to feed nor clothe them well."

Cordelia also had received "many a slap and blow" since she arrived at womanhood, directly from the madam's own hand.

One day, smarting under cruel treatment, she appealed to her mistress in the following strain: "I stood by your mother in all her sickness and nursed her till she died! I waited on your niece, night and day for months, till she died. I waited upon your husband all my life, in his sickness especially, and shrouded in death, etc., yet I am treated cruelly." The words had little impact on the old woman.

Her mistress, at one time, was the owner of about 500 slaves, but within the last few years she had greatly lessened the number by sales.

She stood very high as a lady, and was a member of the Episcopal Church.

To punish Cordelia, on several occasions, she had been sent to one of the plantations to work as a field hand. Fortunately, however, she found the overseers more compassionate than her mistress, though she received no particular favors from any of them.

Asking her to name the overseers, etc., she did so. The first was "Marks, a thin-visaged, poor-looking man, great for swearing." The second was "Gilbert Brower, a very rash, portly man." The third was "Buck Young, a stout man, and very sharp." The fourth was "Lynn Powell, a tall man with red whiskers, very contrary and spiteful." There was also a fifth one, but his name was lost.

Thus Cordelia's experience, though chiefly confined to the "great house," extended occasionally over the corn and tobacco fields, among the overseers and field hands generally. But under no circumstances could she find it in her heart to be thankful for the privileges of slavery.

After leaving her mistress she learned, with some pleasure, that a perplexed state of things existed at the boardinghouse; that her mistress was seriously puzzled to imagine how she would get her shoes and stockings on and off; how she would get her head combed, get dressed, be attended to in sickness, etc., as she (Cordelia) had been compelled to discharge these offices all her life.

Most of the boarders, being slaveholders, naturally sympathized in her affliction; and some of them went so far as to offer a reward to some of the colored servants to gain knowledge of Cordelia's whereabouts. Some charged the servants with having a hand in her leaving, but all agreed that "she had left a very kind and indulgent mistress" and had acted very foolishly in running out of slavery into freedom.

A certain doctor of divinity, the pastor of an Episcopal church in this city and a friend of the mistress, hearing of her distress, by request or voluntarily, undertook to find out Cordelia's hiding place. Hailing on the street a certain colored man with a familiar face, who he thought knew nearly all the colored people about town, he related to him the predicament of his lady friend from the South, remarked how kindly she had always treated her servants, signified that Cordelia would regret the change, and would be left to suffer among the "miserable blacks downtown," that she would not be able to take care of herself, quoted scripture justifying slavery, and finally suggested that he (the colored man) would be doing a duty and a kindness to the fugitive by using his influence to "find her and prevail upon her to return."

It so happened that the colored man thus addressed was Thomas Dorsey, the well-known fashionable caterer of Philadelphia, who had had the experience of quite a number of years as a slave of the South and had himself once been pursued as a fugitive. Having by his industry in the condition of freedom acquired a handsome estate, he felt entirely qualified to reply to the reverend gentleman, which he did, though in not very respectful phrases, that Cordelia had as good a right to her liberty as either he or her former mistress had; that God had never intended one man to be the slave of another; that it was all false about the slaves being better off than the free colored people; that he would find as many "poor, miserably degraded" of his own color "downtown," as among the "degraded blacks," and concluded by telling him that he would "rather give her a hundred dollars to help her off, than to do anything to make known her whereabouts, if he knew ever so much about her."

What further steps were taken by the discomfited divine, the mistress, or her boardinghouse sympathizers, the Committee was not informed.

But with regard to Cordelia, she took her departure for Canada, in the midst of the Daniel Webster (fugitive) trial, with the hope of being permitted to enjoy the remainder of her life in freedom and peace. Being a member of the Baptist Church, and professing to be a Christian, she was persuaded that, by industry and assistance of the Lord, a way would be opened to the seeker of freedom even in a strange land and among strangers.

Part of this story originally appeared in the *New York Evening Post*, having been contributed by the writer, but without his name then being attached to it.

CHAPTER 13

Robert Brown, alias Thomas Jones, Flees Slavery by Crossing a River on Horseback in the Night.

Being in very desperate straits, resolute slaves sought creative and often dangerous ways to achieve freedom at any cost. In reviewing the more perilous methods resorted to, Robert Brown, alias Thomas Jones, stands second to none, with regard to deeds of bold daring. This hero escaped from Martinsburg, Virginia in 1856. He was a man of medium size, racially mixed, about 38 years of age, could read and write, and was sharp-witted. He had formerly been owned by Col. John F. Franic, whom Robert charged with various offenses of a serious domestic character.

Furthermore, he also alleged that his "mistress was cruel to all the slaves," declaring that "they (the slaves) could not live with her," that "she had to hire servants," etc.

In order to make his escape, Robert swam the Potomac River on horseback on Christmas night, while the cold, wind, storm, and darkness surrounded him. This daring bondman, rather than submit to his oppressor any longer, risked his life for a chance to live free. Where he crossed, the river was about a half a mile wide.

His wife and four children, only five days before he fled, were sold to a trader in Richmond, Virginia for no other offense than simply "because she had resisted" the lustful designs of her master, being "true to her own companion." After this poor slave mother and her children were cast into prison for sale, the husband and some of his friends tried hard to find a purchaser in the neighborhood; but the master refused to sell them to anyone local, and wishing to punish his victims all that he could, he sent them to Richmond.

In this trying hour, the husband resolved to escape at all hazards, taking with him a daguerreotype likeness [photograph] of his wife which he happened to have, as well as a lock of hair from her head and from each of the children, as mementoes of his deep affection for them.

After crossing the river, his wet clothing freezing to him, he rode all night, a distance of about 40 miles. In the morning he left his faithful horse tied to a fence, quite broken down. He then commenced his dreary journey on foot, cold and hungry, in a strange place, where it was quite unsafe to make known his condition and needs. Thus for a day or two, without food or shelter, he traveled until his feet were literally worn out, and in this condition he finally reached Harrisburg, Pennsylvania where he found friends.

From Harrisburg, he was sent to Philadelphia, where he arrived safely on New Year's night, 1857, about two hours before day break. Advance word of his coming had been sent from Harrisburg by telegraph. The trip from Harrisburg to Philadelphia took a week via the Underground Railroad.

The night he arrived was very cold; and the Underground train that morning was about three hours behind schedule. While waiting for it out in the cold, a member of the Vigilance Committee of Philadelphia thought he had been frostbitten. But when he subsequently heard the story of the fugitive's sufferings, his mind changed.

Scarcely had Robert entered the house of one of the Committee members, where he was kindly received, when he took from his pocket his wife's likeness, speaking very touchingly while gazing upon it and showing it. Subsequently, in speaking of his family, he showed the locks of hair referred to, which he had separately rolled up in paper. Unrolling them, he said, "this is my wife's; this is from my oldest daughter, 11 years old; and this is from my next oldest; and this from the next; and this from my infant, only eight weeks old." These mementoes he cherished with the utmost care as the last remains of his affectionate family. At the sight of these locks of hair so tenderly preserved, the member of the Committee could fully appreciate the resolution of the fugitive to plunge into the Potomac and risk his own life to leave those who had caused him so much pain.

His wife, as represented by her photograph, was of fair complexion, attractive, and approximately 33 years of age.

CHAPTER 14

Barnaby Grigby, alias John Boyer, and Mary Elizabeth, His Wife; Frank Wanzer, alias Robert Scott; and Emily Foster, alias Ann Wood, Arrive by Horse and Carriage.

All these persons journeyed together from Loudon County, Virginia, two on horseback and four in a carriage for more than 100 miles. Taking advantage of a holiday and their master's horses and carriage, they started for Canada as though they had never been taught that it was their duty, as servants, to "obey their masters." In this respect, they showed total disregard for the interest of their "kindhearted and indulgent owners."

They left home on Monday, Christmas Eve, 1855, under the leadership of Frank Wanzer, and arrived in Columbia, Maryland the following Wednesday at one o'clock. As willfully as they had made their way along, they had not found it smooth sailing. The biting frost and snow rendered their travel anything but agreeable. Nor did they escape hunger, traveling day and night.

When about 100 miles from home, in the neighborhood of Cheat River, Maryland, they were attacked by "six white men, and a boy" who, doubtless, suspected that their intentions were of a "wicked and unlawful character." The whites took it upon themselves to demand of the travelers an account of themselves. In other words, the assailants positively commanded the fugitives to "show what right" they possessed, to be found in such pleasant condition.

The spokesman amongst the fugitives, assuming a posture of great dignity, told their assailants plainly that "no gentleman would interfere with persons riding along civilly." These "gentlemen," however, were not about to accept this response from the travelers. Having the law on their side, they were determined to force the fugitives to surrender without further discussion.

At this juncture, the fugitives believing that the time had arrived for the practical use of their pistols and knives, pulled them out of their concealment, the young women as well as the young men, and declared they would not be "taken!" One of the white men raised his gun, pointing the muzzle directly towards one of the young women, with the threat that he would shoot. "Shoot! Shoot!! Shoot!!!" she exclaimed, with a double-barreled pistol in one hand and a long knife in the other, utterly unterrified and fully ready for a death struggle. The male leader of the fugitives by this time had "pulled back the hammers" of his "pistols," and was about to fire! Their adversaries, seeing the weapons and the unflinching determination on the part of the travelers to stand their ground, "spill blood, kill, or die," rather than be taken, very prudently "sidled over to the other side of the road," leaving at least four of the victors to travel on their way.

At this moment the four in the carriage lost sight of the two on horseback. Soon after the separation they heard firing, but what the result was, they did not know. They were fearful, however, that their companions had been captured.

The following paragraph, which shortly thereafter appeared in a southern paper, leaves no doubt as to the fate of the two:

"Six fugitive slaves from Virginia were arrested at the Maryland line, near Hood's Mill, on Christmas Day, but, after a severe fight, four of them escaped and have not since been heard of. They came from Loudon and Fauquier Counties."

Though the four who were successful saw no "severe fight," it is not unreasonable to suppose that there was a fight, nevertheless; but not until after the number of the fugitives had been reduced to two, instead of six. As chivalrous as slaveholders and slave catchers were, they knew the value of their precious lives and the fearful risk of attempting a capture, when the numbers were equal.

The party in the carriage, after the conflict, went on their way rejoicing at their good fortune. The young men, one cold night, when they were compelled to take rest in the woods and snow, tried in vain to keep the feet of their female companions from freezing by lying on them; but the frost was merciless and bit them severely, as their feet later very plainly showed.

The following disjointed report was cut from the place:

"Six slaves, four men and two women, fugitives from Virginia, having with them two spring wagons and four horses, came to Hood's Mill, on the Baltimore and Ohio Railroad, near the dividing line between Frederick and Carroll Counties, on Christmas Day. After feeding their animals, one of them told a Mr. Dixon whence they came; believing them to be fugitives, he spread the alarm, and some eight or ten persons gathered round to arrest them; but the negroes drawing revolvers and bowie knives, kept their assailants at bay, until five of the party succeeded in escaping in one of the wagons, and as the last one jumped on a horse to flee, he was fired at, the load taking effect in the small of the back. The prisoner says he belongs to Charles W. Simpson, Esq., of Fauquier County, Virginia, and ran away with the others on the preceding evening."

This report from the ***Examiner***, while it is not wholly correct, provides some insight into the probable fate of one of the two fugitives on horseback.

Why the reporter made such glaring mistakes can only be attributed to the heightened bewilderment and alarm that the "assailants" experienced as a result of the bold defiance of the fugitives. Despite the errors in this report, it was preserved with other records.

These travelers and their previous conditions were individually described as follows: Barnaby was owned by William Rogers, a farmer, who was considered a "moderate slaveholder," although of late "addicted to intemperance." He was the owner of about one "dozen head of slaves," and had besides a wife and two children.

Barnaby's chances for making extra "change" for himself were never favorable; sometimes of "nights" he would manage to earn a "trifle." He was prompted to escape because he "wanted to live by the sweat of his own brow," believing that all men ought to live and benefit from their own toil. This was the only reason he gave for fleeing.

Mary Elizabeth, who was Barnaby's wife, had been owned by Townsend McVee (likewise a farmer), and in Mary's judgment, he was "severe," but she added, "his wife made him so." McVee owned about 25 slaves; "he hardly allowed them to talk, would not allow them to raise chickens" and "only allowed Mary three dresses a year;" the rest she had to get as she could. Sometimes McVee would sell slaves; last year he sold two. Mary said that she could not say anything good of her mistress. On the contrary, she declared that her mistress "knew no mercy nor showed any favor."

It was on account of this "domineering spirit" that Mary was determined to escape.

Frank was owned by Luther Sullivan, "the meanest man in Virginia," he said; he treated his people just as bad as he could in every respect. "Sullivan" added Frank, "would allowance the slaves and stint them to save food and get rich" and "would sell and whip," etc. To Frank's knowledge, his master had sold some 25 head. "He sold my mother and her two children to Georgia some four years previous." But the motive that caused Frank to make his flight was his belief and apprehension that his master had some "pretty heavy creditors who might come on him at any time." Frank, therefore, wanted to be in Canada when these gentry should make their visit. "My poor mother has been often flogged by the master," said Frank. As to his mistress, he said she was "tolerably good."

Emily Foster (subsequently known as Ann Wood) also was owned by McVee and was a sister of Elizabeth. Ann confirmed her sister Elizabeth's statement concerning the character of her master.

The four fugitives were all young and capable. Barnaby was 26 years of age, medium size, and intelligent, his wife was about 24 years of age, quite dark, good-looking, and of pleasant appearance. Frank was 25 years of age, racially mixed, and very smart; Ann was 22, good-looking, and smart.

After their pressing needs had been met by the Vigilance Committee, and after partial recuperation from their hard travel, etc., they were forwarded on to the Vigilance Committee in New York. In Syracuse, Frank (the leader), who was engaged to Ann Wood (Emily Foster), concluded that they should be married on the Underground Railroad, although penniless, rather than to delay the matter a single day longer. Thus, after consulting with her on the matter, the two were accordingly united in marriage at the U.G.R.R. Station in Syracuse, by the superintendent of the Railroad station, Rev. J.W. Loguen. After this joyful event, they proceeded to Toronto, and were gladly received there by the Ladies' Society for aiding colored refugees.

The following letter from Mrs. Agnes Willis, wife of the distinguished Rev.

Dr. Willis, brought the news:

"Toronto, 28 January, Monday evening, 1856
"Mr. Still, "Dear Sir:
"I have very great pleasure in making you aware that the following respectable persons have arrived here in safety without being annoyed in any way after you saw them. The women, two of them, viz: Mrs. Greegsby and Mrs. Graham, have been rather ailing, but we hope they will very soon be well. They have been attended to by the Ladies' Society, and are most grateful for any attention they have received. The solitary person, Mrs. Graves, has also been attended to; also her box will be looked after. She is pretty well, but rather dull; however, she will get friends and feel more at

home as time passes. Mrs. Wanzer is quite well; and also young William Henry Sanderson. They are all of them in pretty good spirits, and I have no doubt they will succeed in whatever business they take up. In the meantime the men are chopping wood, and the ladies are getting plenty of sewing done. We are always glad to see our colored refugees safe here. I remain, dear sir, yours respectfully,

"*Agnes Willis,*

"Treasurer to the Ladies' Society to aid colored refugees."

For a time Frank enjoyed his newly won freedom, happy bride, and bright prospects, but the thought of having left sisters and other relatives in bondage became a source of increasing sadness which tempered his joy. He soon made up his mind to deliver them from freedom or "die in the attempt."

Carefully forming his solitary plans to go South, he resolved to take upon himself the entire responsibility of all the risks to be encountered. He did not reveal a word about his plans to anyone else. With $22 in cash and "three pistols" in his pockets, he departed in the "lightning train" [express train] from Toronto for Virginia. On reaching Columbia, Maryland by this means, he felt it unsafe to go any further by public conveyance and consequently continued his long journey on foot.

As he neared the slave territory he traveled only by night. For two weeks, night and day, he avoided contact with anyone and consequently was compelled to seek shelter each night in the woods. Nevertheless, during this period of time he succeeded in rescuing one of his sisters and her husband, and another friend in the bargain. You can scarcely imagine the amazement of the Vigilance Committee of Philadelphia on his return, as they looked upon him and listened to his "noble deeds of daring" and his triumph. A more brave and satisfied man they had never seen.

He knew what slavery was and the dangers surrounding his mission, but possessing true courage, he foresaw no difficulty he would not dare to overcome. A person of less courage would have imagined, and with good reason, that "I could not pass without running the gauntlet of mobs and assassins, prisons and penitentiaries, bailiffs and constables, etc." That person would most assuredly have kept off the enemy's country, and his sister and friends would have remained in chains.

The following were the persons delivered by Frank Wanzer. Their freedom was his reward for this noble act, and living symbol of his courage and honor. The Committee's brief record made on their arrival reads as follows:

"18 August 1856. Frank Wanzer; Robert Stewart, alias Gasberry Robison; Vincent Smith, alias John Jackson; Betsey Smith, wife of Vincent Smith, alias Fanny Jackson. They all came from Alder, Loudon County, Virginia."

Robert is about 30 years of age, medium size, dark chestnut color, intelligent, and resolute. He was held by the widow Hutchinson, who was also the owner of about 100 others. Robert regarded her as a "very hard mistress" until the death of her husband, which took place the Fall prior to his escape. With the death of her husband came improved treatment of her slaves. But yet "nothing was said about freedom" on her part. Robert believed this silence indicated his owner was still committed to slavery. Since he could foresee no prospect of freedom through her generosity, when Frank approached him with a chance to escape to Canada and his friends there, he could scarcely wait. His dear old mother, Sarah Davis, and four brothers and two sisters, William, Thomas, Frederick, and Samuel, Violet, and Ellen, were all owned by Mrs. Hutchinson. Dear as they were to him, he saw no way to take them with him, nor was he prepared to remain a day longer under the yoke. He decided to accompany Frank, regardless of the risks involved.

Vincent is about 23 years of age, very "likely-looking," dark color, and possesses more than ordinary intelligence.

He was owned by the estate of Nathan Skinner, who was "looked upon" by those who knew him "as a good slaveholder." However, he only had 12 slaves, which he "neither sold nor emancipated." A year and a half before Vincent escaped, his master was called to give an account of his stewardship, and there in the spirit land Vincent was willing to let him remain, without much more to add about him. Vincent left his mother, Judah Smith, and brothers and sisters — Edwin, Angeline, Sina Ann, Adaline, Susan, George, John, and Lewis, all belonging to the estate of Skinner.

Vincent was fortunate enough to bring his wife along with him. She was about 17 years of age, of a brown color, and smart, and was owned by the daughter of the widow Hutchinson. This mistress was said to be a "clever woman."

CHAPTER 15

William Jordon, alias William Price, Escapes from North Carolina Governor Badger and Spends Ten Months in the Swamps before Finding His Way to the Underground Railroad.

Under Governor Badger of North Carolina, William had experienced slavery in its most hateful form. True, he had only been 12 months under the yoke of this man. But William's experience in this short period of time had been very painful.

Prior to coming into the governor's hands, William was held as the property of Mrs. Mary Jordon, who owned large numbers of slaves. Whether the governor was moved by this consideration, or by the fascinating charms of Mrs. Jordon, or both, William was not able to decide. But the governor offered her his hand, and they became united in marriage. By this circumstance, William was brought into his unhappy relations with the chief magistrate of the state of North Carolina. This was the third time the governor had been married. Generally, he was regarded as a man of wealth.

William, being an intelligent "piece of property," had a thorough knowledge of the governor's rules and customs, and he readily answered related questions that were addressed to him. In this way a great amount of interesting information was learned from William concerning the governor and slaves on the plantation, in the swamps, and so on.

The governor owned large plantations, and was interested in raising cotton, corn, and peas, and was also a practical planter. He was willing to trust neither overseers nor slaves any further than he could help.

The governor and his wife were both equally severe towards them and would deprive them shamefully of clothing and food, though they did not get flogged quite as often as some others on neighboring plantations. Frequently, the governor would be out on the plantation from early in the morning until noon, inspecting the operations of the overseers and slaves.

In order to serve the governor, William had been separated from his wife by sale, which was the reason for his escape. He parted with his companion unwillingly. At the time, however, he was promised that he would have some favors shown him; could work "overtime" and earn a little money on the side; and once or twice in the year would have the opportunity to visit his wife. Two hundred miles was the distance between them.

He had not been on the governor's plantation very long before the governor made it clear to him that the idea of his going 200 miles to see his wife was all nonsense, and entirely out of the question. "If I said so, I did not mean it," said his honor, when the slave, on a certain occasion, alluded to the conditions on which he "consented" to leave home, etc.

Against this cruel decision of the governor, William's heart revolted, for he was deeply attached to his wife, and so he made up his mind if he could not see her "once or twice a year even", as he had been promised, he would rather "die," or live in a "cave in the wood," than remain under the governor's yoke. Consequently, he went to the woods. For 10 months before he was successful in finding the Underground Railroad, this young fugitive lived in the swamps, three months in a cave, surrounded by bears, wild cats, rattlesnakes, and the like.

While in the swamps and cave, he was not troubled, however, about ferocious animals and venomous reptiles. He feared only man! From his own story there was no escaping the conclusion that if the choice had been left to him, he would have preferred at any time to have encountered at the mouth of his cave a ferocious bear than his master — the governor of North Carolina. How he managed to survive, and ultimately escape, was listened to with the deepest interest.

After night fell, he would come out of his cave, and, in some instances, would succeed in making his way to a plantation. If he could get nothing else, he would help himself to a pig, or anything else he could convert into food. Also, as opportunity would offer, a friend of his would provide him with some cornmeal and other supplies.

During these 10 months he suffered indescribable hardships, but he felt that his condition in the cave was far preferable to that on the plantation, under the control of the governor. All this time, however, William had a true friend with whom he could communicate, one who was very intent on finding a reliable captain from the North, who would consent to take this "property" for a consideration. At last the friend heard of a certain captain who was then doing quite a successful business in the Underground. This good news was conveyed to William, and afforded him a ray of hope in the wilderness.

William was not disappointed. He subsequently was brought away by Captain F. and turned over to the Committee, whose members rejoiced with him over his significant victory.

William was of a dark color, stout, and knew well the value of freedom, and how to hate and combat slavery. It will be seen by the following letter of Thomas Garrett that William had the good luck to fall into the hands of this trusted friend, who helped him reach Philadelphia:

———

"Wilmington, (Delaware) 12th month (December) 19th, 1855 "Dear Friend, William Still:

"The bearer of this [note] is one of the 21 [slaves who are heading] North; he left home on Christmas Day, one year since, wandered about the forests of North Carolina for about 10 months, and then came here with those forwarded to New Bedford, where he is anxious to go. I have furnished him with a pretty good pair of boots, and gave him money to pay his passage to Philadelphia. He has been at work in the country near here for some three weeks, until taken sick; he is by no means well, but thinks he had better try to get further north, which I hope his friends in Philadelphia will aid him to do. This morning I gave Captain Lambson's wife $20 to help [pay the] fee for a lawyer to defend him. [Captain Lambson had been suspected of having aided in the escape of slaves from the neighborhood of Norfolk, and was in prison awaiting his trial.] She leaves this morning, with her child, for

Norfolk, to be at the trial before the Commissioner on the 24th. Passmore Williamson agreed to raise $50 for him. As none came to hand, and a good chance to send it by his wife, I thought best to advance that much.

"Thy friend, *"Thomas Garrett."*

CHAPTER 16

Joseph Grant and John Speak, Who Arrived in Philadelphia from Mississippi via Liverpool.

It is to be regretted that the full account of these persons has not been fully preserved. Could justice be done them, no account in the history of fugitive slaves may have been more interesting or significant. However, in 1857, when these remarkable travelers came to the notice of the Vigilance Committee of Philadelphia, slavery still seemed likely to last for generations and there was little expectation that these accounts could ever be published or that they would have the historical value which they now possess. As a result, care was not always taken to prepare and preserve accounts. Furthermore, the cases coming to the notice of the Committee were so numerous and interesting that it seemed almost impossible to do them all justice. In many instances the rapt attention paid by friends, when listening to the sad accounts of these passengers, would consume so much time that little opportunity was left to make any record of them. [There also existed the concern that these accounts might fall into the wrong hands and be used against both the former slaves and the abolitionists who had helped them to freedom.]

The accounts of Joseph Grant and John Speak particularly consumed the attention and sympathy of members of the Committee. The story of each was so long and sad that a member of the Committee, in attempting to write it out, found that the two narratives would consume volumes. Since it was not possible to record them fully, a mere fragment of their adventures was recorded in order to insure that the experiences of these heroes would not be lost.

The original names of these adventurers were Joseph Grant and John Speaks. Between two and three years before escaping, they were sold from Maryland to John B. Campbell, a negro trader living in Baltimore, and then to Campbell's brother, another trader in New Orleans, and subsequently to Daniel McBeans and Mr. Henry, of Harrison County, Mississippi.

Both experienced nearly the same struggles and trials, and at times had belonged to the same masters. As a result, this account is confined primarily to the incidents in the career of Joseph. He was about 27 years of age, well-built, quite black, intelligent, and self-possessed in his manner. He was owned in Maryland by Mrs. Mary Gibson, who resided at St. Michael's on the Eastern Shore. She was a nice woman, he said, but her property was under mortgage and had to be sold, and he was in danger of sharing the same fate.

Joseph was a married man, and spoke tenderly of his wife. She promised him when he was sold that she would "never marry," and earnestly asked him, if he "ever met with the luck, to come and see her." She was unaware at that time of the great distance that was to divide them; his feelings on being thus separated need not be stated. However, he had scarcely been in Mississippi three weeks before his desire to return to his wife, and the place of his birth, made him attempt his escape. Accordingly he set off, and crossing a lake 80 miles wide in a small boat, he reached Kent Island. There he was captured by the watchman on the Island, who, with pistols, knife, and sword in hand, threatened if he resisted that death would be his instant fate. Of course, he was returned to his master.

He remained there a few months, but could content himself no longer to endure the ills of his condition. So he again started for home, walked to Mobile, and then succeeded in stowing himself away in a steamboat and was thus conveyed to Montgomery, Alabama, a distance of 550 miles through solid slave territory. Again he was captured and returned to his owners, one of whom always resorted to immediate punishment. On the whole, however, Joseph had been pretty fortunate, considering the magnitude of his offenses.

A third time he summoned courage and steered his course homewards towards Maryland, but as in the preceding attempts, he was again unsuccessful.

In this instance, Mr. Henry, the harsh owner, was exasperated, and concluded that nothing short of stern measures would cause Joe to reform. Said Mr. Henry, "I had rather lose my right arm than for him to get off without being punished, after having put us to so much trouble." Joseph will now speak for himself.

"He (master) sent the overseer to tie me. I told him I would not be tied. I ran and stayed away four days, which made Mr. Henry even more angry. Mr. Beans told the servants if they saw me, to tell me to come back and I should not be hurt. Thinking that Mr. Beans had always stood by his word, I was persuaded and came back. He sent for me in his parlor, talked the matter over, sent me to the steamboat (perhaps the one he tried to escape on). After getting cleverly on board the captain told me, I am sorry to tell you, you have to be tied. I was tied and Mr. Henry was sent for. He came. 'Well, I have got you at last, beg my pardon and promise me that you will never run away again and I will not be so hard on you.' I could not do it. He then gave me 300 lashes well laid on. I was stripped entirely naked, and my flesh was as raw as a piece of beef. He made John (the companion who escaped with him) hold one of my feet which I broke loose while being whipped, and when done made him bathe me in salt and water.

"Then I resolved to 'go or die' in the attempt. Before starting, one week later, I could not work. On getting better we went [escaped] to Ship Island; the sailors, who were Englishmen, were very sorry to hear of the treatment we had received, and counseled us [as to] how we might get free."

The advice was followed, and in due time they found themselves in Liverpool, England. There their stay was brief. Without money and education, and in a strange land, they very naturally wanted to return to their native land. Accordingly their host, the keeper of a sailor's boardinghouse, shipped them to Philadelphia.

Joseph saw many horrible things in New Orleans and Mississippi, among which were the following:

"I have seen Mr. Beans whip one of his slaves to death, at the tree to which he was tied. Mr. Henry would make them lie down across a log, stripped naked, and with every stroke would lay the flesh open. Being used to it, some would lie on the log without being tied.

"In New Orleans, I have seen women stretched out just as naked as my hand, on boxes, and given 150 lashes, with four men holding them. I have helped hold them myself — when released they could hardly sit or walk. This whipping was at the 'Fancy House.'"

The "chain gangs" he also saw in constant operation. Four and five slaves chained together and at work on the streets, cleaning, doing repair work, was a common sight. He could hardly tell Sunday from Monday in New Orleans, the slaves were kept so constantly at work.

CHAPTER 17

William Taylor Escapes from Richmond City

"One Hundred Dollars Reward.

"Ran away from Richmond City on Tuesday, the 2nd of June, a negro man named William N. Taylor, belonging to Mrs. Margaret Tyler of Hanover County. "Said negro was hired to Fitzhugh Mayo, Tobacconist, is quite black, of genteel and easy manners, about five feet ten or eleven inches high, has one front tooth broken, and is about 35 years old.

"He is supposed to have either made his escape north, or attempted to do so. The above reward will be paid for his delivery to Messrs. Hill and Rawlings, in Richmond, or secured in jail, so that I get him again.

"Jas. G. Tyler, Trustee for Margaret Tyler. "June 8th & etc.

"***Richmond Enquirer***, 9 June 1857"

William unquestionably possessed a good share of common sense, and enough dislike for slavery to convince him to seek his freedom.

The advertisement of James G. Tyler was not altogether accurate with regard to his description of William; but notwithstanding, in handing William down to posterity, the description of Tyler has been adopted instead of the one included in the records by the Vigilance Committee of Philadelphia. However, as a simple matter of fair play, it seems only fitting that the description given by William, while on the Underground Railroad, of his master, should be presented in William's words.

William acknowledged that he was the property of Walter H. Tyler, brother of ex-President Tyler, who was described as follows: "He (master) was about 65 years of age; was a barbarous man, very intemperate, horse-racer, chicken-cock fighter, and gambler. He had owned as high as 40 head of slaves, but he had gambled them all away. He was a doctor, circulated high among southerners, though he never lived agreeably with his wife, would curse her and call her all kinds of names that he should not call a lady. From a boy of nine up to the time I was fifteen or sixteen, I don't reckon he whipped me less than a hundred times. He shot at me once with a double-barreled gun."

William decided to leave "because I worked for him all my lifetime and he never gave me but $2.15 in all his life. I was hired out this year for $200, but when I would go to him to make complaints of hard treatment from the man I was hired to, he would say: '...don't come to me, all I want is my money.'

"Mr. Tyler was a thin raw-boned man, with a long nose, [and looked very much like] the president [his brother]. His wife was a tolerably well-disposed woman in some instances — she was a tall, thin-visaged woman, and stood high in the community. Through her I fell into the hands of Tyler. At present she owns about 50 slaves. His own slaves, spoken of as having been gambled away, came from his father [by inheritance] — he has been married the second time."

Twice William had been sold and bought back, on account of his master's creditors, and for many months had been expecting to be sold again, to meet pressing claims in the hands of the sheriff against Tyler. He, by the way, "now lives in Hanover County, about 18 miles from Richmond, and for fear of the sheriff, makes himself very scarce in that city."

At 14 years of age, William was sold for $800; in 1857 he probably would have brought about $1250; he was a member of the Baptist Church in good and regular standing.

CHAPTER 18

Jeremiah W. Smith and His Wife Julia Arrive from Richmond.

Richmond was a city noted for its activity and enterprise in slave trade. Several slave pens and prisons were constantly kept up to accommodate the trade. And slave auctions were as common in Richmond as dress goods auctions in Philadelphia. Nevertheless, the Underground Railroad brought away large numbers of passengers from Richmond, Petersburg, and Norfolk, many of whom had lived very close to the auction block.

Many of the potential fugitives from these localities were among the most intelligent and "respectable" slaves in the South. Except at times when disheartened by some grave disaster which had befallen the Underground Railroad, as, for instance, when some friendly captain or conductor was discovered and arrested, many of the "thinking slaves" were daily maneuvering and watching for opportunities to escape or aid their friends to do so.

This state of affairs, of course, caused great consternation to the white Virginians. They had preached long and loudly about the contented and happy condition of the slaves — that the chief end of the black man was to worship and serve the white man, with joy and delight, with more willingness and obedience indeed than he would be expected to serve God. So the slaveholders were utterly at a loss to explain the unnatural desire on the part of the slaves to escape to the North where they affirmed they would be far less happy in freedom than in the hands of those so "kind and indulgent towards them."

Despite all this, particularly the more intelligent slaves increasingly distrusted the statements of their masters, especially when they spoke against the North. For instance, if the master was heard to curse Boston, the slave was then convinced that Boston was just the place he would like to go to; or if the master told the slave that the blacks in Canada were freezing and starving to death by the hundreds, his hope of trying to reach Canada and having an opportunity to confront all the risks of starving and freezing grew tenfold stronger. His desire and determination to find a conductor then would become almost painful.

Compared to many slaves, the situations of Jeremiah and Julia Smith were not considered very harsh. They had fared rather better than most slaves in Virginia. Nevertheless, they desired to better their condition, to keep off of the auction block. Jeremiah could claim to have no mixture in his blood, as his color was of such a pure black. He was also shrewd and intelligent. He was about 26 years of age, of medium height, and poor health.

He described his master, James Kinnard, as a "close and severe man." At the same time he was not considered by the community "a hard man." From 15 years of age, Jeremiah had been hired out, for which his owner had received from $50 to $130 per year. His master's practice of hiring Jeremiah to others made it possible for the master to avoid doctors' bills and other expenses. For the last two years prior to his escape, Jeremiah's health had been very tenuous. As a result, the master had been compelled to accept only $50 a year for his services, sick or well. Jeremiah learned that he was to be transferred to his master's farm, with the hope that he could be made more profitable there than he was in being hired out.

His owner had tried to sell him once, perhaps fearing that Jeremiah would otherwise die on his hands. So he was placed in prison and advertised; but Jeremiah had problems with asthma at that time, and no one would buy him.

While these troubles were presenting themselves to Jeremiah, Julia, his wife, was experiencing even more severe problems.

Julia was of a dark brown color, of medium size, and 30 years of age. For 14 years she had been the slave of A. Judson Crane, and under him she had performed the duties of nurse, chambermaid, and so on, "faithfully and satisfactorily," as a certificate furnished her by this owner witnessed. Her master had experienced business failure, and Julia had been given the certificate to help convince others to buy her.

Mrs. Crane, her mistress, had always promised Julia that she should be free at her death. However, as Mrs. Crane was on her journey home from Cape May, where she had been for her health, she died suddenly in Philadelphia; but Julia was not given her freedom. Twice before her mistress' death, she had been sold: once to the trader, Reed, and afterwards to John Freeland,

and again was on the verge of being sold. Freeland, her last owner, thought she was unhappy because she was denied the privilege of going home at night to her husband, but she was nevertheless compelled to be on hand at the beck and call of her master and mistress day and night. So the very day Julia and her husband escaped, arrangements had been made to put her up at auction a third time.

But both Julia and her husband had seen enough of slavery to leave no room to hope that they could ever find peace or rest so long as they remained in bondage. There and then, they resolved to strike out for Canada via the Underground Railroad. By a little good management, berths were obtained for them on one of the Richmond steamers (berths not known to the officers of the boat), and they were safely landed in the hands of the Vigilance Committee of Philadelphia.

The Committee extended to them the usual hospitality in the way of board, accommodations, and free tickets to Canada, and wished them a safe and speedy passage. The passengers departed, exceedingly lighthearted on 1 February 1854.

CHAPTER 19

Charles Thompson, Carrier of the *National American*, Arrives with a Pass.

The following "pass" was brought to the Underground Railroad station in Philadelphia by Charles, and while it relates directly to his escape, it is important also as a specimen of the way the "pass" system was carried on in the dark days of slavery in Virginia:

"Nat. American Office, "Richmond, 20 July 1857

"Permit Charles to pass and repass from this office to the residence of Rev. B. Manly's on Clay St., near 11th, at any hour of the night for one month.

"Wm. W. Hardwick."

It is a very short document, but it used to be very unsafe for a slave in Richmond, or any other southern city, to be found out in the evening without a legal paper of this description. The penalties for being found unprepared to face the police were fines, imprisonment, and floggings. The guardians of the city seemed to obtain great satisfaction in finding either males or females trespassing without a document. It gave them (the police) the opportunity to prove to those they served (the slaveholders) that they were the right men in the right place, guarding their interests. Then again they profited from the fine, keeping it for pocket money. And, likewise, there was always the pleasure of administering the flogging.

But Charles was too alert to be caught without his pass day or night. Consequently he hung onto it, even after starting on his voyage to Canada. He, however, willingly gave it to a member of the Vigilance Committee of Philadelphia at his special request.

In every way, Charles was quite a remarkable man. It gave the Committee great pleasure to meet and assist him, and much practical and useful information was gathered from his story, which was felt to be truthful.

The Committee, feeling assured that this "chattel" must have been the subject of much inquiry and anxiety from the nature of his former position, as a prominent piece of property, as a member of the Baptist Church, as taking "first premiums" in making tobacco, and as a paper carrier in the ***National American*** office, felt called upon to note fully his movements before and after leaving Richmond.

In stature, he was of medium height, was quite dark in color, and had long, bushy hair. He was rather raw-boned and rugged in appearance, though modest and dignified. And he was very intelligent. On his arrival in Philadelphia, even before he had changed the clothing in which he had escaped, a member of the Vigilance Committee remarked to him, with pencil in hand, that he wanted to take down some account of his life.

"Now," said the member of the Committee, "we shall have to be brief. Please answer as correctly as you can the following questions: How old are you?"

"Thirty-two years old the 1st day of last June." "Were you born a slave?"

"Yes."

"How have you been treated?"

"Badly all the time for the last 12 years." "What do you mean by being treated badly?"

"Have been whipped, and they never give me anything; some people give their servants at Christmas a dollar and a half and two dollars, and some five, but my master would never give me anything."

"What was the name of your master?" "Fleming Bibbs."

"Where did he live?"

"In Caroline County, 50 miles above Richmond." "What did he do?"

"He was a farmer."

"Did you ever live with him?"

"Never did; always hired me out, and then I couldn't please him." "What kind of a man was he?"

"A man with a very severe temper; would drink at all times, though [he] would do it slyly."

"Was he a member of any church?"

"Baptist Church, would curse at his servants as if he weren't in any church." "Were his family members of church, too?"

"Yes."

"What kind of family had he?"

"His wife was a tolerable fair woman, but his sons were dissipated, all of them rowdies and gamblers. His sons had children by the servants. One of his daughters had a child by his grandson last April. They are traders, buy and sell."

"How many slaves did he own?"

"Sam, Richmond, Henry, Dennis, Jesse, Addison, Hilliard, Jenny, Lucius, Julia, Charlotte, Easte, Joe, Taylor, Louisa, two more small children, and Jim."

"Did any of them know that you were going to leave?"

"No. I saw my brother Tuesday, but never told him a word about it."
"What put it into your head to leave?"

"It was bad treatment; for being put in jail for sale the 7th of last January; was whipped in jail and after I came out the only thing they told me was that I had been selling newspapers about the streets, and was half free."

"Where did you live then?"

"In Richmond, Virginia; for 22 years I have been living out." "How much did your master receive a year for your hire?" "From $65 to $150."

"Did you have to find [work] yourself?"

"The people who hired me found me. The general rule is in Richmond, for a week's board, 75 cents is allowed; if he gets any more than that [the slave] has to find work himself."

"How about Sunday clothing?" "Find them yourself."

"How about a house to live in?" "Have that to find [for] yourself." "Suppose you have a wife and family."

"It makes no difference, they don't allow you anything for that at all." "Suppose you are sick. Who pays your doctor's bill?"

"He (master) pays that."

"How do you manage to make a little extra money?"

"By getting up before day and carrying out papers and doing other jobs, cleaning up single men's rooms and the like of that."

"What have you been employed at in Richmond?"

"Been working in tobacco factory in general; this year I was hired at a printing office, the *National American*. I carried papers."

"Had you a wife?"

"I did, but her master was a very bad man and was opposed to me, and was against my coming to his place to see my wife, and he persuaded her to take another husband in preference to me. Being in his hands she took his advice."

"How long ago was that?"

"Very near 12 months; she got married last fall." "Had you any children?"

"Yes."

"How many?" "Five."

"Where are they?"

"Three are with Joel Luck, her master; one with his sister Eliza; and the other belongs to Judge Hudgins, of Bowling Green Courthouse."

"Do you ever expect to see them again?" "No, not in my lifetime!"

"Did you ever have any chance of schooling?" "Not a day in my life."

"Can you read?"

"No, sir, nor write my own name." "What do you think of slavery?"

"I think it's a great curse, and I think the Baptists in Richmond will go to the deepest hell, if there is any, for they are so wicked they will work you all day and part of the night, and wear cloaks and long faces, and try to get all the work out of you they can by telling you about Jesus Christ. All the extra money you make they think you will give to hear talk about Jesus Christ. Out of their extra money they have to pay a white man $500 a year for preaching."

"What kind of preaching does he give them?"

"He tells them if they die in their sins they will go to hell; don't tell them anything about their elevation; he would tell [the slaves] to obey their masters and mistresses, for good servants make good masters."

"Did you belong to the Baptist Church?" "Yes, Second Baptist Church."

"Did you feel that the preaching you heard was the true Gospel?"

"One part of it, and one part burnt me as bad as ever insult did. They would tell us that we must take money out of our pockets to send it to Africa, to enlighten the African race. I think that we were about as blind in Richmond as the African race is in Africa. All they want you to have is sense enough to say master and mistress, and run like lightning when they speak to you, to do exactly what they want you to do."

"When you made up your mind to escape, where did you think you would go to?"

"I made up my mind not to stop short of the British protection; to shake hands with the Lion's paw."

"Were you not afraid of being captured on the way, of being devoured by the abolitionists, or of freezing and starving in Canada?"

"Well, I had often thought that I would be in a bad condition to come here, without money and clothes, but I made up my mind to come, live or die."

"What are your impressions from what little you have seen of freedom?"
"I think it is intended for all men, and all men ought to have it."

"Suppose your master was to appear before you, and offer you the privilege of returning to slavery or face death on the spot, which would be your choice?"

"Die right there. I made up my mind before I started."

"Do you think that many of the slaves are anxious about their freedom?"
"The third part of them ain't anxious about it, because the white people have blinded them, telling about the North, they can't live here; telling them that the people are worse off there than they are here; they say that the 'niggers' in the North have no houses to live in, stand about freezing, dirty, no clothes to wear. They all would be very glad to get their time [freedom], but want to stay where they are."

Just at this point of the interview, the hour of midnight reminded us that it was time for bed. Accordingly, Mr. Thompson said, "I guess we had better close," adding, "if I could only write, I could give seven volumes!" Also, he said, "give my best respects to Mr. W.W. Hardwicke and Mr. Perry in the *National American* office, and ask them to pay the two boys who carry the papers for me, for they are as ignorant of this matter as you are."

Charles was duly forwarded to Canada and from the accounts which came from him to the Committee, he was very pleased with his new life. The following letter shows that in freedom, Charles did not forget either his God or his friends:

"Detroit, 17 September 1862 "Dear Brother in Christ:

"It affords me the greatest pleasure imaginable in the time I shall occupy in penning these few lines to you and your dear loving wife; not because I can write them to you myself, but for the love and regard I have for you, for I never can forget a man who will show kindness to his neighbor when in distress. I remember when I was in distress and out of doors, you took me in; I was hungry, and you fed me; for these things God will reward you, dear brother. I am getting along as well as I can expect. Since I have been out here, I have endeavored to make every day tell for itself, and I can say, no doubt, what a great many men cannot say, that I have made good use of all the time that God has given me, and not one week has been spent in idleness. Brother William, I expect to visit you some time next summer to sit and have a talk with you and Mrs. Still. I hope to see that time, if it is God's will. You will remember me, with my wife, to Mrs. Still. Give my best respects to all inquiring friends, and believe me to be yours forever. Well wishes both soul and body. Please write to me sometimes.

"*C.W. Thompson.*"

CHAPTER 20

Abram Galloway and Richard Eden Arrive on a Vessel Loaded with Turpentine.

The Philadelphia branch of the Underground Railroad was not fortunate in having frequent arrivals from North Carolina. The portion of the North Carolina slave population that managed to become initiated in the mysteries of traveling north by the Underground Railroad were sensible enough to find nearer destinations and safer routes than through Pennsylvania. Nevertheless, the Vigilance Committee of Philadelphia occasionally had the pleasure of receiving some heroes from North Carolina who were worthy to be classed among the bravest of the brave.

In proof of this statement, Abram Galloway and Richard Eden are presented. Abram was only 21 years of age, racially mixed, five feet six inches tall, intelligent, and the picture of good health.

"What was your master's name?" asked a member of the Committee. "Milton Hawkins," answered Abram.

"What business did Milton Hawkins follow?" asked the same member.

"He was chief engineer on the Wilmington and Manchester Railroad" (not a branch of the Underground Railroad), responded Richard.

"Describe him," said the member.

"He was a slim-built, tall man with whiskers. He was a man of very good disposition. I always belonged to him; he owned three [slaves]. He always said he would sell before he would use a whip. His wife was a very mean woman; she would whip contrary to his orders."

"Who was your father?"

"John Wesley Galloway," was the prompt response. "Describe your father."

"He was captain of a government vessel; he recognized me as his son, and protected me as far as he was allowed to do so; he lived at Smithfield, North Carolina."

Abram's master, Milton Hawkins, lived at Wilmington, North Carolina. "What prompted you to escape?" he was next asked.

"Because times were hard and I could not come up with my wages as I was required to do, so I thought I would try and do better."

At this juncture Abram explained what he meant by hard times. In the first place he was not allowed to own himself. However, he preferred hiring his time to serving in the usual way. This favor was granted Abram; but he was compelled to pay his master $15 per month for his time, and in addition earn enough to keep himself in clothing, food, pay doctor bills and a head tax of $15 a year, and cover other needs.

Even under this master, who was a man of very good disposition, Abram was not contented. In the second place, he "always thought slavery was wrong," although he had "never suffered any personal abuse." Toiling month after month the year round to support his master and not himself was the one intolerable thought that was always with him.

Abram and Richard were close friends, and lived near each other. Being in similar circumstances, they could share their secret thoughts with each other. Richard was four years older than Abram, with not quite so much Anglo-Saxon blood in his veins, but was equally as intelligent, and was by trade, a "fashionable barber" who was well known to the ladies and gentlemen of Wilmington.

Richard owed service to Mrs. Mary Loren, a widow. "She was very kind and tender to all her slaves. If I was sick," said Richard, "she would treat me the same as a mother would." She was the owner of 20 men, women, and children, who were all hired out, except the children too young for hire. Besides having his food, clothing, and doctor's expenses to meet, he had to pay the "very kind and tender-hearted widow" $12.50 per month, and the head tax to the state, amounting to 25 cents per month.

At this time, Richard was in legal trouble. Contrary to the laws of North Carolina, he had married a free girl. This was an indictable offense, for which the penalty was 39 lashes and imprisonment at the discretion of the judge.

So Abram and Richard decided to try the Underground Railroad. They concluded that liberty was worth dying for, and that it was their duty to strike for freedom even if it should cost them their lives. The next challenge was to find the Underground Railroad. Soon a schooner turned up, which had come from Wilmington, Delaware. Learning that the ports-of-call of this schooner included Philadelphia, they sought to find out whether this captain was "true to freedom." To determine this fact required tact. It had to be done in such a way that even the captain would not really understand what they were up to — if he was not part of the Underground Railroad. In this instance, however, he was the right man in the right place, and very well understood his business, and what they wanted.

Abram and Richard made arrangements with him to bring them away. They learned when the vessel would depart, and that she was loaded with tar, rosin, and spirits of turpentine, among which the captain would hide them.

But a difficulty presented itself. In order that slaves might not be hidden in vessels, the slaveholders of North Carolina had passed a law requiring all vessels going north to be "smoked" [fumigated]. To escape this dilemma the inventive genius of Abram and Richard soon devised a safeguard against the smoke. This safeguard consisted of large silk oilcloth shrouds with drawstrings, which, when pulled over their heads, might be drawn very tightly around their waists while the process of "smoking" was taking place. Additionally, a bladder of water and towels were provided, the latter to be wet and held over their noses to filter the air if they needed more air than held within the silk oilcloth shrouds. In this manner they were determined to defy death in their quest for liberty.

The hour approached for being at the wharf. At the appointed time they were on hand ready to go on the boat; and the captain hid them, according to agreement. They were ready to run the risk of being smoked to death; but as good luck would have it, the law was not carried into effect in this instance, so that the "smell of smoke was not upon them." The effect of the turpentine, however, turned out to be much worse than the smoke would have been. But, as heroes of the bravest type, they continued steadfast in their hiding places, and thus they finally gained their freedom.

The invigorating northern air and the good treatment of the Vigilance Committee helped them recover from their ordeal. Wishing to retain a more complete record of their experiences, a member of the Committee requested one of their silk shrouds and also arranged to have a photograph taken of one of them; and these keepsakes have been valued very highly. According to normal procedures, the needs of Abram and Richard were duly met by the Committee, financially and otherwise, and they were forwarded to Canada. After their safe arrival in Canada, Richard sent the following letter to a member of the Committee:

"Kingston, 20 July 1857 "Mr. William Still, "Dear Friend:

"I take the opportunity of writing a few lines to let you know that we are all in good health and hoping these few lines may find you and your family enjoying the same blessing. We arrived in Kingston safely. Abram Galloway goes to work this morning at $1.75 per day and John Pettifoot is at work for Mr. George Mink and I will open a shop for myself in a few days. My wife will send a daguerreotype [photograph] to your care which you will please send on to me, Richard Edons, to the care of George Mink, Kingston, C.W.

"Yours with Respect, *"Richard Edons."*

Abram, Richard's friend, worked faithfully for John Bull until the Civil War. When that war commenced, Abram returned to North Carolina to help fight the battles of freedom. How well he served, we are not informed. We only know that after the war was over, in the reconstruction of North Carolina, Abram became a member of the state senate. However, he died in office only a few months later.

CHAPTER 21

John Pettifoot Escapes on a Steamer, Hidden Among Pots and Pans.

Mr. Pettifoot had about half African and half Anglo-Saxon blood. His education, with regard to books, was quite limited. He had, however, managed to learn to read and write to some extent. John was to all intents and purposes a rebel at heart and, because of this, he resolved to take a trip on the Underground Railroad to Canada.

Greatly to the surprise of those he was serving, one morning he was called for, but in vain. No one could tell what had become of John — no more than if he had vanished like a ghost. There is no doubt that Messrs. McHenry and McCulloch were under the impression that newspapers and money possessed great power and could, under the circumstances, be used with unfailing effect. The following advertisement is evidence that John was much needed at the tobacco factory.

"One Hundred Dollar Reward:

"For the apprehension and delivery to us of a mulatto man, named John Massenberg, or John Henry Pettifoot, who has been passing as free under the name of Sydney. He is about five feet six or eight inches high, spare-made, bright, with a bushy head of hair, curled under, and a small moustache. Absconded a few days ago from our tobacco factory.

"McHenry & McCulloch."

John was aware that a reward of this kind would most likely be made for him, and that the large quantity of Anglo-Saxon blood in his veins would not save him. He was aware, too, that he was the reputed son of a white gentleman, who was a professional dentist, by the name of Dr. Peter Cards. The doctor, however, had died, so John could see no hope or virtue in having a white father, although a "chivalric gentleman" and a man of high standing among slaveholders while living. John was a member of the Baptist Church too, and hoped he was a good Christian; but he could look for no favors from the church or sympathy on the score of his being a Christian. He knew very well were it known that he had the love of freedom in his heart, or the idea of the Underground Railroad in his head, he would be regarded as having committed the "unpardonable sin."

So John looked to none of these "broken reeds" in Richmond in the hour of his trial, but to God above, whom he had not seen, and to the Underground Railroad, which he hadn't seen either. He nevertheless felt that if God would aid him and he could get a conductor to put him on the right road to Canada, he would be all right.

John Henry Pettifoot, in general, had been "used very well," and had no fault to find, except this year, being hired to McHenry & McCulloch, tobacconists, of Petersburg, Virginia, whom he found rather more oppressive than he agreed for. Feeling that he had "no right" to work for anybody for nothing, he "picked up his bed and walked." His mistress had told him that he was "willed free" at her death, but John was not willing to wait for her "notions to die."

He had a wife in Richmond, but was not allowed to visit her. He left one sister and a stepfather in bondage. Mr. Pettifoot reached Philadelphia by the Richmond line of steamers, stowed away among the pots and cooking utensils. On reaching the city, he at once surrendered himself into the hands of the Vigilance Committee of Philadelphia, and was helped along the U.G.R.R. line by the regular members.

CHAPTER 22

Emanuel T. White Escapes on a Steamer.

Emanuel was about 25 years of age, with seven-eighths white blood in his veins, of medium height, and a very smart and valuable piece of property generally. He had been owned by Aldridge Mandrey, who he described as a "very cruel man", who would "rather fight than eat." "I have licks that will carry me to my grave, and will be there till the flesh rots off my bones," said Emanuel, adding that his master was a "devil," though a member of the Reformed Methodist Church. But his mistress, he said, was a "right nice little woman, and kept many licks off me." "If you said you were sick, he would whip it out of you." Emanuel once tried to escape from Mandrey, and was gone two months, but was captured at Williamsburg, Virginia. He received a severe flogging, and was carried home.

Mandrey then sold Emanuel to Edward H. Hubbert, a ship timber merchant in Norfolk, Virginia. He was under Hubbert's yoke for only five years when Hubbert finally sold Emanuel to a Mr. Grigway of Norfolk. With Emanuel, Mr. G. was pretty well-suited, but his wife was not, he had "too much white blood in him" for her. Grigway and his wife were members of the Episcopal Church.

In this unhappy condition Emanuel found a conductor of the Underground Railroad. A secret passage was secured for him on one of the Richmond steamers, and thus he escaped from his servitude.

The Vigilance Committee of Philadelphia helped him with his needs, and forwarded him on as usual. From Syracuse, where he was breathing quite freely under the protection of the Rev. J.W. Loguen, he wrote the following letter:

"Syracuse, 29 July 1857 "My Dear Friend, Mr. Still:

"I got safe through to Syracuse, and found the house of our friend, Mr. J.W. Loguen. Many thanks to you for your kindness to me. I wish to say to you, dear sir, that I expect my clothes will be sent to Dr. Landa, and I wish, if you please, get them and send them to the care of Mr. Loguen, at Syracuse, for me. He will be in possession of my whereabouts and will send them to me. Remember me to Mr. Landa and Miss Millen Jespan, and much to you and your family.

"Truly Yours, "*Manual T. White.*"

CHAPTER 23

Emeline Chapman, a Young Slave Mother, Flees Slavery,
Leaving Her Young Children Behind —
A Case Intertwined with that of Arrah Weems.

Emeline Chapman arrived by the Underground Railroad from Washington, D.C., after leaving her family behind, and adopting the name of Susan Bell.

Thus for freedom she was willing to forego her name, her husband, and even her little children. It was a serious sacrifice, but she had been threatened with the auction block, and she well understood what that meant. She left her owner, Emily Thompson of Capitol Hill, Washington, D.C., on 30 August 1856. Thompson immediately offered a $300 reward for her capture and return.

Susan Bell had been hired out. Having lived away from her owner, Emeline did not complain of any very hard times. True, she had been kept at work very constantly, and her owner had very faithfully received all her wages. Emeline had not even been allowed enough of her wages to pay for her own clothing, nor was anything left for the support of her two children. Her kind mistress allowed her to seek help elsewhere, as best she could.

Emeline's husband was named John Henry, her little girl she called Margaret Ann, and her infant boy she had named after his father — all were held by slave owners. The love of freedom, in the breast of this spirited young wife and mother, did not extinguish the love she bore to her husband and children, despite what her leaving them might appear to suggest. For it was just this kind of heroic and self-sacrificing struggle that appealed to the hearts of men and compelled attention. Indeed, who could close his eyes and ears to the plaintive cries of such a mother? Who could refrain from providing aid to help free the children of such a heroic parent?

Letter from Susan Bell

"Syracuse, 5 October 1856 "Dear Friend Still:

"I write to you for Mrs. Susan Bell, who was at your city sometime in September last. She is from Washington City. She left her dear little children behind (two children). She is stopping in our city, and wants to hear from her children very much indeed. She wishes to know if you have heard from Mr. Biglow, of Washington City. She will remain here until she can hear from you. She feels very anxious about her children, I will assure you. I should have written before this, but I have been from home much of the time since she came to our city. She wants to know if Mr. Biglow has heard anything about her husband. If you have not written to Mr. Biglow, she wishes you would. She sends her love to you and your dear family. She says that you were all kind to her and she does not forget it. You will direct your letter to me, dear brother, and I will see that she gets it.

"Miss F.E. Watkins left our house yesterday for Ithaca, and other places in that part of the state. Frederick Douglass, Wm. J. Watkins, and others were with us last week; Gerritt Smith with others. Miss Watkins is doing great good in our part of the state. We think much indeed of her. She is such a good and glorious speaker that we are all charmed with her. We have had 31 fugitives in the last 27 days; but you, no doubt, have had many more than that. I hope the good Lord may bless you and spare you long to do good to the hunted and outraged among our brethren.

"Yours truly, "*J.W. Loguen,*

"Agent of the Underground Railroad."

Susan was transported to Syracuse, New York, where she worked and waited for her children to be brought to her. The following brief memorandum was found among the records of the Underground Railroad, dated July 1857:

"A little child of 14 months old was conveyed to its mother, who had been compelled to flee without it nearly 9 months ago."

While the circumstances connected with the coming of this slave child were deeply interesting, no details other than the simple notice above were at that time recorded. Fortunately, however, letters from the good friends who plucked this infant from the jaws of slavery, have been preserved to throw light on this little one, and to show how true-hearted sympathizers with the slave labored amid dangers and difficulties to save the helpless bondman from oppression. It will be observed, that both these friends wrote from Washington, D.C., the seat of the government, where, if slavery was not seen in its worst aspects, the government, in its support of slavery, appeared in a most revolting light.

First Letter

"Washington, D.C., "12 July 1857

"Dear Sir:

"Some of our citizens, I am told, lately left here for Philadelphia, three of whom were arrested and brought back.

"I beg you will inform me whether two others, (one of whom has a wife in Philadelphia), ever reached your city.

"Tomorrow morning Mrs. Weems, with her baby, will start for Philadelphia and see you probably overnight.

"Yours Truly. "*J.B.*"

"J.B." was a trusted and capable conductor of the Underground Railroad in Washington, but was also a practical lawyer at the same time. His lawyer-like letter, in view of the critical nature of the case, contained few words, and those few naturally enough were subject to more than one interpretation.

Doubtless the references to "our citizens" and "three of whom were arrested and brought back" were causing great anxiety to this correspondent, not knowing how soon he might find himself implicated in the "running off," etc. So, while he felt it to be his duty to still aid the child, he was determined, if the enemy intercepted his letter, the enemy would not find much comfort or information. The cause was safe in such careful hands.

The following letters, bearing on the same case, are from another good conductor, who was then living in Washington.

Second Letter

"Washington, D.C. "8 July 1857

"My Dear Sir,

"I write you now to let you know that the children of E. [Emeline Chapman/Susan Bell] are yet well, and that Mrs. Arrah Weems will start with one of them for Philadelphia tomorrow or [the] next day. She will be with you probably in the day train.

"Arrah Weems goes for the purpose of making an effort to redeem her last child, now in slavery. The whole amount necessary is raised, except about $300. She will take her credentials with her, and you can place the most implicit reliance on her statements. The story in regard to the Weems family was published in Frederick Douglass' paper two years ago. Since then the two middle boys have been redeemed and there is only one left in slavery, and he is in Alabama. The master has agreed to take for him just what he gave, $1100. Mr. Lewis Tappan has his [the slave owner's] letter and [the money that has been raised], but not the full amount specified. About $5000 was raised in England to redeem this family, and they are now all free except this one. And there never was a more excellent and worthy family than the Weems family. I do hope that Mrs. W. will find friends who can advance the amount required [to free her third child].

"Truly Yours, "E.L. Stevens

Third Letter

"Washington, D.C. "13 July 1857

"My Friend,

"Your kind letter in reply to mine about Arrah was duly received. As she is doubtless with you before this, she will explain all. I propose that a second journey be made by her or someone else, in order to take the other. They have been a great burden to the good folks here and should have been at home long before this. Arrah will explain everything. I want, however, to say a word in her behalf. If there is a person in the world that deserves the hearty cooperation of every friend of humanity that person is Arrah Weems, who now, after a long series of self-sacrificing labor to aid others in their struggle for their God-given rights, solicits a small amount to redeem the last one of her own children in slavery. Never have I had my sympathies so aroused in behalf of any object as in behalf of this most worthy family. She can tell you what I have done. And I do hope that our friends in Philadelphia and New York will assist her to make up the full amount required for the purchase of the boy.

"After she does what she can in P., will you give her the proper direction about getting to New York and to Mr. Tappan's? Inform him of what she has done, etc. "Please write me as soon as you can as to whether she arrived safely, etc. Give me your opinion, also, as to the proposal about the other. Had you not better keep the little one in P. till the other is taken there? Inform me also where E. is, how she is getting along, etc., who she is living with, etc. "Yours Truly,

"E.L.S."

In this instance, as in the case of "J.B.," the care and anxiety for other persons, besides this child, crying for deliverance, weighed heavily on the mind of Mr. Stevens, as may be concluded from certain references in his letters. Mr. Stevens' love of humanity and freedom for all, even in those dark days of slavery, when it was both unpopular and unsafe to allow the cries of the bondman to awaken the feeling of humanity to assist the suffering, was constantly leading him to take sides with the oppressed. As revealed in this correspondence, it was his constant desire to aid the helpless, who were all around him.

Arrah Weems, who had Susan Bell's child in her care, had known how intensely painful it was to a mother to have her children torn from her by a cruel master and sold. Arrah had had a number of children sold, and was at that very time striving diligently to raise money to redeem the last one of them. And through such kind-hearted friends as Mr. Stevens, the peculiar hardships of this interesting family were brought to the knowledge of thousands of philanthropists in this country and England. As noted, liberal contributions had already been made by friends of the slave on both sides of the ocean.

While Susan Bell's youngest child had not been a conscious sufferer from the wicked system of slavery, it had been the object of very great anxiety and suffering to many others, who had individually imperiled their own freedom for its future. This child, however, was safely brought to the Vigilance Committee of Philadelphia, and was duly forwarded, via friends in New York, to its mother in Syracuse, where she had stopped to work and wait for her little one, left behind when she escaped.

There is no word in the records of the Vigilance Committee on whether Susan Bell's other child was rescued from slavery or freed with the Civil War.

CHAPTER 24

Samuel W. Johnson: Arrival from the *Dispatch* Office.

Sam was doing slave labor at the office of the Richmond sheet. Somehow, he had learned how to read and write a little, and for the news of the day he had quite an ear. Also with regard to his freedom he was quite anxious.

Being ambitious, he hired his time, for which he paid his master $175 per year in regular quarterly payments. Besides paying this amount, he had to find his own board and clothing, and pay his doctor's expenses.

Sam had had more than one owner in his life. The last one, however, he spoke of thus: "His name is James B. Foster, of Richmond, a very hard man. He owns three more slaves besides myself."

In escaping, Sam was obliged to leave his wife, who was owned by Christian Bourdon. His attachment to her, judging from his frequent warm expressions of affection, was very strong. But, as strong as it was, he felt that he could not consent to remain in slavery any longer. Sam had come across a copy of UNCLE TOM'S CABIN, and in reading it, all his notions with regard to "masters and servants" soon underwent an entire change, and he began to cast his eyes around him to see how he might get his freedom.

One who was as alert to opportunities to seek his freedom, and as courageous, as he was, could now and then find a "berth" on a steamer or schooner going north. Thus, Samuel found passage on one of the steamers that went to Philadelphia. On arriving, he was put at once in the charge of the Vigilance Committee of Philadelphia.

While in their hands, he seemed filled with astonishment at his own achievements, and such spontaneous expressions as naturally flowed from his heart thrilled and amazed his new-found friends. It was abundantly clear that Samuel Washington Johnson would do credit to his fugitive comrades in Canada. So the Committee gladly aided him on his journey.

After arriving in Canada, Samuel wrote frequently and intelligently. The following letter to his wife shows how deeply he was attached to her, and, at the same time, what his views were of slavery. The member of the Committee to whom it was sent, with the request that it should be forwarded to her, could not find the opportunity to do so. A copy of it was preserved with other Underground Railroad documents.

Letter from Samuel W. Johnson to his Wife

"My Dear Wife,

"I now embrace this golden opportunity of writing a few lines to inform you that I am well at present enjoying good health and hope that these few lines may find you well also. My dearest wife I have left you and now I am in a foreign land about 1,400 miles from you, but even though, my wife, my thoughts are upon you all the time. My dearest Frances I hope you will remember me now just as same as you did when I was there with you because my mind is with you night and day and the love that I bear for you in my breast is greater than I thought it was. If I had thought I had so much love for you, I don't think I ever could have left. Being I have escaped and have fled into a land of freedom, I can but stop and look over my past life and say what a fool I was for staying in bondage as long.

"My dear wife I don't want you to get married before you send me some letter because I never shall get married until I see you again. My mind doesn't deceive and it appears to me as if I shall see you again. At my time of writing this letter I am destitute of money I have not gotten into a business yet, but when I do I shall write you and also remember you. Tell my mother and brother and all inquiring friends that I am now safe in a free state. I can't tell where I am at present but direct your letters to Mr. William Still in Philadelphia and I will get them. Answer this as soon as you can if you please for if you write the same day you receive this, it will take a fortnight to reach me. No more to relate at present, but still remain your affectionate husband.

"Mr. Still please forward this piece out if you please. "Samuel Washington Johnson."

Whether Samuel ever met with the opportunity of communicating with his wife, the writer cannot say. But of all the trials which slaves had to endure, the separations of husbands and wives were the most difficult to bear. Although feeling keenly the loss of his wife, Samuel's breast swelled with the thought of freedom, as will be seen from the letter which he wrote immediately after landing in Canada:

Second Letter

"St. Catharines, Upper Canada West. "Mr. William Still:

"I am now in safety. I arrived at home safe on the 11th inst at 12 o'clock midnight. So I hope that you will now take it upon yourself to inform me something of that letter I left at your house that night when I left there and write me word how you are and how is your wife. I wish you may excuse this letter for I am so full that I cannot express my mind at all. I have only got $1.50, but I feel as if I had an independent fortune. But I don't want you to think that I am going to be idle because I am on free ground and I shall always work though I have nothing to do yet.

"Direct your letter to the post office as soon as possible, "Samuel W. Johnson."

CHAPTER 25

The Amos, alias Johnson, Family Escape from Baltimore.

Doubtless, in the eyes of a slaveholder, a more "likely-looking" family could not readily be found in Baltimore than the one now being briefly introduced. The mother and her children were owned by a young slaveholder, who went by the name of William Giddings, and resided in Prince George's County, Maryland. Harriet acknowledged that she had been treated "tolerably well in earlier days" for one in her condition; but, as in so many instances in the experience of slaves, latterly, times had changed with her and she was compelled to serve under a new master who often treated her "very severely."

On one occasion, seven years previously, a brother of her owner for a minor offense struck and kicked her so brutally that she was immediately thrown into a fit of sickness, which lasted "all one summer", from this she finally recovered.

On another occasion, about one year prior to her escape, she was seized by her owner and thrust into prison to be sold. In this instance the interference of the uncle of Harriet's master saved her from the auction block. The young master was underage, and at the same time under the guardianship of his uncle. The young master had early acquired an ardent taste for fast horses, gambling, etc. Harriet felt that her chances for the future in the hands of such a brutal master could not be other than miserable.

Her husband had formerly been owned by John S. Giddings, who was said to have been a "mild man." He had allowed Stephen (her husband) to buy himself, and for 18 months prior to the flight, he had been what was called a free man. It should also be further stated in justice to Stephen's master that he was so disgusted with the manner in which Stephen's wife was treated that he went so far as to counsel Stephen to escape with his wife and children. Here at least is one instance where a Maryland slaveholder lends his influence to the Underground Railroad cause.

The counsel was accepted, and the family started on their perilous flight. And, although they encountered trials and difficulties to discourage and beset them, they battled bravely with all these odds and reached the Vigilance Committee of Philadelphia safely.

Harriet was a bright, racially mixed woman, with marked features of character, and well-made. She spoke well and was quite intelligent. She was about 26 years of age. The children also were remarkably fine-looking, but too young to know the horrors of slavery. The Committee at once relieved them of their heavy load of anxiety by encouragement and tangible support, such as food, money, and lodging. After the family had somewhat recovered from the fatigue and travel-worn condition in which they had arrived, and were prepared to resume their journey, the Committee gave them careful instructions for avoiding slave hunters. Also, they were given details about such points on the Underground Railroad where they would be most in danger of going astray, from a lack of knowledge of the way. Then, with indescribable feelings of sympathy, free tickets were provided them, and they, having been conducted to the depot, were sent on their way to Canada.

CHAPTER 26

Elijah Hilton Uses a Pass to Escape from Richmond.

After many years of hard toil for the support of others, the yoke pressed so heavily upon Elijah's shoulders that he could not endure slave life any longer. In the hope of getting rid of his bondage, he began to formulate a plan for his escape to freedom.

In proof of Elijah's account (which follows), the advertisement of Mr. R.J. Christians is presented, as taken from a Richmond paper about the time that Elijah passed through Philadelphia on the Underground Railroad, in 1857.

"Ran away, $500 Reward, Left the Tobacco Factory of the subscriber, on the 14th inst., on the pretence of being sick, a mulatto man, named Elijah, the property of Maj. Edward Johnson, of Chesterfield County. He is about 5 feet 8 or 10 inches high, slightly built, has bushy hair, and a very genteel appearance; he is supposed to be making his way north. The above reward will be paid if delivered at my factory.

"Ro. J. Christians."

From his infancy up to the hour of his escape, not a breath of free air had he ever been permitted to breathe. He was first owned by Mrs. Caroline Johnson,

"a stingy widow, the owner of about 50 slaves, and a member of Dr. Plummer's church." Elijah, at her death, was willed to Major Johnson, who was in the United States service. Elijah spoke of him as a "favorable man," but added, "I'd rather be free. I believe I can treat myself better than he can or anybody else." For the last 19 years he had been hired out, sometimes as waiter, sometimes in a tobacco factory, and for five years in the coal mines.

At the mines he was treated very brutally, but at Cornelius Hall's tobacco factory, the suffering he had to endure seems almost incredible. The poor fellow, with the scars upon his person and the unmistakable earnestness of his manner, only needed to be seen and heard to confirm the truth of his otherwise incredulous story. One time, for refusing to be flogged at Hall's factory, the overseer, in a rage, "took up a hickory club" and laid his head "open on each side." Overpowered and wounded, he was stripped naked and compelled to receive 300 lashes by which he was virtually skinned from head to foot. For six months afterwards he was "laid up."

Last year he was hired out for $180, out of which he received only $5. This year he brought $190. Up to the time he escaped, he had received $2, and the promise of "more at Christmas." He left brothers and sisters, all ignorant of his way of escape.

The following pass brought away by Elijah speaks for itself:

"Richmond, 3 July 1857

"Permit the Bearer Elijah to pass to and from my factory, to Frederick Williams, In the valley, for one month, until 11 o'clock at night.

"*By A.B. Wells, "R.J. Christian.*

"[Pine Apple Factory.]"

As usual, the Vigilance Committee of Philadelphia provided aid to Elijah, and forwarded him on to Canada, from where he wrote back as follows:

"Toronto, Canada West, July "Dear friend,

"In due respect to your humanity and nobility I now take my pen in hand to inform you of my health. I am enjoying a reasonable proportion of health at this time and hope when these few lines come to hand they may find you and your family the same. Dear Sir, I am in Toronto and am working at my old branch of business with many of my friends. I want you to send to Toronto to Mr. Tuehart on Edward St. my clothes. I came from Richmond, Virginia, and expect my things to come to you. So when they come to you then you will send them to Jesse Tuehart, Edward St. no. 43. I must close by saying I have no more at present.

"I still remain your brother, "*Elijah Hilton.*"

CHAPTER 27

Captain F. Transports 21 Passengers to Freedom on His Boat.

Captain F. was certainly no ordinary man. Although he had been living a seafaring life for many years, and the marks of this calling were plainly visible in his manners and speech, he was, unlike the great majority of this class of men, not addicted to intemperance and profanity. On the contrary, he was a man of thought, and possessed, in a large measure, those humane traits of character which lead men to sympathize with suffering humanity wherever encountered.

It must be admitted, however, that the first impressions gathered from a hasty survey of his rough and rugged appearance, his large head, large mouth, large eyes, and heavy eyebrows, with a natural gift at keeping concealed the inner workings of his mind and feelings, were not calculated to inspire the belief that he was fit to be entrusted with the lives of unprotected females and helpless children. It was even less apparent that this man would take pleasure in risking his own life to rescue others from the hell of slavery; or that he would deliberately enter the enemy's domain, and with the faith of a martyr, face the dread slaveholder, with his Bowie knives and revolvers, as well as slave hunters, bloodhounds, lynchings, and penitentiaries, for humanity's sake. But his deeds proved him to be a true friend of the slave. And his skill, bravery, and success stamped him as one of the most daring and heroic captains ever connected with the Underground Railroad.

At the time he was doing most for humanity in resetting bondsmen from slavery, slave laws were actually being very rigidly enforced. To show mercy, in any way, to man or woman, who might be caught assisting a slave to flee from the prison house, was a matter totally out of the question in Virginia. This was perfectly well understood by Captain F. Indeed, he did not hesitate to say that his hazardous operations might any day result in the "sacrifice" of his life. But this point seemed to give him no more concern than wondering which way the wind would blow the next day. He had his own convictions about dying and the future, and he declared that he had "no fear of death," however it might come.

Still, he was not disposed to be reckless or needlessly to imperil his life, or the lives of those he undertook to aid. Nor was he opposed to receiving compensation for his services. In Richmond, Norfolk, Petersburg, and other places where he traded, many slaves were fully aware of their condition. The great slave sales were constant reminders of the further perils they faced.

Then, the various mechanical trades were given to the slaves because the master had no taste to handle and maintain "greasy, northern machines." Then, again, the stores had to be supplied with porters, draymen, etc., from the slave population. In the hearts of many of the more intelligent among the slaves, the men who worked as mechanics, etc., the women as dressmakers, chambermaids, etc., despite all the opposition and hard laws, the spirit of freedom was steadily burning.

It was only necessary for a single reliable and intelligent slave to learn that a man with a boat running north believed in the freedom of others, for that man to become an object of the greatest interest. If an angel had appeared among them, doubtless its presence would have inspired any greater anxiety and hope than did the presence of Captain F.

The class most anxious to obtain freedom could generally manage to acquire some financial means, which they would willingly offer to captains or conductors in the South for making their escape possible. Many of the slaves learned if they could manage to cross the Mason-Dixon line, even though they might be utterly destitute and penniless, that they would then receive aid and protection from the Vigilance Committee of Philadelphia.

Here it may be well to state that, while the Committee gladly received and aided all who might come or be brought to them, they never employed agents or captains to go into the South with a view of enticing slaves or running off with them. So when captains operated, they did so with the full understanding that they alone were responsible for any failures related to their movements.

But, back to Captain F. with his schooner lying at the wharf in Norfolk, Virginia, loaded with wheat, and at the same time with 21 fugitives hidden inside.

While the boat was lying at its mooring, the rumor was flying all over town that a number of slaves had escaped, which created a general excitement a degree less, perhaps, than if the citizens had just experienced a great earthquake. The mayor of the city and a posse of officers with axes and long spears went down to Captain F.'s boat. The fearless commander received the mayor very calmly. The mayor told the captain who he was, and by what authority he appeared on the boat, and what he meant to do.

"Very well," replied Captain F., "here I am and this is my boat, go ahead and search."

His honor with his deputies looked quickly around, and then an order went forth from the mayor to "spear the wheat thoroughly." The deputies obeyed the command, with enthusiasm. But the spears brought neither blood nor groans, and the observant mayor obviously concluded that he was "barking up the wrong tree." But the mayor was not finished.

"Take the axes and go to work" was the next order; and the axe was used with terrible effect by one of the deputies. The deck and other parts of the boat were chopped and split. However, the axe produced no better results on the wood than had the spears in the wheat. Meantime, Captain F. remained completely indifferent, totally composed. Indeed every step they took proved conclusively that they were entirely ignorant how to search a boat.

At this point, with remarkable shrewdness, Captain F. saw how he could still further confuse them by a bold strategic move. As though about out of patience with the mayor's blunders, the captain instantly told the mayor that he had "stood still long enough" while his boat was being "damaged, chopped up," etc.

"Now if you want to search," continued the captain, "give me the axe, and then point out the spot you want opened and I will open it for you very quick." While uttering these words, as only he was capable of doing, in an indignant and defiant manner, and with an expression that declared it did not matter where or when a man died provided he was in the right, he gave emphasis to his words by bringing the axe down on the deck with smashing impact. Splinters flew from the boards. The mayor and his posse seemed, if not dreadfully frightened, completely confounded. And by the time Captain F. had again brought down his axe a second time, with increased power, while demanding where they would have him open next, they looked as though it was time for them to retire. In a few minutes they actually gave up the search and left the boat without finding a person.

Daniel in the lions' den was no safer than were the 21 passengers hidden on Captain F.'s boat. The law had been carried out with a vengeance, but had not ruffled the nerve of this skilled captain. The five dollars were paid for being searched, the amount which was lawfully required of every captain sailing from Virginia. And the captain steered direct for the City of Brotherly

Love. The wind of heaven favoring the good cause; he arrived safely in the vicinity of Philadelphia, within reach of the Vigilance Committee.

The names of the passengers were as follows: Alan Tatum, Daniel Carr, Michael Vaughn, Thomas Nixon, Frederick Nixon, Peter Petty, Nathaniel Gardener, John Brown, Thomas Freedman, James Foster, Godfrey Scott, Willis Wilson, Nancy Little, John Smith, Francis Haines, David Johnson, Phillis Gault, Alice Jones, and Ned Wilson.

These passengers were most "likely-looking articles." A number of them, doubtless, would have commanded the very highest prices in the Richmond slave market. Among them were some good mechanics, one excellent dressmaker, and some "prime" waiters and chambermaids, men and women with brains, some of them displaying remarkable intelligence and decided bravery, just the kind of passengers that gave the greatest satisfaction to the Vigilance Committee.

The interview with these passengers was extremely interesting. Each one gave his or her experience of slavery, the escape, etc., in his or her own way, deeply impressing those who had the privilege of seeing and hearing them, with the fact of the growing spirit of liberty, and the wonderful perception and intelligence possessed by some of the sons of toil in the South. While all the names of these passengers were duly entered on the Underground Railroad records, the number was too large, and the time they spent with the Committee too brief to record more than a few short sketches, as follows:

Alan Tatum

Alan was about 30 years of age, dark, intelligent, and of a good physical build. For the last 14 years he had been owned by Lovey White, a widow and the owner of nine slaves, from whom she derived a comfortable support. This slaveholding madam was a member of the Methodist Church, and was considered in her general appearance, a "moderate slaveholder." For 10 years prior to his escape, Alan had been hiring his time and for this privilege he paid his mistress, the widow, $120 per year. If he happened to be so unfortunate as to lose time by sickness within the year, he was obliged to make that up. In addition he had to pay for his own clothes and other needs.

Although Alan had at first stated that his mistress was "moderate," further on in his story, as he recounted the details of his life, he declared that he was prompted to leave because he disliked his mistress, that "she was mean and without principle." Alan left three sisters, one brother, and a daughter. The names of the sisters and brother were Mary, Ann, Rachel, and William — the daughter, Mary.

Daniel Carr

Daniel was about 38 years of age, dark mulatto, apparently of sound body and mind, and manly. The man to whom he had been compelled to render hard and unpaid labor and call master was known by the name of John C. McBole. McBole lived at Plymouth, North Carolina and was in the steam-mill business. McBole had bought Daniel in Portsmouth, where he had been raised, for $1150 only two years prior to his escape.

Twice Daniel had been sold on the auction block. A part of his life he had been treated hard. Two unsuccessful attempts to escape were made by Daniel, after being sold to North Carolina; for this offense, he was on one occasion stripped naked and flogged severely. This did not cure him. Prior to his joining Captain F.'s party, he had fled to the swamps, and lived there for three months, surrounded with wild animals and snakes.

Daniel had a wife in Portsmouth. He succeeded in making his way from the swamp to pay her a private visit. It was there, to his unspeakable joy, that he made the acquaintance of Captain F., who was delighted to give him passage to the North.

Daniel, after being sold, had been allowed only one opportunity during two years to visit his wife; being thus debarred he resolved to escape. His wife, whose name was Hannah, had three children, all slaves. Their names were Sam, Dan, and "baby." The name of the latter was unknown to him.

Michael Vaughn

Michael was about 31 years of age, with superior physical proportions, and no lack of common sense. His color was without paleness, dark and unfading, and his manly appearance was quite striking. Michael belonged to a lady, whom he described as a "very disagreeable woman." "For all my life I have belonged to her, but for the last eight years I have hired my time. I paid my mistress $120 a year; a part of the time I had to find my board and all my clothing."

Michael left a wife and one child in slavery, but they were not owned by his mistress. Before escaping, he felt afraid to share the secret of his contemplated escape, because he felt that there was no possible way for him to help her escape; on the other hand, she might be so excited by his plan, as to give it away. His wife's name was Esther. His continuing love for her is expressed in the following letter:

"New Bedford, 22 August 1855 "Dear Sir:

"I send you this to inform you that I expect my wife to come that way. If she should, you will direct her to me. When I came through your city last fall, you took my name in your office, which was then given you, Michael Vaughn; since then my name is William Brown, No. 130 Kempton Street. Please give my wife and child's name to Dr. Lundy, and tell him to attend to it for me. Her name is Esther, and the child's name Louisa.

"Truly yours, "*William Brown.*"

Michael worked in a foundry. In church fellowship he was connected with the Methodists — his mistress was with the Baptists.

Thomas Nixon

Thomas was about 19 years of age, of a dark hue, and quite intelligent. He had little reason for leaving, except that he was "tired of staying" with his "owner." As he feared he might be sold some day, he thought that he might as well save his owner the trouble. Thomas belonged to a Mr. Bockover, a wholesale grocer at No. 12 Brewer Street. Thomas left behind him his mother and three brothers. His father was sold away when he was an infant, and Thomas never saw him again. Thomas was a member of the Methodist Church; his master was of the same persuasion.

Frederick Nixon

Frederick was about 33 years old, and was exceptional both physically and mentally. He had a more urgent excuse for escaping than Thomas; he declared that he fled because his owner wanted "to work him hard without allowing him any chance, and had treated him rough." Frederick was also one of Mr. Bockover's slaves; he left his wife, Elizabeth, in bondage with four children. They were living in Eatontown, North Carolina. Had he remained in Norfolk he had not the slightest prospect of being reunited with his wife and children. He had been separated from them for about three years and it had been a year since he had even seen them. This painful state of affairs only increased his desire to leave those who caused their separation.

Peter Petty

Peter was about 24 years old, and wore a happy countenance; he was a person of agreeable manners, and was pretty smart. He acknowledged that he had been owned by Joseph Boukley, Hair Inspector. Peter said Mr. Boukley was "rowdyish in his habits, was deceitful and sly, and would sell his slaves any time. He kept them in hard bondage — something like the children of Israel." This was his simple excuse for fleeing. He hired his time from his master, for which he was compelled to pay $156 a year. When he lost time by sickness or rainy weather, he was required to make up the deficiency, and to also find his clothing.

He left a wife, Lavinia, and one child, Eliza, both slaves. Peter communicated to his wife his secret intention to leave, and she agreed to his going. He left his parents also. All his sisters and brothers had been sold. Peter would have been sold, too, but his owner was under the impression that he was "too good a Christian" to violate the laws by running away. Peter's master was quite a devoted Methodist, and was attached to the same church that Peter attended.

While on the subject of religion, Peter was asked about the kind and character of preaching that he had been accustomed to hearing; whereupon he gave the following graphic example: "Servants obey your masters; good servants make good masters; when your mistress speaks to you don't pout

out your mouths; when you want to go to church ask your mistress and master," etc. Peter declared that he had only heard one preacher speak against slavery, and that "one was obliged to leave suddenly for the North." He said that a Quaker lady spoke in meeting against slavery one day, which resulted in an outbreak, and final breaking up of the meeting.

Phillis Gault

Phillis was a widow, about 30 years of age; the blood of two races flowed in about equal proportions through her veins. From her personal appearance, refinement, manners, and intelligence, others might assume that she had possessed superior advantages. But the facts in her history proved that she had been made to feel very keenly the horrifying effects of slavery — not in the field, for she had never worked there — nor as a common drudge, for she had always been required to fill higher roles. She was a dressmaker — but not without fear of the auction block. This dreaded destiny was the motive that caused her to escape with the 20 others.

Death had robbed her of her husband at the time that the fever raged so fearfully in Norfolk. This sad event deprived her of the hope she had of being purchased by her husband, as he had intended. She was haunted by the constant thought of again being sold, as she had once been, and as she had witnessed the sale of her sister's four children after the death of their mother.

Phillis was, to use her own striking expression, in a state of "great horror" and she felt that nothing would relieve her but freedom. After having fully pondered the prospect of her freedom and the only mode offered by which she could escape, she consented to endure bravely whatever suffering and trial might come. As was the case with thousands of other slaves, she gained her freedom.

She remained several days in the family of a member of the Committee of Philadelphia, favorably impressing all who saw her. As she had formed a very high opinion of Boston, from having heard it so thoroughly reviled in Norfolk, she desired to go there. The Committee made no objections, gave her a free ticket, and helped her reach her destination. From that time to the present, she has sustained a good Christian character, and as an industrious, upright, and intelligent woman, she has been and is highly respected by all who know her. The following letter is characteristic of her:

"Boston, 22 March 1858 "My Dear Sir,

"I received your photograph by Mr. Cooper and it afforded me much pleasure to do, so I hope that these few lines may find you and your family well as it leaves me and little Dicky at present. I have no interesting news to tell you more than there is a great revival of religion through the land. I almost forgot to thank you for your kindness and our little Dick he is very wild and goes to school and it is my desire and prayer for him to grow up a useful man.

"I wish you would try to gain some information from Norfolk and write me word how the times are there, for I am afraid to write. I wish you would see the doctor for me and ask him if he could carefully find out anyway that we could steal little Johnny for I think to raise nine or ten hundred dollars for such a child is outrageous. Just at this time I feel as if I would rather steal him than to buy him.

"Give my kind regards to the doctor and his family. Tell Miss Margaret and Mrs. Landy that I would like to see them out here this summer again to have a nice time in Cambridge. Miss Walker, who spent the evening with me in Cambridge, sends much love to you and Mrs. Landy. Give my kind regards to Mrs. Still and children and receive a portion for yourself. I have no more to say at present but remain yours respectfully.

"*Flarece. P.G.*

"When you write, direct your letters to Mrs. Flarece P. Gault, No. 62 Pinkhey."

CHAPTER 28

John Henry Hill Makes a Desperate Resistance at a Slave Auction and Escapes after Hiding for Nine Months.

John Henry, at the time of his escape, was 25 years of age; he was at least six feet tall and remarkably well-proportioned in every respect. He was of a rather brown color, with marked intelligence. By trade, John was a carpenter, and was considered a competent workman. The year prior to his escape, he hired his time, for which he paid his owner $150. This amount John had fully paid up the last day of the year.

John Henry was a young man of steady habits, and a husband and father. He also was strongly attached to the ideas of liberty. His owner, John Mitchell, evidently observed these traits in his character, and concluded that he was a dangerous piece of property to keep, that his worth in money could be more easily managed than the man himself. Consequently, his master unceremoniously, without giving John any advance indication that he was to be sold, took him to Richmond and directly to the slave auction on the first day of January (the great annual sale day).

Just as John was being taken into the building, efforts were made to place handcuffs on him. The thought flashed through his mind that he was about to be sold on the auction block, and he grew terribly desperate. "Liberty or death" was the watchword of that awful moment.

Without a moment's hesitation, he turned on his enemies with his fists, knife, and feet, so tiger-like, that he actually put four or five men to flight, his master among the number. John then wheeled and ran, and was soon out of sight of his pursuers. He quickly found a hiding place. This was the last hour of John Henry's slave life, but not, however, of his struggles and sufferings for freedom. Before a final chance to escape presented itself, nine months would elapse. The mystery as to where he hid, and how he fared, is told in his own words:

"Nine months I was trying to get away. I was secreted for a long time in a kitchen of a merchant near the corner of Franklyn and 7th Streets at

Richmond, where I was well taken care of by a lady friend of my mother. When I got tired of staying in that place, I wrote myself a pass to pass myself to Petersburg; here I stopped with a very prominent Colored person, who was a friend to freedom [and] stayed here until two white friends told other friends if I was in the city to tell me to go at once, and stand not upon the order of going, because they had heard [of] a plot [to capture me]. I wrote a pass [and] started for Richmond. Reached Manchester, got off the cars [and] walked into Richmond; once more got back into the same old den; stayed here from the 16th of Aug. to 12th Sept. On the 11th of September at 8:00 P.M. a message came to me that there had been a stateroom taken on the steamer City of Richmond for my benefit, and I assured the party that it would be occupied if God be willing. Before 10:00 the next morning, on the 12th, a beautiful September day, I arose early, wrote my pass for Norfolk, left my old den with many a goodbye, turned out the back way to 7th St., then to Main, down Main...to old Rockett's and after about 20 minutes of delay I succeed in reaching the stateroom. My conductor was very much excited, but I felt as composed as I do at this moment, for I had started from my den that morning for liberty or for death providing myself with a brace of pistols."

A private berth was arranged for him on the steamship brought on safely to Philadelphia. While in the city, he enjoyed the hospitality of the Vigilance Committee of Philadelphia, and the greetings of a number of friends. The thought of his wife and two children left in Petersburg, however, caused him much anxiety. Fortunately, they were all free; therefore, he was not without hope of getting them. Moreover, his wife's father (Jack McCraey) was a free man, well-known, and very well-to-do; it was unlikely that he would allow his daughter and grandchildren to suffer. In this respect, Hill's condition was quite favorable, compared with that of most slaves leaving their wives and children behind.

Many letters from John Henry show how his thoughts and concerns were focused on the oppressed. He displayed remarkable intelligence and ability with the pen, considering that he had had no chance to acquire book knowledge. After having fled for refuge to Canada and having become a free man under the government of Great Britain, he was still not satisfied because his thoughts and concerns were with other oppressed people.

"Change your name." "Never tell anyone how you escaped." "Never let anyone know where you came from." "Never think of writing back, not even to your wife; you can do your kin no good, but may do them harm by writing." "Take care of yourself." "You are free, well, be satisfied then." "It will do you no good to fret about your wife and children; that will not get them out of slavery." Such was the advice often given to the fugitive. Men who had been slaves themselves, and some who had aided in the escape of individuals, sometimes urged these sentiments on men and women whose hearts were almost breaking over the thought that their dearest family members and best friends were in chains in the prison house. Perhaps it was thoughtlessness on the part of some, and a wish to inspire due caution on the part of others, that prompted this advice. Doubtless some did soon forget their friends, for they may have seen no way by which they could readily communicate with them, or help them achieve freedom. Perhaps slavery had dealt with them so cruelly that little hope was left in them.

However, fugitives constantly expressed strong love and attachment for their relatives and friends left in the South. But few probably are aware how deeply these feelings were cherished in the breasts of this people. Even if separated from their loved ones for forty, fifty, or sixty years, their sympathy and love continued as warm and unwavering as ever. Children left to the cruel mercy of slaveholders could never be forgotten. Brothers and sisters could not refrain from weeping over memories of their separation on the auction block; of having seen innocent children, and feeble and defenseless women in the grasp of a merciless tyrant, pleading and crying in vain for pity.

The following letters from John Henry illustrate the strong affections and attachments of fugitive slaves. John Henry never forgot those with whom he had been a fellow sufferer in slavery. He never forgot the oppression that they were enduring, and longed to do something to aid and encourage those who were striving to get their freedom. He wrote many letters in behalf of others, as well as for himself, the tone of which was always marked by the most zealous devotion to the slave, a high sense of the value of freedom, and unshaken confidence that God was on the side of the oppressed. He never failed to express hope that the day was not far distant when the slave power would be "suddenly broken and that without remedy."

Despite the literary imperfections of these letters, they add an important insight into the feelings of the former slave. Of course, slaves were not allowed book learning. Virginia even imprisoned white women for teaching free colored children the alphabet. Who has forgotten the imprisonment of Mrs. Douglass for this offense? In view of these facts, no apology is needed for Mr. Hill's grammar or spelling.

First Letter

"Toronto,

"4 October 1853 "Dear Sir:

"I take this method of informing you that I am well, and that I got to this city all safe and sound, though I did not get here as soon as I [had] expected. I left your city on Saturday and I was on the way until the Friday following. I got to New York the same day that I left Philadelphia, but I had to stay there until Monday evening. I left that place at six o'clock. I got to Albany next morning in time to take the half past six o'clock train for Rochester, where I stayed until Wednesday night. The reason I stayed there so long [was that] Mr. Gibbs [had] given me a letter to Mr. Morris at Rochester. I left that place Wednesday, but I only got five miles from that city that night. I got to Lewiston on Thursday afternoon, but too late for the boat to this city. I left Lewiston on Friday at one o'clock, got to this city at five.

"Sir, I found this to be a very handsome city. I like it better than any city I ever saw. It is not as large as the city that you live in, but it is a very large place—much more so than I expected to find it. I seen the gentleman that you gave me the letter to. I thought him [to be] much of a gentleman.

"I got into work on Monday. The man whom I am working for is named Myers; but I expect to go to work for another man by name of Tinsly, who is a master workman in this city. He says that he will give me work next week and everybody advises me to work for Mr. Tinsly as there [is more security] in him.

"Mr. Still, I have been looking and looking for my friends for several days, but have not seen nor heard of them. I hope and trust in the Lord Almighty that all things are well with them.

"My dear sir, I would feel so much better satisfied if I could hear from my wife. Since reaching this city I have telegraphed to friend Brown to send my things to me, but I have not heard a word from no one at all. I have written to Mr. Brown two or three times since I left the city. I trust that he has gotten my wife's letters, that is if she has written.

"Please direct your letters to me, near the corner Sarah and Edward Street, until I give you further notice. You will tell friend B. how to direct his letters, as I forgot when I wrote to him, and ask him if he has heard anything from Virginia. Please let me hear from him without delay for my very soul is troubled about my friends whom I expected to have seen here before this hour. Whatever you do please to write. I shall look for your paper shortly.

"Believe me sir to be your well wisher. "*John H. Hill.*"

Second Letter:

Expressions of gratitude — The Custom House refuses to charge him duty. He is greatly concerned for his wife.

"Toronto,
"30 October 1853 "My Dear Friend:
"I now write to inform you that I have received my things all safe and sound, and also have shook hands with the friend that you send on to this place [and] one of them is stopping with me. His name is Chas. Stuert; he seems to be a tolerable smart fellow. I received my letters. I have taken this friend to see Mr. Smith. However, will give him a place to board until he can get to work. I shall do everything I can for them....

Mr. Still, I am under...obligation to you for your kindness. When shall I ever repay? S. speak very highly of you. I will [tell] you what [the] Customhouse master said to me. He asked me when he presented my effects, "Are these your effects?" I answered yes. He then asked me if I was going to settle in Canada. I told him I was. He then asked me of my case. I told [him] all about it. He said, "I am happy to see you and all that will come." He ask me how much I had to pay for my paper. I told him [a] half dollar. He then told me that I should have my money again. He arose from his seat and got my money. So my friend you can see the people and tell them all this is a land of liberty and believe they will find friends here. My best love to all.

"My friend, I must call upon you once more to do more kindness for me — that is to write to my wife as soon as you get this, and tell her when she gets ready to come she will pack and consign her things to you. You will give her some instructions, but not to your expense, but to her own. When you write direct your letter to Phillip Ubank, Petersburg, Virginia. My box arrived here the 27th.

"My dear sir, I am in a hurry to take this friend to church, so I must close by saying I am your humble servant in the cause of liberty and humanity.

"*John H. Hill.*"

Third Letter:

Canada is highly praised — The Vigilance Committee is implored to send all the fugitives there.

"So I ask you to send the fugitives to Canada. I don't know much of this province but I believe that there is room enough for the colored and whites of the United States. We want farmers [and] mechanics of all qualifications; if they are not made we will make them, if we cannot make the old, we will make our children.

"Now concerning the city of Toronto, this city is beautiful and prosperous...

[a] great many wooden cottages more than what should be but I am in hopes there will be more of the brick and stone. But I am not done about your Republicanism. Our masters have told us that there was no living in Canada for a Negro but if it may please your gentlemanship to publish these facts that we are here able to earn enough bread and money enough

to make us comfortable. But I say give me freedom, and the United States may have all her money and her luxuries; yes give [me] liberty or death. I'm in America, but not under such a government that I cannot express myself, speak, think or write. So as I am able, and if my master had allowed me to have an education, I would make them American slaveholders feel me. Yes I would make them tremble when I spoke, and when I take my pen in hand their knees smote together.

"My dear sir, suppose I was an educated man. I could write you something worth reading, but you know we poor fugitives who have just come over from the South are not able to write much on no subject whatsoever, but I hope by the aid of my God I will try to use my midnight lamp, until I can have influence upon American slavery. If someone would say to me, that they would give my wife bread until I could be educated I would stop my trade this day and take up my books.

"But a crisis is approaching when essential requisite to the American slaveholders when blood, death, or liberty will be required at their hands. I think our people have depended too long and too much on false legislature, let us now look for ourselves. It is true that...however, the Englishman is our best friend but we as men ought not to depend upon her [protest] with the Americans because she loves her commercial trade as [much as any] nations do.

"But I must say, we look up and acknowledge the power of greatness and honor of old England, and believe that while we sit beneath the silken folds of her flag of perfect liberty, we are secure, beyond the reach of the aggressions of the bloodhounds and free from the despotism that would wrap around our limbs by the damnable slaveholder. ...like spoiled children [we] depend upon her, but [not] upon ourselves.... And as one means of strengthening ourselves, we should agitate the emigration to Canada.

"I here send you a paragraph which I clipped from the weekly Globe. I hope you will publish it so that Mr. Williamson may know that men are not chattel here but rather they are men and if he wants his chattel let him come here after it or his thing. I want you to let the whole United States know we are satisfied here because I have seen more pleasure since I came here then I saw in the U.S. the 24 years that I served my master. Come poor distressed men [and] women and come to Canada where colored men are free. Oh how sweet the word does sound to me, yes, when I contemplate of these things; [but] my very flesh creeps [and] my heart throbs when I think of my beloved friends whom I left in that cursed hole. Oh my God what can I do for them or shall I do for them? Lord help them. Suffer them to be no longer depressed beneath the brute creation but may they be looked upon as men made of the [same] bone and blood as Anglo-Americans. May God in his mercy give liberty to all in this world. I must close as it is a late hour at night. I remain your friend in the cause of liberty and humanity.

"John H. Hill, a fugitive.

"If you know anyone who would give me an education, write and let me know for I am in want of it very much.

"Yours with respect, "*J.H.H.*"

Fourth Letter

He rejoices over the arrival of his wife, but at the same time, his heart is bleeding over a dear friend whom he had promised to help before he left slavery.

———

"Toronto,
"29 December 1853 "My Dear Friend:
"It affords me a good deal of pleasure to say that my wife and the children have arrived safe in this city. But my wife had very bad luck. She lost her money and the money that was belonging to the children, the whole amount was $35. She had to go to Niagara Falls and telegraph me to come after her. She got to the falls on Saturday and I went after her on Monday. We saw each other once again after so long an absence, you may know what sort of meeting it was, joyful times of course. My wife [is] satisfied here, and she was pleased during her stay in the city....

"Mr. Still, I hold in my hand a letter from a friend [in the] South, who calls me to [reminds me of] a promise that I made to him before I left. My dear sir, this letter has made my heart bleed since I received it. He also desires of me to remember him to his beloved brethren [and] to pray for him and his dear friends who are in slavery. I shall present his letter to the churches of this city...Mrs. Hill sends her love to your wife and yourself.

"I sincerely hope that our friends from Petersburg have reached your city before this letter is dated. I must close by saying, that I, sir, remain [your] humble and obedient servant,

"*J.H.H.*"

Fifth Letter

He is now earnestly appealing on behalf of a friend in slavery, trying to obtain aid and assistance with which this particular friend can obtain freedom.

———

"Toronto,

"8 March 1854

"My Dear Friend Still:

"We will once more trouble you upon this great cause of freedom, as we know that you are a man that is never fatigued in such a glorious cause. Sir, what I wish to say is this: Mr. Forman has received a letter from his wife dated the 29th. She stated to him that she was ready at any time, and that everything was right with her, and she hoped that he would lose no time in sending for her for she was ready and waiting for him. Well friend Still, we learned that Mr. Minkens could not bring her on account of her child. We are very sorry to hear such news, however, you will please read this letter with care, as we have learned that Minkens cannot do what we wish to be done; we propose another way.

"There is a white man that sails from Richmond to Boston [and] that man is very safe, he will bring F.'s wife with her child. So you will do us a favor [if you take it] upon yourself to transcribe from this letter what we shall write. There is a Colored gentleman that works on the basin...this man's name is Esue Foster. He can tell Mrs. Forman all about this sailor. So you can place the letter in the hands of M. to take to Forman's wife [and] she can read it for herself. She will find Foster at Ladlum's warehouse on the basin, and when you write call my name to him and he will trust it. This Foster is a member of the old Baptist Church. When you have done all you can do let us know what you have done; if you hear anything of my uncle let me know."

Sixth Letter

He grieves over his uncle's fate, who was suffering in a dungeon-like place of concealment daily waiting for the opportunity to escape.

"Toronto,
"18 March 1864 "My Dear Still:
"Yours of the 15th reached on the 11th, found myself and family very well, and not to delay no time in replying to you, as there was an article in your letter which aroused me very much when I read it; that was you praying to me to be cautious how I write down South. Be so kind as to tell me in your next letter whether you have at any time apprehended any danger in my letters whatsoever, in those bound southward; if there have been, allow me to beg 10,000 pardons before God and man, for I [do not mean] to throw any obstacle in the way of those whom I left in the South, but to aid them in every possible way. I have done as you requested, to warn friends of the danger of writing South.

"I have told all you said in yours that Mr. Minkens would be in your city very soon, and you would see what you could do for me. Do you mean or do you speak in reference to my dear uncle? I am hoping that you will use every effort to get him from the position in which he now stands. I know how he feels at this time, for I have felt the same when I was a runaway. I was bereft of all participation with my family for nearly nine months, and now that poor fellow is placed in the same position. Oh God help I pray, what a pity it is that I cannot do him no good, but I sincerely hope that you will not get fatigued at doing good in such cases, nay, I think otherwise of you, however, I say no more on this subject at present, but leave it for you to judge.

"On the 13th you made some remarks concerning friend Forman's wife; I am satisfied that you will do all you can for her release from slavery, but as you said you feel for them, so do I, and Mr. Forman comes to me very often to know if I have heard anything from you concerning his wife.

"God Save the Queen. All my letters southward have passed through your hands with an exception of one.

"*John H. Hill.*"

Seventh Letter

Death has taken away one of his children and he has cause to mourn; in his grief he recounts his struggles for freedom, and his hating to leave his wife and children.

"Toronto,
"14 September 1854 "My Dear Friend Still:
"This is the first opportunity that I have had to write you since I received your letter of the 20th July. There has been sickness and death in my family since your letter was received. Our dear little child has been taken from us, one whom we loved so very dear. But the almighty God knows what is best for us all.

"Louis Henry Hill was born in Petersburg, Virginia on 7 May 1852, and died in Toronto on 19 August 1854, at five o'clock P.M.

"Dear Still, I could say much about the times and incidences that have taken place since the coming of that dear little angel just spoken of. It was 12 months and 3 days from the time that I took departure of my wife and child to proceed to Richmond to await a conveyance up to the day of his death.

"It was Thursday the 13th that I left Richmond. It was Saturday the 15th that I landed to my great joy in the city of Philadelphia. Then I put out for Canada. I arrived in this city on Friday the 30th and to my great satisfaction, I found myself upon Britain's free land, not only free for the white man but for all.

"This day, 12 months ago, I was not out of the reach of the slaveholders, but this 14th day of September, I am as free as your President Pierce — only I have not been free so long. However, the 30th of the month I will have been free only 12 months.

"It is true that I have to work very hard for comfort but I would not exchange with 10,000 slaves that are equal with their masters. I am happy, happy.

"Give love to Mrs. Still. My wife laments her child's death too much. Will you be so kind as to see Mr. Brown and ask him to write to me, and if he has heard from Petersburg, Virginia.

"Yours truly, "*J.H. Hill*."

Eighth Letter

Great joy over an arrival. Twelve months praying for the deliverance of an uncle who has been in a hiding place, while the slave hunters are daily expected. Strong appeals for aid, etc.

"Toronto,

"7 January 1855 "My Dear Friend:

"It is with much pleasure that I take this opportunity of addressing you with these few lines hoping when they reach you they may find yourself and family enjoying good health as they leave us at present.

"And it is with much happiness that I can say to you that Mrs. Mercer arrived in this city yesterday. Mr. Mercer was at my house late in the evening, and I told him that when he went home if he hears anything from Virginia, that he must let me know as soon as possible. He told me that if he went home and found any news there he would come right back and inform me thereof. But little did he expect to find his dearest [wife] there. You may judge what a meeting there was with them, and may God grant that there may be some more meetings with our wives and friends.

"I had been looking for someone from the old sod for several days, but I was in good hopes that it would be my poor uncle. But the poor fellow he is yet groaning under the sufferings of a horrid system, expecting every day to receive his doom. Oh, God, what shall I do, or what can I do for him? I have prayed for him more than 12 months, yet he is in that horrid condition. I can never hear anything directly from him or any of my people.

"Once more I appeal to your humanity. Will you act for him, as if you was in slavery yourself, and I sincerely believe that he will come out of that condition? Mrs. M. have told me that she given some directions how he could be gotten at, but friend Still, if this conductor should not be successful this time, will you remind him of the poor slave again. I hope you will as Mrs. Mercer have told the friend what to do I cannot do more, therefore I must leave it to the mercy of God and your exertion.

"The weather has been very mild ever since the 23rd of Dec. I have thought considerable about our condition in this country, seeing that the weather was so very favorable to us. I was thinking a few days ago, that nature had giving us a country and adopted all things suitable.

"You will do me the kindness of telling me in your next [letter] whether or not the 10 slaves have been brought out from North Carolina....

"Yours most respectfully, "*John H. Hill.*

"P.S. Every fugitive regretted to hear of the death of Mrs. Moore. I myself think that there are no other to take her place.

"Yours, "*J.H.H.*"

If the sentiments in the above letters do not indicate an uncommon degree of natural intelligence, a clear perception of the wrongs of slavery, and a just appreciation of freedom, where shall we look for the signs of intellect and manhood?

Note: After the Civil War, John Henry Hill became a Justice of the Peace in Petersburg, Virginia.

CHAPTER 29

Hezekiah Hill — Uncle of John Henry Hill — Escapes on a Steamer after 13 Months in the Wilderness.

Driven by the love of freedom, Hezekiah resolved that he would work no longer for nothing; that he would never be sold on the auction block; that he no longer would obey the bidding of a master; and that he would rather die than be a slave. This decision, however, had only been entertained by him a short time prior to his escape.

For a number of years Hezekiah had been laboring under the pleasing thought that he should succeed in obtaining freedom through purchase, having had an understanding with his owner on this objective. At different times he had paid on account for himself payments totaling $1900, $600 more than he was to have paid according to the first agreement. Although so shamefully defrauded in the first instance, he concluded to bear the disappointment as patiently as possible and get out of the lion's mouth as best he could.

He continued to work on and save his money until he had actually come within $100 of paying $2000. At this point, instead of getting his free papers, as he firmly believed that he should, to his surprise one day he saw a notorious trader approaching the shop where he was at work. The errand of the trader was soon known; he was being sold.

Hezekiah asked if he could get his coat; going to the other end of the shop where it was hanging, he seized it and ran. He was pursued but not captured. This took place in Petersburg, Virginia, about 1 December 1854. On the night of the same day of his escape from the trader, Hezekiah walked to Richmond and was hidden there under a floor by a friend. He was a tall man, of powerful muscular strength, about 30 years of age, just in the prime of his manhood with enough courage and daring for two men.

A heavy reward was offered for him, but the hunters failed to find him in this hiding place under the floor. He strongly hoped to get away soon. On several occasions he made efforts, only to be disappointed. At different times at least two captains had agreed to provide passage to Philadelphia, but someone always got ahead of him. Two or three times he even managed to reach the boat on the river, but had to return to his miserable place under the floor. Some were under the impression that he was an exceedingly unlucky man, and for a time captains feared to bring him. But his courage sustained him unwaveringly.

Finally at the end of his 13th month in hiding, a private passage was obtained for him on the steamship Pennsylvania, and with a seven-year-old slave boy (the son of the man who had hidden him), though placed in a very hard berth, he arrived safely in Philadelphia. The Vigilance Committee of Philadelphia, which had waited for him so long that they had despaired of his ever coming, was overjoyed with his final success. Hezekiah's joy may be imagined, but never described. None but one who had been in similar straits could have felt the same.

He had left his wife Louisa, and two little boys, Henry and Manual. His passage cost $100.

Hezekiah, needing rest to recover from his ordeals, remained in Philadelphia several days, and then went on to Canada rejoicing. After arriving there he returned the following letter:

———

"Toronto, 24 January 1856 "Mr. Still:

"This is to inform you that myself and [the] little boy arrived safely in this city this day the 24th, at 10:00, after a very long and pleasant trip. I had a great deal of attention paid to me while on the way.

"I owe a great deal of thanks to yourself and friends. I will just say here that when I arrived at New York, I found Mr. Gibbs sick and could not be attended to there. However, I have arrived alright.

"You will please give my respects to your friend that writes in the office with you, and to Mr. Smith, also Mr. Brown, and the friends, Mrs. Still in particular.

"Friend Still, you will please send the enclosed to John Hill at Petersburg. I want him to send some things to me. You will be so kind as to send your direction to them, so that the things come to your care. If you do not see a convenient way to send it by hands, will you please direct your letter to Phillip Ubank at Petersburg.

"Yours Respectfully, "*H. Hill.*"

CHAPTER 30

James Hill Escapes on a Boat after Hiding on Land for Three Years.

For three years James Hill suffered in a place of concealment before he found the opportunity to make his escape. When he decided to seek his freedom, he was well under 21 years of age. A courageous young man with unfailing spirit, he remained hidden in Richmond, Virginia for three years in resistance to the slave establishment.

Such heroes in the days of slavery did much to make the slave system insecure, and to keep alive the spirit of freedom in liberty-loving hearts the world over — wherever such deeds of noble daring were made known. But of James' heroism, little can be reported here, because the notes that were made by the Vigilance Committee of Philadelphia concerning his adventure were never transferred from the loose slips of paper on which they were first written to the regular record book.

However, an important letter from the friend who had been hiding him, written a short time before he escaped (on a boat), gives some idea of his condition:

———

"Richmond, Virginia, 16 February 1861 "Dear Brother Still:

"I received a message from Brother Julius Anderson asking me to send the bundle on, but I have no way to send it. I have been waiting and truly hoping that you would make some arrangement with some person, and send for the parcel. I have no way to send it, and I cannot communicate the subject to a stranger. There is a way by the New York line, but they are all strangers to me, and of course I could not approach them with this subject for I would endanger myself greatly. This business is left to you and to you alone to attend to in providing the way for me to send on the parcel, if you only make an arrangement with some person and let me know the said person and the article which is to be sent on, then I can send the parcel. Unless you do make an arrangement with some person, and assure them that they will receive the funds for delivering the parcel this business cannot be accomplished. It is in your power to try to make some provision for the article to be sent, but it is not in my power to do so; the bundle has been on my hands now going on three years, and I have suffered a great deal of danger, and am still suffering the same. I have understood sir that there was no difficulty about the money, that you had it in your possession, ready for the bundle whenever it is delivered. But sir as I have said I can do nothing now. Sir I ask you please through sympathy and feelings on my part and his try to provide a way for the bundle to be sent and relieve me of the danger in which I am in. You might succeed in making an arrangement with those on the New York steamers for they do such things but please let me know the man that the arrangement is made with, please give me an answer by the bearer.

"Yours truly friend, "*C.A.*"

At last, the long, dark night passed away, and this young slave safely made his way to freedom, and proceeded to Boston, where he now resides. While the Committee was looked to for aid in the deliverance of this poor fellow, it was painful to feel that it was not in their power to answer his prayers — not until after his escape was it possible to do so. But his escape to freedom gave them a satisfaction which no words can well express.

CHAPTER 31

William B. White, Susan Brooks, alias Susan Cooke, and William Henry Atkins Stowed Away Aboard the City of Richmond.

If it were not for their hope of liberty, these fugitives could hardly have endured their unfortunate positions.

William B. White

William had been compelled to earn bread and butter, clothing and luxuries, houses and land, education and ease for H.B. Dickinson of Richmond. William hurt frequently, but what could he do? Complaint from a slave was a crime of the deepest kind. So William worked away silently, but, nevertheless, continued to think.

William was about 36 years old, of dark chestnut color, medium size, and pleasant manners. His owner was a tobacco manufacturer who held some 30 slaves in his own right, besides hiring a great many others. William was regularly employed by day in his master's tobacco factory. He was likewise employed as one of the carriers of the ***Richmond Dispatch***, the time allotted to fill the duties of this office was before sunrise in the morning. It is only just to state, in favor of his master, that William was himself the receiver of a part of the pay for this night work. It was by this means William purchased clothing and certain other necessaries.

From William's report of his master, he was by no means among the worst of slaveholders in Richmond; he did not himself flog, but the overseer was allowed to conduct this business when it was considered necessary. For a long time William had cherished a strong desire to be free, and had gone so far on several occasions as to make unsuccessful attempts to accomplish this end. At last he was apprised of his opportunity to carry his wishes into practice a few moments before the hour for the starting of the Underground Railroad train.

Being on the watch, he accepted the privilege, and left without looking back. True he left his wife and two children, who were free, and a son also who was owned by Warner Toliver, of Gloucester County, Virginia. The Vigilance Committee of Philadelphia received him as a true and honest friend of freedom, and, as such, aided him.

Susan Brooks

Susan was also a passenger on the same ship that brought William B. White. She was from Norfolk, Virginia. Her toil, body, and strength were claimed by Thomas Eckels, Esq., a man of wealth and likewise a man of intemperance. For 16 years, Susan had been able to hire her time, for which she was required to pay five dollars per month. As she had the reputation of being a good cook and chambermaid, she was employed steadily, sometimes on boats. This sum may therefore be considered reasonable.

Owing to the death of her husband, about a year prior to her escape, she had suffered greatly, so much so that on two or three occasions, she had fallen into alarming fits a fact by no means agreeable to her owner, as he feared that the traders on learning about her failing health would underrate her on this account. But Susan was rather thankful for these signs of weakness, as she was thereby enabled to develop her plans and thus to elude detection.

Having a son who had gone on ahead to Canada about six months before, Susan felt that she had strong ties in the good land. Every day she remained in bondage, the ropes bound her more tightly, and "weeks seemed like months, and months like years," so disgusting had the peculiar institution become to her in every way. In this state of mind, she saw no option but to seek a hiding place until she had an opportunity to make her escape via the Underground Railroad.

So for four months, like a true and earnest woman, she endured a great "fight of affliction," in her horrible hiding place. But the thought of freedom enabled her to keep her courage up, until the welcome news was conveyed to her that all things were ready, providing that she could get safely to the boat on which she was to be secreted away. How she succeeded in reaching the boat, the record book of the Vigilance Committee of Philadelphia fails to explain.

One of the methods, which used to succeed very well in skillful and brave hands, was this: In order to avoid suspicion, the woman intending to make her secret escape approached the boat with a clean, ironed shirt on her arm, bare headed and in her usual working dress, looking good-natured of course, and as if she were simply conveying the shirt to one of the men on the boat. The attention of the officer on the watch would not for a moment be attracted by a custom so common as this. Thus, safely on the boat, the man whose business it was to put this piece of property in the most safe Underground Railroad hiding place, if he saw that everything looked favorable, would quickly arrange matters without being missed from his duties. In numerous instances, officers were outwitted in this way.

Susan left one sister, named Mary Ann Tharagood, who also hoped to "come away very much." Susan was a woman of dark color, round build, medium height, and about 40 years of age when she escaped in 1854.

William Henry Atkins

William Henry was also a fellow passenger on the same boat with William White and Susan Cooke. These might be set down as first-class Underground Railroad travelers. Henry was a very likely-looking article. He was smart, about six feet tall, racially mixed, and was owned by a Baptist minister.

For some cause not stated in the record books of the Vigilance Committee of Philadelphia, not long before leaving, Henry had received a notice from his owner that he should hunt himself a new master as soon as possible. This was a business for which Henry had no enthusiasm. His present owner, he concluded, was bad enough, and it did not occur to him that finding another would make the matter much better.

In thinking over his options, he was "taken sick." He felt the need for a little time to reflect upon matters involving his freedom. So when he was called upon one day to go to his regular toil, the answer was, "I am sick, I am not able to budge hardly." The excuse worked and Henry attended faithfully to his "sick business," for the time being, while on the other hand, the Baptist minister waited patiently all the while for William to get well enough to hunt for a new master.

What had to be done, needed to be done quickly before his master's patience was exhausted. William soon had matters arranged for traveling north. He had a wife, Eliza, for whom he felt the greatest affection, but as he viewed matters at that time, he concluded that he could really do more for her in Canada than he could in Norfolk. He saw no chance, either under the Baptist minister or under a new master, to help her. His wife was owned by Susan Langely.

When the hour for his escape arrived, Henry, having considered all the risks and costs, was in his place on the boat with his face turned towards Canada.

How he looked at matters after reaching Canada, the following letters from Henry will clearly reveal:

First Letter

"St. Catharines, 4 August 1854 "My Dear Sir:

"It is with pleasure that I now take my pen to inform you that I am well... and I hope that these few lines may find you enjoying good health, and will you please be so kind as to send a letter down home for me if you please to my wife. The reason that I beg the favor of you I have written to you several times and never receive an answer. She [doesn't] know where I am and I would like her to know, if it is possible. [Her name is] Elizeran Atkins, and when you write will you please send me all the news? Give my respect to all the family and also to Mr. Lundey and his family and tell him to please send me those books if you please the first chance you can get. Mrs. Wood sends her love too.

"Mr. Still, answer this as soon as on hand, the boys all send their love to all, the reason why I send for an answer right away [is] I expect to leave this [place] and go up west next month, not to stay, but to get some land. I have no more at present. I remain your friend.

"*W.H. Atkins.*"

Second Letter

"St. Catharines, C.W., 5 October 1854 "Mr. William Still:

"Dear Friend,

"I take the liberty to address to you a few lines in behalf of my wife, who is still at Norfolk, Virginia. I have heard by my friend Richmond Bohm, who arrived lately, that she was in the hands of my friend Henry Lovey (the same who had me in hand at the time I started). I understood that she was about to make her start this month, and that she was only waiting for me to send her some means. I would like for you to communicate the substance of this letter to my wife, through friend Henry Lovey, and for her to come on as soon as she can. I would like to have my wife write to me a few lines at the first opportunity. She could write to you in Philadelphia, 31 North Fifth Street. I wish to send my love to you and your family and would like for you to answer this letter with the least possible delay in the care of Hiram Wilson.

"Very respectfully yours, "*W.H.*

"P.S. I would like for my friend Henry Lovey to send my wife right on to Philadelphia; not to stop for want of means, for I will forward means on to my friend Wm. S. My love to my father and mother, my friend Lovey, and to all my inquiring friends. If cannot find it convenient to write, please forward this by the boat.

"*H.W.A.*"

CHAPTER 32

Four Arrivals, 31 May 1856.

About 31 May 1856, an exceedingly anxious state of feelings existed with the active Vigilance Committee of Philadelphia. In the course of 24 hours, four arrivals came to hand from different localities. The circumstances connected with the escape of each party being so unusual, there was scarcely ground for any other conclusion than that disaster was imminent, if not impossible, to be averted.

It was a day long to be remembered. Aside from the danger, however, a more encouraging hour had never presented itself in the history of the Underground Railroad. The courage, which had so often been shown in the face of great danger, continued to convince members of the Vigilance Committee that there were heroes and heroines among these passengers, fully entitled to the applause and recognition of the liberty-loving citizens of the City of Brotherly Love. The very idea of having to walk for days and nights in succession, over strange roads, through byways and valleys, over mountains and marshes, especially where women and children were concerned, was enough to invoke the admiration and respect of all.

Being familiar with such cases, the Committee was delighted beyond measure to observe how wisely and successfully each of these parties had managed to overcome their difficulties.

Charlotte Giles and Harriet Eglin: Escape in Deep Mourning

Giles and Eglin were owned by Captain William Applegarth and John Delahay. Neither of these girls had any great complaints to make on the score of ill-treatment endured. But each contrived to get a mourning suit, with heavy black veils, and thus dressed, apparently absorbed with grief, a friend passed them to the Baltimore depot (a hard place to pass, unless aided by an individual well-known to the railroad company). There they took a direct course for Philadelphia.

While seated in the passenger car (where slaves and masters both belonged) before leaving Baltimore, who should enter but the master of one of the girls! In a very excited manner, he hurriedly approached Charlotte and Harriet, who were apparently weeping, and peeping under their veils, to question them.

"What is your name?" exclaimed the excited gentleman. "Mary, sir," sobbed Charlotte.

"What is your name?" he asked of the other mourner. "Lizzie, sir," was the faint reply from Harriet.

On rushed the excited gentleman, as if moved by steam through the cars, looking for his property. Not finding it, he passed out of the cars, and, to the delight of Charlotte and Harriet, soon disappeared. Fair businessmen would be likely to look at this conduct on the part of the two girls in the light of a "sharp practice." In military talk it might be regarded as excellent strategy. Be this as it may, the Underground Railroad passengers arrived safely at the Philadelphia station and were gladly received.

A brief stay in the city was thought prudent in case the hunters were in pursuit.

They were, therefore, retained in safe quarters.

White Lady and a Small Child Traveling with a Black Coachman

In the meantime, Arrival No. 2 reached the Committee. It consisted of a black man, a white woman, and a child about 10 years old. This case created considerable surprise, even though quite a number of passengers that were fair enough to pass for white, with just a slight tinge of colored blood in their veins, even sons and daughters of some of the First Families of Virginia — had on various occasions come over the U.G.R.R.

But this party was unusual. An explanation was sought, which resulted in discovering that the party was from Leesburg, Virginia; that David, the black man, was about 27 years of age, intelligent, and was owned, or claimed, by Joshua Pusey. David had no taste for slavery; indeed, he felt that it would be impossible for him to adapt to a life of servitude for the special benefit of others. He had, already, as he thought, been dealt with very wrongfully by Pusey, who had deprived him of many years of the best part of his life, and would continue thus to wrong him, if he did not make a resolute effort to get away.

After considering various plans, he determined not to run off as a slave with his "budget on his back" but to "travel as a coachman," under the "protection of a white lady." In planning this pleasant scheme, David was not blind to the fact that neither he nor the "white lady," with whom he proposed to travel, possessed either horse or carriage.

But his master happened to have a vehicle that could be used on this occasion. David reasoned that as Joshua, his so-called master, had deprived him of his just dues for so many years, he had a right to borrow, or take without borrowing, one of Joshua's horses for the expedition. The plan was submitted to the lady, and was approved, and a mutual understanding here entered into that she should hire a carriage, and also take her little girl with them. The lady was to assume the proprietorship of the horse, carriage, and coachman. In so doing all dangers would be, in their judgment, averted.

The scheme was ready to be put into action. The time for departure was fixed and the carriage was hired. David secured his master Joshua's horse, and off they started in the direction of Pennsylvania. White people being so accustomed to riding, and colored people to driving, the party looked very commonplace. No one suspected them, that they were aware of, while passing through Virginia.

On reaching Chambersburg, Pennsylvania, in the evening, they drove to a hotel, and the lady alighted, holding by the hand her well-dressed and nice-looking little daughter, bearing herself with as independent an air as if she had owned 20 boys such as her coachman. She did not hesitate to enter and request accommodations for the night, for herself, daughter, coachman, and horse. Being politely told that they could be accommodated, all that was necessary was that the lady should continue her act to the best advantage possible. The same duty also rested with weight upon the mind of David.

The night passed safely and the morning was ushered in with bright hopes, which were overcast only for a moment. Breakfast having been ordered and eaten, to the lady's surprise, just as she was in the act of paying the bill, the proprietor of the hotel hinted that he thought that matters "looked a little suspicious." He then said plainly that he "believed that an Underground Railroad movement" was taking place before his very eyes; but being an obliging hotel keeper, he assured her at the same time that he "would not betray them."

At that moment, as at any other railroad when things threaten to come to a halt, they could do nothing more than make their way out of the peril as best they could. One thing they decided to do immediately was to "leave the horse and carriage," and try other modes of travel. They concluded to take the regular railroad passenger cars. In this way they reached Philadelphia. While still in Harrisburg, they had sought and received instructions how to find the Vigilance Committee of Philadelphia.

What relations had previously existed between David and this lady in Virginia, the Committee did not know. It looked more like the time spoken of in the Book of Isaiah, where it is said, "And a little child shall lead them," than anything that had ever been previously witnessed on the Underground Railroad.

The Underground Railroad never imposed any restrictions based on race, color, or previous condition. All were welcome to its immunities, white or black, when the object to be gained favored freedom, or weakened slavery. As the sole aim apparent in this case was freedom for the slave, the Committee received these travelers as regular Underground Railroad passengers.

Three Young Men Escape from Baltimore

Arrival No. 3 was Charles H. Ringold, Robert Smith, and John Henry Richards, all from Baltimore. Their ages ranged from 20 to 24 years. They were in appearance from that class of slaves considered most profitable to men who were in the business of buying and selling slaves. Charles and John were owned by James Hodges, and Robert by Wm. H. Normis, living in Baltimore. This is all that the records contain of them.

The exciting and hectic time when they were in charge of the Committee probably precluded time to write out a more detailed account of them, as was often the case.

Four Large and Two Small Hams

With the above three arrivals on hand, it may be seen how great the danger to which all concerned were exposed on account of the bold open manner in which these parties had escaped from the land of the institution. Nevertheless, a feeling of very great pleasure existed in view of the success of these new and adventurous modes of traveling. Indulging in reflections of this sort, the writer on going from his dinner that day to the antislavery office, to his surprise found a police officer waiting for him.

This officer was on the mayor's police force. Before many moments had been allowed to pass, the officer, evidently burdened with the importance of his mission, began to state his business substantially as follows:

"I have just received a telegraphic dispatch from a slaveholder living in Maryland informing me that six slaves had escaped from him, and that he had reason to believe that they were on their way to Philadelphia, and would come in the regular train direct from Harrisburg. I am requested to be at the depot on the arrival of the train to arrest the party, for whom a reward of $1800 is offered. Now I am not the man for this business. I would have nothing to do with the contemptible work of arresting fugitives. I'd rather help them off. What I am telling you is confidential. My object in coming to the office is simply to notify the Vigilance Committee so that they may be on the lookout for them at the depot this evening and get them out of danger as soon as possible. This is the way I really feel about them; but I shall telegraph back that I will be on the lookout for them."

While the officer was giving this information he was listened to most attentively, and every word he uttered was carefully weighed. An air of truthfulness, however, was apparent; nevertheless he was a stranger and there was cause for great caution. During the interview an unopened telegraphic dispatch which had come to hand during the writer's absence lay on the desk. Impressed with the belief that it might shed further light on the officer's story, the first opportunity that was offered, it was seized and opened. It read as follows:

"Harrisburg, 31 May 1856 "Wm. Still, N. 5th St.:

"I have sent via at two o'clock four large and two small hams. "*Jos. C. Bustill.*"

Now there was no room for further doubt, but much need for vigilance. Although the dispatch was not given to the police officer, he was told that it was about the same party, and that they would be looked after. The telegram would hardly have been understood by the officer, had he been permitted to read it, so carefully was it worded.

In one particular detail, related to the depot where they were expected to arrive, the officer was in the dark. His dispatch pointed to the regular train, and, of course, to the depot at Eleventh and Market Streets. The Underground Railroad dispatch, on the contrary, pointed to a totally different location of the city: Broad and Callowhill Streets, "Via," i.e., Reading.

As notified, that evening the "four large and two small hams" arrived, and turned out to be of the very finest quality, just such as any trader would have paid the highest market price for. Being mindful of the great danger of the hour, on the occasion this was more a time for anxiety and watchfulness than for cheering and rejoicing over the brave passengers.

Therefore, to provide for them in the usual manner was not possible. In this critical hour, it fell to a member of the Committee, for the safety of all parties, to find new and separate places of accommodation, especially for the six known to be pursued. To be stored other than with private families would not do. Three or four families were contacted at once; however, after learning of the danger much sympathy was expressed, but one after another made excuses and refused. This was painful, for the parties had plenty of house space, were identified with the oppressed race, and on public meeting occasions made loud professions of devotion to the cause of the fugitive. The memory of those refusals is still fresh in mind.

Accommodations were finally obtained for a number of the fugitives with a widow woman (Ann Laws), whose resources to help were far less than at the places where refusals had been made. But Mrs. L. was kindhearted, and nobly showed a willingness to do all that she could for their safety. Of course the Committee felt bound to bear whatever expense might necessarily be incurred. Here some of the passengers were kept for several days, in strict secrecy, long enough to give the slave hunters full opportunity to tire from their search and give up the chase in despair.

Some among the former arrivals also had to be similarly kept for the same reasons. Through careful management all were assisted and cared for. While much interesting information was obtained from these several arrivals, the incidents connected with their lives in slavery and when escaping were only briefly written out. Of this fourth arrival, however, the following details should be highly gratifying to the friends of freedom, and wherever the labors of the Underground Railroad may be appreciated.

Furthermore, people near Hagerstown, Maryland may like to know how these "articles" got off so successfully, the circumstances of their escape having doubtless created some excitement in that region of the country.

Arrival No. 4.: Charles Bird, George Dorsey, Angeline Brown, Albert Brown, Charles Brown, and Jane Scott

Charles was 24 years of age, quite dark, of quick motion, and ready speech, and in every way appearing as though he could take care of himself. He had been a farm laborer. This calling he decided to leave, not because he disliked farming, but simply to get rid of David Clargart, who professed to own him, and compelled him to work without pay "for nothing." While Charles spoke favorably of Clargart, who was described as not a hard man, nevertheless Charles was so decidedly opposed to slavery that he felt compelled to look out for himself. Serving another man on the no-pay principle, at the same time liable to be flogged and sold at the pleasure of another, Charles felt it was worse than heathenism viewed in any light whatsoever. He was prepared, therefore, to leave without delay. He had four sisters in the hands of Clargart, but he could do nothing for them but leave them to the hands of fate.

The next on the list was George Dorsey, a comrade of Charles. He was a young man, of medium size, mixed blood, intelligent, and a brave fellow as will soon be obvious.

In order to get over the road as expeditiously as possible, the party took their master's horses and wagon and moved off at a rate that would not arouse attention. About nine miles from home, their carriage broke down. In this condition, they were encountered by a couple of white men. The white men approached them, unceremoniously seized the horses by the reins, and were evidently about to assume authority.

The white men undoubtedly thought that the boys would surrender at once. Instead of doing so, the boys used their large clubs, which they had brought with them, and struck the white men with all their might. The effect of the clubs brought the white men down in the road, in an attitude resembling two men dreaming.

The victorious passengers, seeing that the smashed-up carriage could be of no further use to them, quickly decided to unhitch the horses and continue their escape on horseback. Each horse was required to carry three passengers. So up they mounted and off they galloped with the horses' heads turned directly towards Pennsylvania.

No further difficulty presented itself until they had traveled some 40 miles. Here the poor horses broke down and had to be abandoned. The fugitives were hopeful, but mindful that considerable difficulty and hardship awaited them. For one whole week they had to fare as they could, out in the woods, over the mountains, etc. How they overcame the trials in this situation we cannot describe here. Suffice it to say, they managed to reach Harrisburg and found assistance as already noted.

George and Angeline (who was George's sister) with her two boys had a considerable amount of white blood in their veins, and belonged to a wealthy man by the name of George Schaeffer, who was in the milling business. They were of one mind in describing him as a hard man. "He would often threaten to sell, and was very hard to please." George and Angeline left their mother and 10 brothers and sisters.

Jane was a well-grown girl, smart, and good-looking, with a fine brown skin, and was also owned by Schaeffer.

Letters from Some of These Passengers

Letters from the enterprising Charlotte and Harriet (Arrival No. 1) brought the good news that they had found good homes in western New York, and valued their freedom highly. Three out of quite a number of letters received from them from time-to-time are enclosed below:

First Letter

"Sennett, June 1856 "Mr. William Still: "Dear Sir:
"I am happy to tell you that Charlotte Gildes and myself have got along thus far safely. We have had no trouble and found friends all the way along, for which we feel very thankful to you and to all our friends on the road since we left. We reached Mr. Loguen's in Syracuse, on last Tuesday evening and

on Wednesday two gentlemen from this community called and we went with them to work in their families. What I wish you would do is to be so kind as to send our clothes to this place if they should fall into your hands. We hope our uncle in Baltimore will get the letter Charlotte wrote to him last Sabbath, while we were at your house, concerning the clothes. Perhaps the best would be to send them to Syracuse to the care of Mr. Loguen and he will send them to us. This will more certainly ensure our getting them. If you hear anything that would be interesting to Charlotte or me from Baltimore, please direct a letter to us to this place, to the care of Reverend Charles Anderson, Sennett, Cayuga County, New York. Please give my love and Charlotte's to Mrs. Still and thank her for her kindness to us while at your house.

"Your affectionate friend, "*Harriet Eglin.*"

Second Letter

"Sennett, 31 July 1856 "Mr. Wm. Still:

"My Dear Friend:

"I have just received your note of the 29th and allow me, dear sir, to assure you that the only letter I have written is the one you received, an answer to which you sent me. I never wrote to Baltimore, nor did any person write there for me, and it is with indescribable grief that I hear what your letter communicates to me, of those who you say have gotten into difficulty on my account. My cousin Charlotte, who came with me, got into a good place in this vicinity, but she could not content herself to stay here but just one week, she then went to Canada, and she is the one who by writing (if anyone), has brought this trouble upon those to whom you refer in Baltimore.

"She has written me two letters from Canada, and by neither of them can I ascertain where she lives, her letters are mailed at Suspension Bridge, but she does not live there as her letters show. In the first she does not even sign her name. She has evidently employed some person to write, who is nearly as ignorant as herself. If I knew where to find her I would find out what she has written.

"I don't know but she has told where I live, and may yet get me and my friends here in trouble too, as she has some in other places. I don't wish to have you trouble yourself about my clothes, I am in a place where I can get all the clothes I want or need. Will you please write me when convenient and tell me what you hear about those who I fear are suffering as the result of their kindness to me? May God, in some way, grant them deliverance. Oh the misery the sorrow which this cursed system of slavery is constantly bringing upon millions in this land of boasted freedom!

"Can you tell me where Sarah King is, who was at your house when I was there? She was going to Canada to meet her husband. Give my love to Mrs. Still and accept the same yourself. Your much indebted & obliged friend,

"*Harriet Eglin.*"

The "difficulty" about which Harriet expressed so much regret in the above letter was in reference to a letter supposed to have been written by her friend Charlotte to Baltimore about her clothing. It had been intercepted, and in this way, a clue was obtained by one of the owners as to how they escaped, who aided them, and so on. On the strength of the information thus obtained, a well-known black man named James Adams was immediately arrested and put in prison at the insistence of one of the owners, and also a suit was at the same time instituted against the railroad company for damages. These events caused a huge excitement in Baltimore.

As to Adams, the prospect looked simply hopeless. Many hearts were sad in view of the doom which they feared would fall upon him for obeying a humane impulse (he had put the girls on the cars).

But with the railroad company it was a different matter; they had money, power, friends, etc., and could defy the courts. In the course of a few months, when the suit against Adams and the railroad company came up, the railroad company proved in court, in defense, that the prosecutor [the slave owner] had entered the cars in search of his runaway, had seen and spoken to the two young women in "mourning" the day they escaped, looking expressly for the identical parties, for which he was seeking damages before the court, and that he had declared to the conductor, on leaving the cars, that the said "two girls in mourning were not the ones he was looking after," or, in other words, that "neither" belonged to him. This positive testimony satisfied the jury, and both the railroad company and poor James Adams escaped with the verdict of not guilty.

Third Letter

"Sennett, 28 October 1856 "Dear Mr. Still:

"I am happy to tell you that I am well and happy. I still live with Rev. Mr. Anderson in this place, I am learning to read and write. I do not like to trouble you too much, but I would like to know if you have heard anything more about my friends in Baltimore who got into trouble on our account. Do be pleased to write me if you can give me any information about them. I feel bad that they should suffer for me. I wish all my brethren and sisters in bondage were as well off as I am. The girl that came with me is in Canada, near the Suspension Bridge. I was glad to see Green Murdock, a colored young man, who stopped at your house about six weeks ago; he knew my folks at the South. He has got into a good place to work in this neighborhood. Give my love to Mrs. Still, and believe me your obliged friend,

"*Harriet Eglin.*

"P.S. I would like to know what became of Johnson, the man whose foot was smashed by jumping off the cars. He was at your house when I was there. [Johnson was an unfortunate young fugitive, who, while escaping, saw his master or pursuer in the cars, and jumped from the train.]

"*H.E.*"

CHAPTER 33

Charles Gilbert Flees Slavery by Hiding up a Tree, under a Floor, and in a Thicket, Disguising Himself as a Woman, and Stowing Away on a Steamer.

In 1854 Charles was owned in the city of Richmond by Benjamin Davis, a notorious negro trader. Charles was quite a "likely-looking article," not too black or too white, but rather of a nice "gingerbread color." Davis was of the opinion that this "article" would bring him a tip-top price. For two or three months the trader advertised Charles for sale in the papers, but for some reason or other Charles did not command the high price that was demanded.

While Davis was doing what he could to sell Charles, Charles was contemplating how he might escape. Being uncommonly shrewd he learned about a captain of a schooner from Boston who might help him, and approached him in hopes of securing passage. The captain showed a willingness to help him for the sum of $10, provided Charles could manage to get to Old Point Comfort, where the captain would pick him up. The Point was about 160 miles from Richmond.

A man of ordinary nerve would have declined this condition without hesitation. However, Charles had no intention to let any offer slip away. Indeed he felt that he must make an effort. If he failed, he could not see how his lot could be made more miserable by attempting to flee. Fully aware of all the consequences, he made his hazardous escape, and, to his great satisfaction, reached Old Point Comfort safely. In that locality he was well-known, unfortunately too well-known, for he had been partly raised there and many of his relatives and acquaintances were still living there. These facts were evidently well-known to the trader, who unquestionably had snares set in order to entrap Charles, should he seek shelter among his relatives.

Charles had scarcely reached his old home before he learned that the hunters and watch dogs of slavery were eagerly watching for him. Even his nearest relatives, through fear of consequences, had to hide their faces from him. None dared to offer him a night's lodging, scarcely a cup of water, for fear that such an act might be discovered by the hunters, whose fiendish hearts would have found pleasure in dispensing the most dire punishments to those guilty of thus violating the laws of slavery. The prospect, if not utterly hopeless, was decidedly discouraging. The way to Boston was entirely closed. A "reward of $200" was advertised for his capture.

For the first week after arriving at Old Point, Charles entrusted himself to a young friend who went by E.S. The fear of the pursuers drove him from his hiding place by the end of the week. Then he sought shelter, not from relatives or churchgoers, but under a large hotel, where he tried living for a while. Having watched his opportunity, he managed to reach Higee Hotel, a very large house without a cellar, which was erected on pillars three or four feet above the ground. One spot near the cistern presented a hiding place that gave him some protection under the circumstances. He at once willingly occupied this dark and gloomy spot rather than return to slavery. He remained in this refuge for four weeks.

Of course, Charles could not live without food, but to communicate with man or woman would inevitably subject him to danger. Charles' experience in the neighborhood of his old home left no reason for him to hope that he would be likely to find friendly aid anywhere under the shadow of slavery. As a result of these fears and realities, he obtained his food from the "slop tub", securing this diet in the darkness of night after all was still and quiet around the hotel. To use his own language, the meals thus obtained were often "sweet" to his taste.

One evening, however, he was greatly alarmed by the approach of an Irish boy who came under the hotel to hunt chickens. While prowling around in the darkness he appeared to be making his way unconsciously toward the very spot where Charles was hiding. What could Charles do? He snarled like a savage dog and issued a furious growl, which he hoped would frighten the boy half out of his senses, and cause him to leave Charles' hiding spot. The boy fled. However, the boy's father, hearing about the attack of the vicious dog, swore that he would kill the animal.

Charles overheard the threat, and immediately knew that he could no longer remain in safety in his present quarters. That night he left for Bay Shore. Here he decided to pass a day in the woods, but he did not feel that the woods offered adequate hiding places. But where else could he go? It occurred to him that he would be much safer up a tree than hiding in the bushes and undergrowth. He therefore climbed up a large acorn tree, passing an entire day in deep meditation there.

No gleam of hope appeared, yet he would not let himself even think of returning to bondage. In this dilemma, he remembered a poor washerwoman named Isabella — a slave who had charge of a washhouse, and he decided to seek her assistance. Leaving the woods he proceeded to the washhouse and was kindly received by Isabella. But she had no idea what to do with him or where to hide him. However, the education that Charles had been receiving at the expense of the slave hunters made it much easier for him than for her to see how he could be accommodated. He was not accustomed to the comforts of a room. Of course he could not expect such comforts now. Like many another escaping from the relentless tyrant, Charles could envision methods which to his venturesome mind would offer hope, however desperate they might appear to others.

He thought that he might be safe under the floor. To Isabella the idea was strange, but her sympathies were strongly with Charles, and she readily agreed to accommodate him under the floor of the washhouse. Isabella and a friend of Charles by the name of John Thomas were the only persons who knew of this arrangement. The kindness of these friends, shown by their willingness to do anything in their power to aid and bring comfort to Charles, was proof to him that his efforts and sufferings had not been altogether in vain.

He remained under the floor for two weeks, accessible to kind voices and friendly encouragement. At the end of this time his peace was again disturbed by reports from without that people were beginning to become suspicious of the washhouse. How this happened neither Charles nor his friends could guess. But the arrival of six police officers whom he could hear talking very plainly in the house, whose errand was actually to search for him, convinced him that he had never for a single moment been in greater danger. The officers not only searched the house, but they offered his friend, John Thomas, $25 reward if he would only put them on Charles' track. John professed to know nothing; Isabella was equally ignorant. Discouraged with their efforts on this occasion, the officers gave up the hunt and left the house.

Charles, however, had had enough of the accommodations beneath the floor. He left that night and returned to his old quarters under the hotel. Here he stayed one week, at the end of which time the need for fresh air was so great that he resolved to go out at night and spend a day in the woods. He had knowledge of a place where the undergrowth and bushes were almost impenetrable. To rest and refresh himself in this thicket he felt would be a great comfort to him.

Without serious difficulty he reached the thicket, and while pondering over the all-absorbing matter as to how he should ever manage to make his escape, an old man approached. Now while Charles had no reason to think that he was sought by the old man, Charles knew that it would neither be safe nor desirable to allow him to come nearer. Charles, remembering that his trick of playing the dog had worked well before, thought that it might also work well in the thicket. So he again tried his power at growling and barking hideously for a moment or two; the old man reversed his course at once. Charles could hear him distinctly retreating, and at the same time cursing the dog. The owner of the place had the reputation of keeping "bad dogs," so the old man poured out a dreadful threat against "Stephens' dogs," and was soon out of the sight of the one in the thicket.

Notwithstanding his success in frightening off the old man, Charles felt that the thicket was by no means a safe place for him. He concluded to make another change. This time he sought a marsh; two hours' stay there was sufficient to satisfy him that that too was no place to stay, even for a single night. He, therefore, left immediately. A third time, he returned to the hotel, where he remained another two days.

His appeals had at last reached the heart of his mother, she could no longer bear to see him struggling, and suffering, and not render him aid, whatever the consequences might be. If she at first feared to lend him a helping hand, she now resolutely worked with a view of saving money to help him. His prospects began to brighten.

A passage was secured for him on a steamer bound for Philadelphia. Another day and a night must elapse before he could be received on board.

The joyful anticipations which now filled his head left no room for fear; indeed, he could scarcely contain himself he was so filled with joy. In this state of mind he concluded that nothing would afford him more pleasure before leaving than to spend his last hours at the washhouse.

Charles made his way to the washhouse, without any fear of hunters in his mind. Charles had scarcely been three hours in this place, however, before several police officers came in search of him. Two of them talked with Isabella, asked her about her "boarders," etc.; in the meanwhile, one of them, uninvited, made his way upstairs. It so happened that Charles was in this very portion of the house. His case now seemed more hopeless than ever. The officer upstairs was separated from him simply by a thin curtain. Women's garments hung all around. Instead of fainting or surrendering, in the twinkling of an eye, Charles' inventive mind led him to dress himself in female attire. Here, to use his own language, a "thousand thoughts" rushed into his mind in a minute.

The next instant Charles was going downstairs in the presence of the officers, his old calico dress, bonnet, and wig attracting no further attention than simply to elicit the following simple questions:

"Whose gal are you?" "Mr. Cockling's, sir." "What is your name?" "Delie, sir."

"Go on then!" said one of the officers, and on Charles went to take passage on the steamer, a passage which his mother had obtained for him for the sum of $30.

In due time, he succeeded in getting on the steamer, but he soon learned that its course would not take him directly to Philadelphia, but that it was scheduled to stop first at Norfolk, Virginia. Although disappointed, he made up his mind to be patient. He was delayed in Norfolk four weeks.

From the time Charles first escaped, his owner (Davis, the negro trader) had kept a standing reward of $550 advertised for his recovery. This showed that Davis was willing to risk heavy expenses to recover Charles as well as gave evidence that he believed him still to be hiding either around Richmond, Petersburg, or Old Point Comfort. In this belief he was not far from being correct, for Charles spent most of his time in either of these three places, from the day of his escape until the day that he finally embarked.

Charles was to leave his mother, with no hope of ever seeing her again, but she had purchased herself and was called free. Her name was Margaret Johnson. Three brothers likewise were always in his thoughts, Henry, Bill, and Sam (half brothers and all slaves). But the hope of freedom outweighed every other consideration, and he was prepared to give up even his life in an attempt to live as a free man.

Charles arrived in Philadelphia by steamer from Norfolk on 11 November 1854. The Richmond papers bear witness to the fact that Benjamin Davis advertised several months for Charles Gilbert prior to this date, as has been stated above.

This story was written down just as Charles told it, directly after his arrival, with no thought of magnifying a single incident. On the contrary, much that was of interest in the story had to be omitted. Instead of being exaggerated in any way, not half of the details and events were recorded. Had the idea then been entertained that the narrative of this young slave warrior was to be brought to light in the manner and time that it now is, a far more thrilling account of his adventures might have been written.

Other black men who knew both Davis and Charles, as well as one man ordinarily knows another, rejoiced at seeing Charles in Philadelphia, and they listened with perfect faith to his story. So marvelous were the incidents of his escape that his sufferings in slavery prior to his heroic struggles to throw off the yoke were among the facts omitted from the records.

CHAPTER 34

Jim Bowlegs, alias Bill Paul,
Arrives after `Five or Six Years' of Failed Attempts in the South.

In 1855 a traveler arrived with the name of Jim Bowlegs, who, on examination, was found to possess very extraordinary characteristics. Some portions of his history were most remarkable. His schooling could only have been gathered on plantations under brutal overseers; while fleeing; in swamps; in prisons; or on the auction block; etc.; in which conditions he was often found.

Despite having never benefitted from books nor human kindnesses, his native intelligence as it regarded human nature was extraordinary. His resolution and perseverance never faltered. In all respects he was a remarkable man. He was a young man, weighing about 180 pounds, and was uncommonly muscular and strong. He was born in the state of Georgia, Oglethorpe County, and was owned by Dr. Thomas Stephens, of Lexington.

On reaching the Vigilance Committee of Philadelphia, his story was told many times. Hour after hour was occupied by friends listening to the simple narrative of his struggles for freedom. An account of "Jim" was forwarded in a letter to M.A. Shadd, then the editor of the ***Provincial Freeman***. This account has been preserved, and is included here as it appeared in the columns of that paper:

Though this poor fugitive [a young man 26 years old by the name of 'Jim,' who fled from near Charleston, South Carolina] was utterly ignorant of letters, his natural good sense and keen perception qualified him to arrest the attention and interest the heart in a most remarkable degree.

His master, frequently finding him unavailable because of his tendency to run away, would gladly have offered him for sale. He was once taken to Florida for that purpose; but traders generally were pretty shrewd, and on inspecting him, would almost invariably pronounce him a "rascal", because he would never fail to eye them sternly as they inspected him. The obedient and submissive slave is always recognized by hanging his head and looking at the ground, when looked at by a slaveholder. This lesson Jim had never learned, and so he was judged not to be trusted.

His head and chest, and indeed his entire structure, was as solid as a rock, indicating that he was physically no ordinary man. And since he was not under the spirit of "non-resistance," he had occasionally been found to be a very formidable customer.

His father was a full-blooded Indian, brother to the noted Indian Chief, Billy Bowlegs; his mother was quite black and of pure African blood.

For five or six years, the greater part of Jim's time was occupied in trying to escape, and in being in prison for sale to punish him for running away.

His mechanical genius was exceptional as was his knowledge of geography. He could make shoes or do carpenter's work very handily, though he had never had the chance to learn how. As to traveling by night or day, he was always road-ready and, having an uncommon memory, could give exceedingly good accounts of what he had observed on his trips.

When he entered a swamp and had occasion to take a nap, he took care first to decide upon the posture he must take, so that if come upon unexpectedly by the hounds and slave hunters, he might know in an instant which way to steer to defeat them. He always carried a "special liquid," which he had prepared, to prevent hounds from scenting him, which he said had never failed. As soon as the hounds came to the place where he had rubbed his legs and feet with the liquid, they could follow him no further, but howled and turned immediately.

CHAPTER 35

Edward Davis, the Saltwater Fugitive.

The facts in his exceptional case were incontestably established in the **Philadelphia Register** of 20 April 1854, from which the following account is taken:

"The steamship Keystone State, which arrived at this port [Philadelphia] on Saturday morning, had just entered Delaware Bay when a man was discovered secreted outside of the vessel and under the guardrail. When brought from his hiding place, he was found to be a fugitive slave who had hidden himself there before the vessel left Savannah on Wednesday, and had remained in that place from the time of departure!

"His position was such that the water swept over and around him almost constantly. He had some bread in his pocket, which he had intended for subsistence until he could reach a land of liberty. It was saturated with seawater and dissolved to a pulp.

"When our readers remember the high winds of Friday, and the sudden change to cold during that night, and the fact that the fugitive had remained in that situation for three days and nights, we think it will be conceded that he fully earned his liberty, and that the "institution," which was so intolerable that he was willing to run the risk of almost certain death to escape from it, held no very great attractions for him. But the poor man was doomed to disappointment. The captain ordered the vessel to put into Newcastle, where the fugitive, hardly able to stand, was taken on shore and put in jail, where he now awaits the order of his owner in Savannah."

The following particulars appeared in the same newspaper on the 21st:

"The Keystone State case — Our article yesterday morning brought us several letters of inquiry and offers of contributions to aid in the purchase from his master of the unfortunate inmate of Newcastle Jail. In answer to the former, we would say that the steamer Keystone State left Savannah at 9 A.M. last Wednesday. It was about the same hour the next morning that the men engaged in heaving lead heard a voice from under the guards calling for help. A rope was obtained, and the man was retrieved from his dangerous and suffering situation. He was well cared for immediately, a suit of dry clothes was furnished him and he was given a share of the contents of the boat pantry. On arriving at Newcastle, the captain had him placed in jail, for the purpose, as we are informed, of taking him back to Savannah.

"To those who have offered contributions so liberally, we answer that the prospect is that only a small amount will be needed, enough to pay a lawyer to sue out a writ of habeas corpus. The saltwater fugitive claims to be a free man, and a native of Philadelphia. He gives his name as Edward Davis, and says that he formerly lived at No. 5 Steel's Court, that he was a pupil in Bird's School, on Sixth Street, above Lombard, and that he has a sister living at Mr. Diamond's, a distiller, on South Street. We are not informed why he was in Georgia, from which he took such an extraordinary means to attempt his escape. If the above assertion be true, we apprehend little trouble in restoring the man to his former home. The claim of the captain to take him back to Savannah will not be listened to for a moment by any court. The only claim the owners of the Keystone State or the captain can have on Saltwater Davis, is for half passenger fare, he came half the way as a fish. A gentleman who came from Wilmington yesterday assures us that the case is in good hands at Newcastle."

The Abduction, Enslavement, and Escape of Davis and the Attempts to Reduce Him to Slavery Again

The case of Saltwater Davis, who made such a bold stroke to regain his liberty by imperiling his life on board the steamer, detailed account of his abduction and sale as a slave in the states of Maryland and Georgia, and some of his adventures up to the time of reaching Delaware. His own story is substantially as follows:

He left Philadelphia on 15 September 1851, and went to Harrisburg. Intending to go to Hollidaysburg, he took a canal boat for Havre de Grace, where he arrived the next day. There he hired on board the schooner Thomas and Edward (an oyster boat) of Baltimore. He went from Havre de Grace to St. Michael's, for oysters, then to Baltimore, and then to Havre de Grace again.

He then was hired to a Mr. Sullivan, who kept a grocery store, to do jobs. While there, a constable named Smith took him before a magistrate named Graham, who fined him $15 or $20 for violating the law in relation to free negroes coming into the state. He was not able to pay this fine, and Smith took him to Bell Air prison. Sheriff Gaw wrote to Mr. Maitland in Philadelphia, to whom he referred, and received an answer that Mr. Maitland was dead and none of the family knew him. He remained in that prison nearly two months. He then had a trial in court before a Judge Grier, who sentenced him to be sold to pay his fine and expenses, which amounted to $50.

After a few days and without being offered at public sale, he was taken out of jail at two o'clock in the morning and carried to Campbell's slave pen, in Baltimore, where he remained several months. While there, he was employed to cook for some 50 or 60 slaves, being told that he was working out his fine and jail fees. After being there about six months, he was taken out of prison and handcuffed by Winters, who took him and two or three other slaves to Washington and then to Charleston, South Carolina. Here Winters left them, and they were taken by steamboat to Savannah. While on board the boat, he learned that he and the other two had been sold to Mr. William Dean, of Macon, where he stayed two days, and was taken from that place to the East Valley Railroad.

Subsequently he was sent to work on the Possum Tail Railroad. Here he was worked so hard that in one month he lost his health. The other two men taken on with him failed before he did. He was then sent to Macon, and then to the cotton plantation again.

During the time he worked on the railroad he had allowed himself one peck of corn meal, four pounds of bacon, and one quart of molasses per week. He cooked it himself at night, for the next day's use. He worked at packing cotton for four or five months, and in the middle of November 1852, was sent back to the railroad, where he was again set to wheeling.

He worked at "task work" two months, being obliged to wheel 16 square yards of dirt and rock per day. At the end of two months he broke down again, and was sick. They tried one month to cure him, but did not succeed. In July 1853, he was taken to an infirmary in Macon. Dr. Nottinghan and Dr. Harris, of that institution, both stated that his was the worst case of the kind they had ever seen. He remained at the infirmary two months and partially recovered.

He told these physicians the story of how he had been wronged, and they subsequently tried to buy his freedom. One of his legs was drawn up so that he could not walk well, and they offered $400 for him, which his master refused. The doctors wanted him to attend their patients, which were mostly slaves. While in Georgia he was frequently asked where he came from, being found more educated than the common run of slaves.

On the 12th of March he ran away from Macon and went to Savannah. There he hid in a stable until Tuesday afternoon at six o'clock, when he hid himself on board the Keystone State. At nine o'clock the next morning the Keystone State left with Davis hidden over the guardrail, as was previously stated.

The following documents relate what happened next:

Copy of First Order of Commitment

"New Castle County, vis., State of Delaware. "To Wm. R. Lynam, Sheriff of said county,

"Davis (Negro) is delivered to your custody for further examination and hearing for traveling without a pass, and supposed to be held a Slave to some person in the State of Georgia.

"Witness the hand and seal of John Bradford, one of the Justices of the Peace for the County of New Castle, the 17th day of March 1854.

"*John Bradford, J.P.*"

Copy of Discharge

"To Wm. R. Lynam, Sheriff of New Castle County: You will discharge Davis from your custody, satisfactory proof having been made before me that he is a free man.

"*John Bradford, J.P.*

"Witnesses — Joanna Diamond, John H. Brady, Martha C. Maguire."

Copy of Order of Re-Commitment

"New Castle County, ss., the State of Delaware to Wm. R. Lynam, and to the Sheriff or keeper of the Common Jail of said county, Whereas Davis hath this day been brought before me, the subscriber, one of the Justices of the Peace, in and for the said county, charged upon the oath of Robert Hardie with being a runaway slave, and also as a suspicious person, traveling without a pass, these are therefore to command you, the said Wm. R. Lynam, forthwith to convey and deliver into the custody of the said Sheriff, or keeper of the said jail, the body of the said Davis, and you the said Sheriff or receiver of the body of the said Davis into your custody in the said jail, and him there safely keep until he be thence delivered by due course of the law.

"Given under my hand and seal at New Castle this 21st day of March, A.D. 1854.

"*John Bradford, J.P.*"

On 4 April, the marshal of Macon called at the jail in New Castle, and demanded Davis as a fugitive slave, but the sheriff refused to give him up until a fair hearing could be had according to the laws of the state of Delaware. The marshal returned to Georgia, intending to bring the claimant on the next trip.

While it was evident that the Delaware authorities had no desire to deliver up a man whose freedom was clearly proved, further steps would be needed to secure Davis' freedom. A trial would probably be held before U.S. Commissioner Guthrie, and there was expectation that it would be a fair one. However, the friends of right and justice were well aware that such a trial would be expensive, and that the imprisoned man had been so long deprived of his liberty that he would have little or no money to pay for his own defense. These were some of the challenges that lay ahead.

CHAPTER 36

Samuel Green, alias Wesley Kinnard, Receives Ten Years in the Penitentiary for Having a Copy of *Uncle Tom's Cabin*.

The Underground Railroad passenger answering to the name of Samuel Green left Indian Creek, Chester County, Maryland where he had been held as a slave by Dr. James Muse. One week had elapsed from the time he set out until his arrival in Philadelphia.

Although he had never enjoyed school privileges of any kind, he was very bright. He had absorbed all he could from his daily experiences and observations as a slave, and had managed to learn to read and write a little, despite laws that prohibited these activities for slaves. Sam was about 25 years old and was a blacksmith. Before running away, his general character for sobriety, industry, and religion had evidently been considered good; but, in seeking his freedom and running away to obtain it, he had sunk far below the utmost limit of forgiveness or mercy in the estimation of the slaveholders of Indian Creek.

During his interview with the Vigilance Committee of Philadelphia, he calmly gave a brief description of his master, which was entered on the record book substantially as follows: "Dr. James Muse is thought by the servants to be the worst man in Maryland, inflicting whipping and all manner of cruelties upon the servants."

While Sam gave reasons for this sweeping charge, which left no room for doubt on the part of the Committee members, it was not considered necessary to retain those details, which surely justified Sam's decision to take passage on the Underground Railroad.

For several years, Sam was hired out by the doctor to do blacksmithing, and daily wore the yoke of unpaid labor. At this time, through the kindness of Harriet Tubman (sometimes called "Moses" among the blacks), the "light of the Underground Railroad and Canada" suddenly filled his mind. At the time, these things were new to him, but he was too intelligent and liberty-loving not to heed the valuable information which this sister of humanity imparted. From that moment, he was in love with Canada and a decided admirer of the Underground Railroad. Harriet Tubman was a shrewd and fearless agent and well understood the entire route from that part of the country to Canada. The previous spring, she had paid a visit to the very neighborhood in which Sam lived, expressly to lead her own brothers out of "Egypt." She succeeded in laying the groundwork. To Sam this was cheering and glorious news, and he made up his mind that before long Indian Creek should have one less slave and that Canada should have one more citizen. Vigilantly, he watched for an opportunity to carry out his idea. In due time, good fortune opened the way, and to Sam's satisfaction he reached Philadelphia without encountering any peculiar difficulties.

The Committee aided him in the usual manner. Letters of introduction were given him, and he was duly forwarded on his way. He had left his father, mother, and one sister behind. Samuel and Catharine were the names of his parents. Thus far, Sam's escape would seem not to affect his parents, nor was it apparent that there was any other reason his owner should seek revenge upon them.

Sam's father was an old local preacher in the Methodist Church — and was much respected as an inoffensive, industrious man. He earned his bread by the sweat of his brow, and attempted to move along the narrow road allotted colored people — enslaved or free — without exciting the ill will of the pro-slavery power in his community. But the high-handed actions of his son aroused bitterness among the slaveholders, bringing the father under suspicion and hate. But for the moment, the eye of slavery could do nothing more than watch for an occasion to pounce upon him. And it was not long before the desired opportunity presented itself.

Moved by parental affection, the old man decided to pay a visit to his boy, to see how he was faring in a distant land, and among strangers. He quietly visited his son in Canada, where he found him to be an industrious, sober, and righteous young man — following in his own footsteps. The old man's heart was delighted with what his eyes saw and his ears heard in Canada.

During the best portion of his days, Sam's father had faithfully worn the badge of slavery, had afterwards purchased his freedom, and thus become a free man. He innocently believed that he was doing no harm in availing himself not only of his "God-given rights" [freedom], but of the rights that he had also purchased by the hard toil of his own hands [the rights that came along with freedom].

But the enemy was lurking in ambush for him. To his utter shock, not long after he returned from his visit to his son, "a party of gentlemen from the New Market district went at night to Green's house and conducted a search, where they found the hour had arrived to bring vengeance upon poor Samuel Green [the father]. The course pursued and the result may be seen in the following statement taken from the Cambridge (Maryland) ***Democrat*** of 29 April 1857, as communicated by the writer, Sam Green:

"The case of the state against Sam Green (free negro) indicted for having in his possession, papers, pamphlets and pictorial representations, having a tendency to create discontent, etc., among the people of color in the state, was tried before the court on Friday last.

"This case was of great importance, and has created in the public mind a great deal of interest — it being the first case of the kind ever having occurred in our country.

"It appeared, in evidence, that this Green has a son in Canada to whom Green made a visit last summer. Since his return to this county, suspicion has fastened upon him, as giving aid and assisting slaves who have since run away and reached Canada, and several weeks ago, a party of gentlemen from New Market district went at night to Green's house and searched it, whereupon was found a volume of ***Uncle Tom's Cabin***, a map of Canada, several schedules of routes to the North, and a letter from his son in Canada, detailing the pleasant trip he had, the number of friends he met with on the way, with plenty to eat, drink, etc., and concludes with a request to his father that he shall tell certain other slaves, naming them, to come on. These slaves, it is well known, did leave shortly afterwards, and have reached Canada. The case was argued with great ability, the counsel on both sides displaying a great deal of ingenuity, learning, and eloquence. The first indictment was for having the letter, map, and route schedules in his possession.

"Notwithstanding the mass of evidence given to show the prisoner's guilt in unlawfully having in his possession these documents and the nine-tenths of the community in which he lived believing that he had a hand in the running away of slaves, it was the opinion of the court that the law under which he was indicted was not applicable to the case and that a verdict of not guilty must be rendered accordingly.

"Samuel was immediately arraigned upon another indictment, for having in his possession ***Uncle Tom's Cabin***, and he was tried; in this case the court has not yet rendered a verdict, but holds it under curia till after the

Somerset County court. It is to be hoped that the court will find the evidence in this case sufficient to bring it within the scope of the law under which the prisoner is indicted (that of 1842, chap. 272), and that the prisoner may meet his due reward, be that what it may.

"That there is something required to be done by our legislators for the protection of slave property is evident from the variety of constructions put upon the statute in this case, and we trust that at the next meeting of the Legislature there will be such amendments, as to make the law on this subject perfectly clear and comprehensible to the understanding of every one.

"In the language of the assistant counsel for the state, 'Slavery must be protected or it must be abolished.'"

From the same newspaper, dated 20 May, the terrible doom of Samuel Green, is announced in the following words:

"In the case of the state against Sam Green (free negro), who was tried at the April term of the Circuit Court of this county for having in his possession abolition pamphlets, among which was a copy of **Uncle Tom's Cabin**, was sentenced to the penitentiary for the term of 10 years, until the 14th of May 1867."

The son, a refugee in Canada, hearing the distressing news of his father's sad fate in the hands of the relentless "gentlemen," often wrote to know if there was any prospect of his deliverance. The following letter is an example of his correspondence:

"Alford, 22, 1857 "Dear Sir,

"I take my pen in hand to request a favor of you if you can by any means without doing injustice to yourself or your business grant it, as I believe you to be a man that would sympathize in one's condition.... [I am enclosing] a letter that states...that my father has been betrayed in the act of helping some friend to Canada and the law has convicted and sentenced him to the state's prison for 10 years. His white friends offered $2000 to redeem him but they would not settle for less than $3000. I am in Canada and it is a difficult thing to get a letter to any of my friends in Maryland so as to get proper information about it, if you can... get any intelligence from Baltimore City, the information that you think proper as regards the event and the best method to redeem him, then please write soon as you can. You will oblige your friend and direct your letter to Salford Post Office, C.W.

"*Samuel Green.*"

In this dark hour the friends of the slave could do little more than sympathize with this heart-stricken son and grey-headed father. The aged follower of the rejected and crucified had to, like Him, bear the "reproach of many" and make his bed with the wicked in the penitentiary. Doubtless there were a few friends in his neighborhood who sympathized with him, but they were powerless to aid the old man.

But thanks to fate, the Civil War, by which so many captives were freed, also unlocked Samuel Green's prison doors and he was allowed to go free.

CHAPTER 37

Sam Nixon, alias Dr. Thomas Bayne, Arrives on a Schooner.

Few could be found among the Underground Railroad passengers who had a stronger dislike for the slave labor system, or the recognized terms of "master" and "slave," than Dr. Thomas "Sam" Bayne. Nor were many to be found who were more fearless and independent in expressing their sentiments.

Dr. Bayne's place of bondage was in the city of Norfolk, Virginia, where he was held to service by Dr. C.F. Martin, a dentist of some celebrity. While with Dr. Martin, Sam learned all aspects of dentistry, and was often required by his master, the doctor, to fulfill professional engagements, both at home and at a distance, when it did not suit the pleasure or convenience of Dr. Martin to appear in person. In the "mechanical department," especially, Sam was called upon to execute the most difficult tasks. This was not the testimony of Sam alone; various individuals who were with him in Norfolk, but had moved to Philadelphia, and were living there at the time of his arrival, fully corroborated his statements.

The master's professional practice, according to Sam's calculation, was worth $3000 per year. Fully $1000 of this amount, in the opinion of Sam, was the result of Sam's own services. Not only was Sam of great service to the doctor in the mechanical and practical branches of his profession, but he helped keep books and medical records as well. The doctor frequently would have Sam at his books instead of a bookkeeper. The doctor obviously considered Sam to be a valuable "article."

Of course, Sam had never received an hour's schooling in his life, but being very perceptive and having high self-esteem, he learned very quickly. Had the doctor attempted to keep Sam in ignorance, the doctor would have found it a labor beyond his power. But there is no reason to suppose that Dr. Martin was opposed to Sam's learning to read and write. Furthermore, we are pleased to note that no charges of ill treatment are found recorded against Dr. M. in the narrative of Sam. True, Sam had been sold several times in his younger days, and consequently had been made to feel keenly the evils of slavery, but nothing of this kind was charged against the doctor. Dr. M. may be described as a pretty fair man, for nothing is known to the contrary, with the exception of depriving Sam of the just reward of his labor. Furthermore, the doctor did not keep Sam so closely confined to dentistry and bookkeeping that he had no time to attend occasionally to outside activities.

In fact, Sam was quite active and successful as an Underground Railroad agent, and rendered important aid in various directions. Indeed, Sam had good reason to suspect that the slaveholders were watching him, and that if he remained in the South much longer, he would most likely find himself in "hot water up to his eyes." Wisdom dictated that he should "pull up stakes" and depart while the way was open. He knew the captains who were then in the habit of taking similar passengers, but he had some fears that they too might not be able to pursue the business much longer.

In contemplating the change which he was about to make, Sam felt it necessary to keep his movements strictly private. He did not feel at liberty even to tell his wife and child of his plans, fearing that it would do them no good, and might prove his utter failure. His wife's name was Edna and his daughter was called Elizabeth; both were slaves and owned by E.P. Tabb, Esq., a hardware merchant of Norfolk.

No mention is made on the books of ill treatment in connection with his wife's servitude; it may therefore be inferred, that her situation was not unduly hard. It must not be supposed that Sam was not truly attached to his wife. He gave abundant proof of true devotion to his wife, notwithstanding the secrecy of his arrangements for flight. Being naturally hopeful, he concluded that he could better succeed in securing his wife's freedom after obtaining freedom himself, than in undertaking the task beforehand.

The captain that took Sam had two or three other Underground Railroad male passengers to bring with him, for whom arrangements had been previously made, and no more could be brought that trip. At the appointed time, the passengers were at the disposal of the captain of the schooner, which was to bring them out of slavery into freedom. Fully aware of the dangerous consequences should he be detected, the captain, faithful to his promise, hid them in the usual manner, and set sail northward.

However, instead of landing his passengers in Philadelphia, as was his intention, for some reason or other (the schooner may have been disabled), he landed them on the New Jersey coast, not far from Cape Island. He gave them instructions on how to reach Philadelphia. Sam had friends in the city, and immediately wrote to them about the distress he and his fellow passengers were facing. In making their way in the direction of Philadelphia, they reached Salem, New Jersey, where they were discovered to be strangers and fugitives, and were directed to Abigail Goodwin — a Quaker lady, an abolitionist, long noted for her devotion to the cause of freedom, and one of the most liberal and faithful friends of the Vigilance Committee of Philadelphia.

This friend's opportunities of witnessing fresh arrivals had been rare, and perhaps she had never before come in contact with a "chattel" as smart as Sam. Consequently she was much embarrassed when she heard his story, especially when he talked of his experience as a "dentist." She was inclined to suspect that he was a "shrewd impostor" that needed "watching" instead of aiding. But her humanity forbade her from making a hasty decision on this point. She was soon persuaded to aid him, despite her apprehensions.

While resting a day or two in Salem, Sam's letter was received in Philadelphia. In the meantime, Friend Goodwin received a letter written by a member of the Committee, asking her to make inquiries concerning the stray fugitives and informing her why they happened to be coming in her direction. While Abigail Goodwin's mind was much relieved by the letter she received, she was still in some doubt, as will be seen by the following excerpt from a letter she wrote:

Letter from A. Goodwin

"Salem, 3 mo, 25, 1855 "Dear Friend:

"Thine of the 22nd came to hand yesterday noon. I do not believe that any of them are the ones thee wrote about, who wanted Dr. Lundy to come for them, and promised they would pay his expenses. They had no money, the minister said, but were pretty well off for clothes. I gave him all I had and more, but it seemed very little for four travelers, only a dollar for each, but they will meet with friends and helpers on the way. He said they expected to go away tomorrow. I am afraid [because] it's so cold, and one of them had a sore foot, they will not get away; it's dangerous staying here. There has been a slave hunter here lately, I was told yesterday, in search of a woman; he tracked her to our Alms house, she had lately been confined and was not able to go, he will come back for her and his infant, and will not wait long I expect. I want much to get her away first, and if one had a C.C. Torney here no doubt it would be done; but she will be well guarded. How much I wish the poor thing could be hidden in some safe place until she is able to travel northward; but where that could be it's not easy to see. I presume the Carolina freed people have arrived before now. I hope they will meet many friends, and be well provided for. Mary Davis will be then paid, her cousins have sent her $24, as it was not wanted for the purchase money, it was to be kept for them when they arrive. I am glad thee did keep the $10 for the fugitives.

"Samuel Nixon is now here, just come, a smart young man, they will be after him soon. I advised him to hurry on to Canada; he will leave here tomorrow, but [doesn't] say that he will go straight to the city. I would send this by him if he did. I am afraid he will loiter about and be taken ... I could not hear much of what he said, some who did don't like him at all, think him an impostor, a great brag, said he was a dentist ten years. He was asked where he came from, but would not tell till he looked at the letter that lay on the table and that he had just brought back. I don't feel much confidence in him, don't believe he is the one thee alluded to. He was asked his name, he looked at the letter to find it out. Says nobody can make a better set of teeth than he can. He said they will go on tomorrow in the stage, he took down the number and street of the Anti-Slavery Office, you will be on your guard against imposition, he kept the letter thee sent from Norfolk. I had then no doubt of him, and had no objection to it. I now rather regret it. I would send it to thee if I had it, but perhaps it is of no importance.

"He wanted the names taken down of nine more who expected to get off soon and might come here. He told us to send them to him, but did not seem to know where he was going to. He was well-dressed in fine broadcloth coat and overcoat, and has a very active tongue in his head.

"But I have said enough, don't want to prejudice thee against him, but only be on thy guard, and do not let him deceive thee, as I fear he has some of us here.

"With kind regards, "*A. Goodwin.*"

———

In due time Samuel and his companions reached Philadelphia, where a cordial welcome awaited them. The confusion and difficulties into which they had fallen, by having to travel an indirect route, were fully explained, and to the hearty merriment of the Committee and strangers, the dilemma of their good Quaker friend Goodwin at Salem was alluded to. After a rest of a day or two in Philadelphia, Samuel and his companions left for New Bedford.

Sam and the other refugees were told that Canada would be the safest place for them; but it was in vain to attempt to convince Sam that Canada or any other place on this continent was quite equal to New Bedford. His heart was there, and there he was resolved to go, and there he did go too, bearing with him his resolute mind, determined, if possible, to work his way up to an honorable position at his old trade, dentistry, and that too for his own benefit.

Aided by the Committee, the journey was made safely to the desired haven, where many old friends from Norfolk were found. Here our hero was known by the name of Dr. Thomas Bayne and no longer Sam. In a short time the doctor commenced his profession in a humble way, while, at the same time, he deeply interested himself in his own improvement, as well as the improvement of others, especially those who had escaped from slavery as he had. Then, too, since black men were voters and, therefore, eligible to hold an office in New Bedford, the doctor's natural ambition and intelligence led him to take an interest in politics, and before he was a citizen of New Bedford four years, he was elected a member of the City Council.

He was also an outspoken advocate of the cause of temperance, and was likewise a ready speaker at antislavery meetings held by his race. Some idea of his abilities, and the interest he took in the Underground Railroad, education, and related causes, may be gathered from the following letters:

First Letter

"New Bedford, 23 June 1855 "W. Still:

"Sir,

"I write you this to inform you that I have received my things and that you need not say anything to Bagnul about them, I see by the paper that the Underground Railroad is back in operation, since the Saless Party was betrayed two weeks ago by that captain. We in Massachusetts are very anxious to know the name of that captain ... Others started last Saturday night. They are all my old friends and we are waiting their arrival, we hope you will look out for them. They may come by way of Salem, New Jersey, if they are not overtaken. They are from Norfolk.

"Times are very hard in Canada. Two of our old friends have left Canada and come to Bedford for a living. Everything is so expensive and wages so low. They cannot make a living (owing to the Civil War) and others are expected shortly, let me hear from Saless and his party. Get the name of the captain that betrayed him and let me know if Mrs. Goodwin of Salem are [still] at the same place, John Austin is with us. Lightfoot is well and remembers you and [your] family. My business is getting better since getting an office. Send me a Norfolk paper or any other to read when convenient.

"Let me hear from those people as soon as possible. They consist of woman and child, and two or three men belonging to Marsh Bottmore, L. Slosser, and Herman & Co, and Turner, all of Norfolk, Virginia.

"Truly yours, "*Thos. Bayne.*

"Direct to Box No. 516, New Bedford, Massachusetts. Don't direct my letters to my office. Send them to my box. My office is 66 1/2 William St., the same street the post office is on and near the city market."

The doctor, feeling his educational deficiency, devoted himself to study, including such difficult subjects as medicine, etc., as the following letters will show:

Second Letter

"New Bedford, January 1860
"No. 22, Cheapside, opposite City Hall.
"My Dear Friend,
"Yours of the 3rd reached me safely in the midst of my misfortune. I suppose you have learned that my office and other buildings burned during the recent fire. My loss is $550, and was insured for $350.

"I would have written you before, but I have been to Rhode Island for some time. Upon my return, the fire took place before I had had time to examine the books that you sent, and this accounts for my delay. In regard to the books I am under many obligations to you and all others for so great a piece of kindness, and shall ever feel indebted to you for the same. I shall esteem them very highly for two reasons: First, the way in which they come, that is through and by your vigilance as a colored man helping a colored man to get such knowledge as will give the lie to our enemies. Secondly, their contents being just the thing I needed at this time. My indebtedness to you and all concerned for me in this direction is inexpressible.

"There are some other books the doctor says I must have, such as the Medical Dictionary, Physician's Dictionary, and a work on anatomy. These I will have to get, but any work that may be of use to a student of anatomy or medicine will be thankfully received. You shall hear from me again soon.

"Truly Yours, "*Thos. Bayne.*"

Third Letter

"New Bedford, 18 March 1861 "Mr. William Still:

"Dear Sir,

"Dr. Powell called to see me and informed me that you had a medical lexicon (dictionary) for me. If you have such a book for me, it will be very thankfully received, and any other book that pertains to the medical or dental profession. I am quite limited in means as yet and in want of books to continue my studies. The books I need most at present are those that discuss midwifery, anatomy, etc. But any book or books in either of the above mentioned cases will be of use to me. You can send them by express, or by any friend that may chance to come this way, but by express will be the safest way to send them. Times are quite dull. This leaves me well and hope it may find you and family the same. My regards to your wife and all others.

"Yours, etc., "*Thomas Bayne,*

"22 Cheapside, opposite City Hall."

Thus, the doctor continued to labor and improve his skills until the Civil War removed the institution of slavery from the nation. As soon as the way opened for his return to his old home, New Bedford no longer had sufficient attractions to retain him. With all its faults, "Old Virginia" offered decided incentives for his return. Accordingly he went directly to Norfolk, from where he had escaped.

Upon his return, he found everything in the utmost confusion and disorder, except where the military was in control. As soon as the time drew near for reorganizing, elections, and so on, the doctor ran for a seat in Congress, and was found to be a very difficult candidate to beat. Indeed, in the initial election returns, his name was among the elected; but subsequent counts indicated he had lost by a very small margin.

At the time of the doctor's escape, in 1855, he was 31 years old, a man of medium size, about as purely black as could be found, and full of self-esteem, courage, and determination.

CHAPTER 38

Robert McCoy, alias William Donar, and Elizabeth Frances, alias Ellen Saunders, Arrive on a Steamer.

In October 1854, the Vigilance Committee of Philadelphia received by steamer, directly from Norfolk, Virginia, Robert McCoy and Elizabeth Frances.

Robert McCoy

For the last 16 years prior to his escape, Robert constantly had been in the clutches of the negro trader Hall. Therefore, he had possessed very favorable opportunities to observe the trader's conduct in his wicked business, as well as to witness the effects of the auction block upon all ages, tearing apart the dearest ties despite the piteous wails of children and parents. But no attempt will be made to record the deeds of this dealer in human flesh. Those stories, fresh from the lips of one who had just escaped, were extremely painful. Furthermore, many of the details are too revolting to be published. In lieu of this fact, except the above allusions to the trader's business, this sketch will only refer to Robert's condition as a slave and as a traveler on the Underground Railroad.

Robert was a man of medium size, racially mixed but dark, and in possession of more than ordinary intelligence. His duties had been confined to the house, and not to the slave pen. In general, he had managed, doubtless through much shrewdness, to avoid very severe outrages from the trader. On the whole, he had fared "about as well" as was possible for a slave.

Yet, in order to free himself from his "miserable" life, he was willing, as he declared, to suffer almost any sacrifice. Indeed, his conduct proved the sincerity of this statement, as he had actually been concealed five months in a place in the city where he could not possibly avoid continuous suffering of the most trying kind.

His resolve to be free just became stronger as a result of this ordeal. The trader had threatened to sell Robert, and to prevent it, Robert "took off." He successfully eluded the keen scent and grasp of the hunters, who made a diligent effort to recapture him.

Although a young man, only about 28 years of age, his health was by no means good. His system had evidently been considerably shattered by slavery, and symptoms of consumption, together with chronic rheumatism, were making rapid headway against the physical man. Under his various ills, he declared, as did many others from the land of bondage, that his faith in God afforded him comfort and hope. He was obliged to leave his wife, Eliza, in bonds, not knowing whether they should ever meet again on earth, but he was somewhat hopeful that the way would open for her escape also.

After reaching Philadelphia, where his arrival had been anticipated for some time by the Vigilance Committee, his immediate needs were met, and in due time he was forwarded to New Bedford, Massachusetts, where he felt he would be happy in freedom. He had been in New Bedford only one month, when his prayers and hopes were realized with regard to the deliverance of his wife. On hearing of the good news of her coming, he wrote as follows:

"New Bedford, 3 November 1859 "Dear Sir:

"I embrace this opportunity to inform you that I received your letter with pleasure, I am enjoying good health and hope that these few lines will find you enjoying the same blessing. I rejoice to hear from you and I feel very much indebted to you .... I rejoice to hear of the arrival of my wife, and hope she is not sick from the rolling of the sea and if she is not, please send her on here Monday with a ... rifle to guard her up to my residence. I thank you kindly for the good that you have done for me. Give my respects to Mrs. Still, tell her I want to see her very bad and you also. I would come but I am afraid yet to venture. I received your letter the second, but about the first of spring I hope to pay you a visit or next summer. I am getting something to do every day. I will write on her arrival and tell you more. Mr. R. White sends his love to you and your family and says that he is very much indebted to you ... and also he desires to know whether his clothes have arrived yet or not, and if they are, please express them on to him or by Mrs. Donar. Not anymore at present.

"I remain your affectionate brother, "*William Donar.*"

Elizabeth Frances

Along with Mrs. Donar, and similarly hidden, was Elizabeth Frances, alias Ellen Saunders. She was a single young woman, about 22, with as pleasant a countenance as one would wish to see. Her manners were equally agreeable. Perhaps her joy over her achieved victory added somewhat to her personal appearance.

She had, however, belonged to the more favored class of slaves. She had neither been overworked nor badly abused. Elizabeth was the property of a lady a few shades lighter than herself (Elizabeth was of mixed blood), by the name of Sarah Shephard, of Norfolk. In order to increase her financial return from Elizabeth's labor, the mistress resorted to hiring her out for a given sum per month. Against this usage Elizabeth made no significant complaint. Indeed the only serious charge she brought was to the effect that her mistress had sold her mother away to a place in the far South, when Elizabeth was only ten years old. Shephard had also sold a brother and sister to a foreign southern market.

These acts awakened Elizabeth to her condition and began her planning for her own freedom. By the time she had reached womanhood, she had developed a strong resolve to escape. Thus growing to hate slavery in every way and manner, she was prepared to make a desperate effort to be free. Having saved $35, she was willing to give every cent of it (although it was all she possessed) for assistance to escape from Norfolk to Philadelphia.

After reaching Philadelphia, having suffered severely while coming, she was invited to remain until she had recovered. When she had recovered, she left for New Bedford, Massachusetts, which she reached without difficulty and was cordially welcomed. The following letter, expressing her appreciation for aid received, was forwarded soon after her arrival in New Bedford:

"New Bedford, Mass., 16 October 1854 "Mr. Still:

"Dear Sir,

"I now take my pen in my hand to inform you of my health which is good at present, all except a cold I have got, but I hope when these few lines reach you, you may be enjoying good health. I arrived in New Bedford Thursday morning safely and what little I have seen of the city I like it very much and my friends were very glad to see me. I found my sister very well. Give my love to Mrs. Still and also your dear little children. I am now out at service. I do not think of going to Canada now. I think I shall remain in this city this winter. Please tell Mrs. Still I have not met any person who has treated me any kinder than she did since I left. I consider you both to have been true friends to me. I hope you will think the same of me. I feel very thankful to you indeed. It might been supposed, out of sight, out of mind, but it is not so. I never forget my friends. Give my love to Florence. If you come to this city I would be very happy to see you. Kiss your dear little children for me. Please answer this as soon as possible, so that I may know you received this. No more at present.

"I still remain your friend, *"Ellen Saunders."*

Eliza McCoy

Eliza McCoy, the wife of Robert McCoy, whose narrative was previously recorded (above), and who was left to wait in hope when her husband escaped, soon followed him to freedom. It is a source of great satisfaction to be able to present her narrative in so close proximity to her husband's.

He arrived about the first of October — she about the first of November the following year. Her testimony described her sufferings as a slave on the auction block, and in a place of concealment seven months, waiting and praying for an opportunity to escape. But it was thought sufficient to record only a very brief outline of her active slave life, which consisted of the following notable features. Eliza had been owned by Andrew Sigany of Norfolk. She was about 38 years old, racially mixed, and a woman whose appearance would readily command attention and respect anywhere outside of the barbarism of slavery. She stated that her experience in the cruel hands of slavery had been very trying, and that she had "always wanted to be free." Her language was unmistakable on this point.

Neither mistress nor servant was satisfied with each other; the mistress was so "queer" and "hard to please" that Eliza became "sick" of trying to please her, an angel would have failed with such a woman. Matters continued to grow worse and worse, and Eliza increasingly contemplated a more pleasant atmosphere in the North.

When she went into hiding, she was determined to endure her chosen discomfort until she could finally find a way to leave the South. The martyrs in olden times who lived in "dens and caves of the earth" could hardly have fared worse than some of these wayworn travelers.

After an opportunity to rest and recover, which was needed by one who had suffered so severely until her arrival in Philadelphia, she was forwarded to her anxiously waiting husband in New Bedford.

CHAPTER 39

Lear Green Escapes in a Chest.

"One Hundred and Fifty Dollar Reward. Ran away from the subscriber, on Sunday night, 27th, my negro girl, Lear Green, about 18 years of age, black complexion, round-featured, good-looking, and ordinary size; she had on and with her, when she left, a tan-colored silk bonnet, a dark plaid silk dress, a light muslin delaine, also one watered silk cape and one tan-colored cape. I have reason to be confident that she was persuaded off by a negro man named William Adams, black, quick-spoken, five feet ten inches high, a large scar on one side of his face, running down in a ridge by the corner of his mouth, about four inches long, barber by trade, but works mostly about taverns, opening oysters, etc. He has been missing about a week; he had been heard to say he was going to marry the above girl and ship to New York, where it is said his mother resides. The above reward will be paid if said girl is taken out of the state of Maryland and delivered to me; or $50 if taken in the state of Maryland.

"*James Noble,*

"m26-3t.

"No. 153 Broadway, Baltimore."

Lear Green, as advertised in the **Baltimore Sun** by James Noble, won for herself a strong claim to a high place among the heroic women of the 19th century. In regard to description and age the advertisement is quite accurate, although her master might have added that her countenance was one of peculiar modesty and grace. Furthermore, instead of being "black," she was of a "dark-brown color."

Of her bondage, Lear made the following statement: She was owned by James Noble, a "butter dealer" of Baltimore. He fell heir to Lear by the will of his wife's mother, Mrs. Rachel Howard, by whom she had previously been owned. Lear was but a mere child when she came into the hands of

Noble's family. She, therefore, remembered little about her old mistress. Her young mistress, however, had made a lasting impression upon her mind, for she was very exacting and oppressive in regard to the tasks she made Lear perform. Her mistress never granted her any liberties. While confronting these circumstances, a young man by the name of William Adams proposed marriage to Lear. She was inclined to accept this offer, but disliked the idea of being encumbered with the chains of slavery and the duties of a family at the same time.

After discussing this with her mother as well as William Adams, she decided that she must be free in order to fill the station of a wife and mother. For a time, dangers and difficulties arose which defied all hope of escape. While every pulse was beating strong for liberty, only one chance seemed to be left, the trial of which required as much courage as it would to endure the cutting off the right arm or plucking out the right eye.

A strong, old chest, such as sailors commonly used, was acquired. A quilt, a pillow, and a few articles of clothing, as well as a small quantity of food and a bottle of water were put into it, along with Lear. The chest was then tied with strong ropes, and stowed among the ordinary freight on one of the Ericson steamers.

The mother of William Adams, who was free, agreed to come as a passenger on the same boat. The rules of the Ericson line assigned colored passengers to the deck. In this instance it was exactly where this guardian and mother desired to be, as near the chest as possible. Once or twice, during the silent watches of the night, she was drawn irresistibly to the chest, and could not refrain from untying the rope and raising the lid a little, to see if the poor child was still alive, and at the same time to give her a breath of fresh air.

After she had passed 18 hours in the chest, the steamer arrived at the wharf in Philadelphia, and in due time the living freight was brought off the boat. At first, it was delivered to a house in Barley Street, which was occupied by friends of the mother. Subsequently, the chest and freight were moved to the residence of the writer, in whose family she remained several days under the protection and care of the Vigilance Committee.

The desire for liberty that was demonstrated by Lear made the efforts of the most ardent friends, who were in the habit of aiding fugitives, seem feeble at best.

Of all the heroes in Canada or elsewhere, who had purchased their liberty through downright bravery, none deserved more praise than Lear Green.

She remained for a time in Philadelphia, and was then forwarded to Elmira, New York. There she was married to William Adams. They never went to Canada, but took up their permanent residence in Elmira. She was given only about three years to enjoy freedom before she died.

About the time of Lear's death, her mother-in-law also died in Philadelphia. The impressions made by both mother and daughter can never be forgotten. The chest in which Lear escaped was preserved by the writer as was a photograph taken of her while she was in the chest. The chest and photograph remained as a memorial to her courage and her wish to live in freedom.

CHAPTER 40

Isaac Williams, Henry Banks, and Kit Nickless.

Rarely have three travelers encountered more difficulties in escaping from the house of bondage. Much dramatic material might have been gathered from the incidents of their lives and travels. However, all that we can introduce here is the brief account recorded at the time of their stay at the Philadelphia station of the Underground Railroad, while they were on their way to Canada in 1854.

The three journeyed together. They had been slaves together in the same neighborhood. Two of them had shared the same den and cave in the woods, and had been shot, captured, confined in the same prison, and had broken out of prison and again escaped.

Isaac was a stout young man, about 26 years of age, possessing a good degree of physical and mental ability. Indeed his intelligence did not allow his submission to the requirements of slavery, rendered him unhappy, and led him to seek his freedom. He owed services to D. Fitchhugh up to within a short time before he escaped. Against Fitchhugh he made grave charges, saying that he was a "hard, bad man." It is only fair to add that Isaac was similarly regarded by his master, so both were dissatisfied with each other.

The master had the advantage over Isaac because he could sell Isaac. Isaac, however, decided to turn the table on his master by running off. But the master moved quickly and sold Isaac to Dr. James, a negro trader. The trader anticipated making a good profit out of his investment; Isaac determined that he should be disappointed, indeed, that he should lose every dollar that he paid for him.

While the doctor was determining where and how he could get the best price for him, Isaac was planning how and where he might safely get beyond his reach. But Isaac's time for planning and acting was growing exceedingly short. He daily expected to be sent south. In this situation he made his condition known to a friend of his who was in precisely the same situation, the friend recently had been sold to the same trader James, just as Isaac had been. No argument was needed to convince his friend and fellow servant that if they meant to be free they would have to escape immediately.

That night, Henry Banks and Isaac Williams started for the woods together, preferring to live among reptiles and wild animals than remain any longer at the disposal of Dr. James. For two weeks they successfully escaped their pursuers. The woods, however, were being hunted in every direction, and one day the pursuers came upon them, shot them both, and carried them to King George's County Jail. The jail was an old building and had weak places in it; but the prisoners decided to make no attempt to break out while suffering badly from their wounds. So they remained one month in confinement. As they recovered, their brave spirits grew more and more daring.

Again they decided to strike out for freedom, but they had no idea where to go except back to the woods. Of course they had heard, as most slaves had, of hiding in caves, and pretty well understood all the measures which had to be resorted to when entering upon so hazardous an undertaking.

They concluded, however, that the risks of the cave could not make their condition any worse.

Having discovered how they could break jail, they were not long in accomplishing their purpose. Again they were out and off to the woods. This time they went far into the forest, and there they dug a cave. With great pains, they completely concealed their hiding spot. In this den they stayed three months. Now and then they would manage to secure a pig. A friend also would occasionally bring them a meal. Their sufferings were fearful; but, great as they were, the thought of returning to slavery never occurred to them. And the longer they stayed in the woods, the greater became their determination to be free. In the belief that their owner had about given up his search, they decided to take the North Star as their pilot, and began their way to free land.

Kit, an old friend in time of need, who had helped them during their concealment in their cave, was told of their plan. Kit fully appreciated the risks they would be taking, but indicated that he would like to join them in the undertaking. Kit was badly treated by his master, who was called General Washington, a common farmer, hard drinker, and brutal fighter, which Kit's poor back fully proved by the marks it bore. Isaac and Henry were very willing for him to join them.

In leaving their respective homes they broke family ties of the tenderest nature. Isaac had a wife, Eliza, and three children — Isaac, Estella, and Ellen — all owned by Fitchhugh. Henry was only 19, single, but left parents, brothers, and sisters, all owned by different slaveholders. Kit had a wife, Matilda, and three children, Sarah Ann, Jane Frances, and Ellen, all slaves.

CHAPTER 41

Pete Matthews, alias Samuel Sparrows, Arrives from Virginia.

Up to the age of 35, "Pete" had worn the yoke of slavery under William S. Matthews of Oak Hall, near Temperanceville, Virginia. Pete said that his "master was not a hard man," but the man to whom he "was hired, George

Matthews, was a very cruel man. I might as well be in the penitentiary as in his hands," was his statement.

One day, a short time before Pete "took off," an ox broke into the vegetable patch, helped himself to choice delicacies to the full extent of his roomy stomach, and badly damaged the garden in general. Pete's attention being attracted by the ox, he chased the ox out of the garden and gave the ox what he considered an appropriate "scolding." At this liberty taken by Pete, the master became furious. He got his gun and threatened to shoot Pete. "Open your mouth if you dare, and I will put the whole load into you," said the enraged master. He took out a large dirk-knife, and attempted to stab Pete, but Pete managed to keep out of his way.

Nevertheless, the violence of the master did not abate until he had beaten Pete over the head and body until he was weary, inflicting severe injuries.

A great change took hold of Pete's mind. He was now ready to adopt any plan that might hold out even the least encouragement for escape. Having about four dollars in his possession, he felt that he could not afford to employ a conductor on the Underground Railroad to help him escape. But he had a good pair of legs, and, he figured, with the help of a pistol he could face any two or three slave catchers. Pete knew a man who had a pistol for sale. He went to the man and told him that he wished to purchase it. For one dollar the pistol became Pete's property.

He now had three dollars left, but he was determined to make that amount meet his needs.

The last cruel beating had brought him to a point of desperation. On top of this, he remembered how he had been compelled to work hard night and day under Matthews. Furthermore, Pete had a wife whom his master prevented him from visiting; and these were not among the least offenses with which Pete charged his master. Fully bent on leaving, the following Sunday was fixed by Pete as the date for his departure.

The time arrived and Pete bade farewell to slavery. He followed the North Star, with his pistol in hand ready for action. After traveling about 200 miles from home he unexpectedly had an opportunity to use his pistol. To his astonishment, he suddenly came face-to-face with a former master, whom he had not seen for a long time. Pete desired no friendly exchange with him whatever. However, Pete saw that his old master recognized him and was determined to stop him.

Pete held on to his pistol, but took off in the opposite direction as fast as his tired legs would take him. As he was running, Pete cautiously cast a glance over his shoulder to see what had become of his old master. To his amazement, he found that a regular chase was being made after him. The need to double his pace was quite obvious. In this hour of peril, Pete's legs saved him.

After this notable race, Pete had more confidence in his legs than he had in his old pistol, but he held on to the gun until he reached Philadelphia, where he left it in the possession of the secretary of the Vigilance Committee. Considering it worth saving simply as a relic of the Underground Railroad, the gun was carefully retained.

Pete was now christened Samuel Sparrows. He was furnished with clean clothes, a ticket, and letters of introduction, and made his way toward Canada, looking quite respectable. Undoubtedly he felt even better than he looked; free air had a powerful effect on such passengers as Samuel Sparrows.

Pete's escape occurred about 1 October 1855. Pete may be described as a man of unmixed blood, well-made, and intelligent.

CHAPTER 42

John Atkinson Escapes on a Ship from a 'Worthless Sot'.

John was a slave under James Ray of Portsmouth, Virginia, whom he declared to be "a worthless sot." His character was fully described, but it is too disgusting to relate here. John was racially mixed, but dark, 31 years of age, well-formed, and intelligent. For some years before escaping he had been in the habit of hiring his time for $120 per year. Daily toiling to support his drunken and brutal master was a hardship that John felt keenly, but he was compelled to submit up to the day of his escape.

During John's life he had suffered many abuses from his oppressor and only a short while before freeing himself, he was threatened with being sold. This caused him to take the first daring step towards Canada, to leave his wife, Mary, without bidding her goodbye, or saying a word to her about his intention of fleeing.

John came as a private passenger on one of the Richmond steamers, and was indebted to the steward of the boat for his accommodations. Having been received by the Vigilance Committee of Philadelphia, he was cared for and sent on his way to Canada. There he found employment, and asked for nothing but his wife, and clothing, both left in Virginia. On these two points he wrote several times with considerable feeling.

Some slaves who hired their time in addition to the payment of their monthly hire, purchased nice clothes for themselves, which they usually valued highly, so much so, that after escaping they would not be content until they had tried every possible scheme to secure them. They would write back continually, either to their friends in the North or South, hoping by these means to obtain their clothing.

Frequently the persons who rendered them assistance in the South would be entrusted with all their effects, with the understanding that such valuables would be forwarded to a friend or to the Vigilance Committee at the earliest opportunity. The Committee strongly urged fugitives not to write back to the South (through the mails) because their letters may get others into serious trouble. All such letters were liable to be intercepted by authorities and slave owners in order to discover the names of those who had aided them on the Underground Railroad. To reduce this risk to others in the South, the Vigilance Committee often agreed to be taxed with demands to rescue clothing as well as wives and children, belonging to those they had already helped.

The following letters are typical examples of a large number which came to the Committee concerning clothing:

First Letter

"St. Catharines, 4 September "Dear Sir,

"I now embrace this favorable opportunity of writing you a few lines to inform you that I am quite well and arrived here safe, and I hope that these few lines may find you and your family the same. I hope you will intercede for my clothes and as soon as they come please send them to me, and if you have not time, get Dr. Lundy to look out for them, and when they come be very careful in sending them. I wish you would copy off this letter and give it to the steward, and tell him to give it to Henry Lewy and tell him to give it to my wife. Brother sends his love to you and all the family and he is overjoyed at seeing me arrive safe, he can hardly contain himself; also he wants to see his wife very much, and says when she comes he hopes you will send her on as soon as possible. Jerry Williams' love, together with all of us. I had a message for Mr. Lundy, but I forgot it when I was there.

"No more at present, but remain your ever grateful and sincere friend, "*John Atkinson.*"

Second Letter

"St. Catharines, C.W., 5 October 1854 "Mr. Wm. Still:
"Dear Sir,
"I have learned from my friend, Richmond Bohm, that my clothes were in Philadelphia. Will you have the kindness to see Dr. Lundy and if he has my clothes in charge, or knows about them, for him to send them on to me immediately, as I am in great need of them. I would like to have them put in a small box, and the overcoat I left at your house to be put in the box with them, to be sent to the care of my friend, Hiram Wilson. On receipt of this letter, I desire you to write a few lines to my wife, Mary Atkins, in the care of my friend, Henry Lowey, stating that I am well and hearty and hoping that she is the same. Please tell her to remember my love to her mother and her cousin, Emelin, and her husband, and Thomas Hunter; also to my father and mother. Please request her to write to me immediately, for her to be of good courage, that I love her more than ever. I would like her to come on as soon as she can, but for her to write and let me know when she is going to start.

"Affectionately Yours, "*John Atkins.*
"W.H. Atkinson, Fugitive, October 1854"

CHAPTER 43

Harriet Shephard, Her Five Children, and Others Escape with Their Master's Horses and Carriages.

One morning about 1 November 1855, the sleepy, slaveholding neighborhood of Chestertown, Maryland was doubtless deeply excited on learning that 11 slaves, 4 horses, and 2 carriages were missing. It is reasonable to suppose that the first report must have produced a shock about as stunning as an earthquake. Abolitionists were more reviled than ever. And curses and threats were dispensed by a deeply agitated community for days in succession.

Harriet Shephard, the mother of five children, could not bear the thought of her offspring being compelled to wear the miserable yoke of slavery, as she had been compelled to do. By her own personal experience, Harriet could very well judge what their fate would be when reaching man and womanhood. She declared that she had never received "kind treatment." It was not on this account, however, that she was prompted to escape. She was motivated to save her children from the same experiences.

Anna Maria, Edwin, Eliza Jane, Mary Ann, and John Henry were the names of the children for whom she was willing to make any sacrifice. They were young, and unable to walk, and she was penniless and unable to hire a conveyance, even if she had known anyone who would have been willing to risk the law to take them on a night's journey. She had to rely on her own resources. She then decided to seize the horses and carriages belonging to her master, and use these to liberate her children.

Knowing others who also wanted to escape to Canada, she consulted with others, both males and females, and they mutually decided to travel together.

It is not likely that they knew much about the roads; nevertheless they reached Wilmington, Delaware without difficulty, and ventured up into the heart of the town in carriages, looking as innocent as if they were going to meeting to hear an old-fashioned southern sermon, "Servants, obey your masters." Of course, the distinguished travelers were immediately reported to Thomas Garrett, who coolly transacted the affairs of the Underground Railroad in these vicinities.

On this occasion, there was little time for deliberation and great need for quick action. Garrett immediately decided that the fugitives must leave the horses and carriages, and be gotten out of Wilmington by other means as quickly as possible. With the courage and skill so characteristic of Garrett, the fugitives, under escort, were soon on their way to Kennett Square (a hotbed of abolitionists and stockholders of the Underground Railroad), which they reached safely. When they reached Kennett Square, a meeting was being held at the Long Wood Meetinghouse. They were invited to stay for a while at the meeting, after which they remained all night with one of the Kennett friends. Early the next morning, they were brought to Downingtown. Later that day, within a short distance of Kimberton, they reached the assistance of friend Lewis.

After receiving friendly aid and advice while there, they were forwarded to the Vigilance Committee in Philadelphia. Here further aid was given them. Since danger was quite obvious, they were divided into smaller groups and disguised, so that they might safely be sent on to Canada by means of one of the regular trains. Considering the condition of the slave mother and her children and friends, all concerned rejoiced that they had had the courage to use their master's horses and vehicles as they did.

CHAPTER 44

Washington Somlor, alias James Moore, Arrives on a Steamer.

Few could tell of having been eyewitness to outrages more revolting and disgraceful than Washington Somlor. He arrived by the steamer Pennsylvania, directly from Norfolk, Virginia in 1855. He was 32 years of age — a man of medium size and great intelligence. A merchant by the name of Smith owned Washington. Eight and a half months before escaping, Washington had hidden in order to escape both his master and the auction block. Smith believed in selling, flogging, cobbing, paddling, and otherwise torturing his slaves, in order to make the slaves feel his power. He thus tyrannized about 25 slaves.

Being a passionate man, when in a brutal mood, Smith made his slaves suffer unmercifully. Washington said, "On one occasion, about two months before I went into hiding, he had five of the slaves (some of them women) tied across a barrel, lashed with the cowhide and then cobbed, this was a common practice."

Such treatment was so inhuman and so incredible, that the Vigilance Committee of Philadelphia hesitated at first to believe his statement, and only yielded when facts and evidences were given which seemed indisputable.

The first effort to escape was made on the steamship of ice obstruction in the river, the steamer had to return. How Washington felt at having his hopes broken may be imagined but can scarcely be described.

Despite his great danger, when the steamer returned to Norfolk, he was able to get off the boat, under the watch of police officers, and again return to his hiding place. Here he waited patiently for spring. It came. Again the opportunity for another escape was presented, and it was seized unhesitatingly. This time, his faith was rewarded with success. He came through safely to the satisfaction of the Vigilance Committee as well as his own.

Although closely hidden in Norfolk, he had, through friends, some contact with the outside world. Among other items of information which came to his attention was a report that his master was being pressed by his creditors, and had all his slaves advertised for sale. An item still more sad also reached his ear, to the effect that his wife had been sold away to North Carolina, and thus separated from her two-year-old child. The child was given as a present to a niece of the master.

Washington spent a short time in Philadelphia in order to recuperate, after which he went to Canada where he could live as a free man.

CHAPTER 45

James Griffin, alias Thomas Brown, Arrives from Baltimore.

James was a farm hand under the yoke of Joshua Hitch, who lived on a farm about 17 miles from Baltimore. James spoke rather favorably of Hitch; indeed, it was through a direct act of kindness on the part of his master that he got the opportunity to make his escape. It appeared from his story that his master's affairs had become increasingly difficult, and the sheriff was making frequent visits to his house. This sign was interpreted to mean that James, if not others, would have to be sold before long.

The master was very perplexed as to which way to turn. He owned only three other adult slaves besides James, and they were females. One of them was his chief housekeeper, and with them all his relations were of such a nature as to lead James and others to think and say that they "were all his wives." To use James's own language, "he had three slave women; two were sisters, and he lived with them all as his wives; two of them he was very fond of," and desired to keep them from being sold if possible. The third, he concluded he could not save, she would have to be sold. In this dilemma, the master was good enough to allow James a few days' holiday for the purpose of finding himself a good master. Expressing his satisfaction and appreciation, James, armed with full authority from his master to select a new master, started for Baltimore.

On reaching Baltimore, however, James carefully steered clear of all slaveholders, and shrewdly turned his attention to the matter of getting an Underground Railroad ticket for Canada. After making a few inquiries without success, he decided to make his way north by walking at night. He thought his feet and legs were in good order, and his faith and hope were strong enough to move a mountain. Besides, several days still remained in which he was permitted to look for a new master, and these he decided could be profitably spent in making his way toward Canada.

Off he started, at a rapid pace; at the end of the first night's journey, he had made good headway, but at the expense of his feet.

His faith was stronger than ever. So he rested the next day in the woods, concealed, of course, and the next evening started with fresh courage and renewed perseverance. Finally, he reached Columbia, Pennsylvania. And there he found friendly hands reached out to help him, particularly with a more speedy and comfortable mode of travel advised. He was directed to the Vigilance Committee in Philadelphia, from whom he received friendly assistance, including advice and other help for reaching Canada.

James was 31 years of age, rather a fine-looking man, of a chestnut color, and intelligent. He had been a married man, but for two years before his escape, he had been a widower, that is, his wife had been sold away from him to North Carolina, and in that space of time he had received only three letters from her; he had given up all hope of ever seeing her again. He had two little boys living in Baltimore, whom he was obliged to leave. Their names were Edward and William. What became of them afterwards was never known at the Philadelphia station.

James's master was a man of about 50 years of age, who had never been lawfully married, yet had a number of children on his place who were of great concern to him in the midst of other pressing embarrassments. Of course, the Committee never learned how matters were settled after James left, but, in all probability, the wives, Nancy and Mary (sisters) and Lizzie, with all the children, had to be sold.

CHAPTER 46

Owen, Otho, and Benjamin Taylor and Their Families Flee on Horseback.

About the end of March 1856, Owen Taylor and his wife, Mary Ann, and their little son, Edward, together with a brother and his wife and two children, and a third brother, Benjamin, arrived from near Clear Springs, nine miles from Hagerstown, Maryland. They all left their home, or rather escaped from the prison house, on Easter Sunday, and came to Harrisburg, where they were assisted and directed to the Vigilance Committee in Philadelphia. A more interesting party had not reached the Committee for a long time.

The three brothers were intelligent, heroic, and resolved to obtain freedom not only for themselves, but for their wives and children, desperately in earnest. They had carefully calculated the cost of this struggle for liberty, and had fully made up their minds that if interfered with by slave catchers, somebody would have to bite the dust. They had pledged themselves never to surrender alive. Their travel-worn appearance, their attachment to each other, the joy that the tokens of friendship afforded them, and the description they gave of incidents on the road, made an impression not soon to be forgotten.

In the presence of a group like this, Sumner's great and eloquent speech on the barbarism of slavery seemed almost cold and dead, the mute appeals of these little ones in their mother's arms, the unlettered language of these young mothers, striving to save their offspring from the doom of slavery, the resolute and manly bearing of these brothers expressed in words full of love of liberty, and of the determination to resist slavery to the death, in defense of their wives and children, this was Sumner's speech enacted before our eyes.

Owen was about 31 years of age, but had experienced a great deal of trouble. He had been married twice, and his first wife was believed still to be alive. She, with their little child, had been sold in the Baltimore market about three years before, the mother being sent to Louisiana, the child to South Carolina. Father, mother, and child were parted with no hope of ever seeing each other again in this world. After Owen's wife was sent South, he sent her his likeness and a dress; the latter was received, and she was greatly delighted with it, but he never heard of her having received his photograph. He wrote to her, but he was not sure that she received his letters. Finally, he came to the conclusion that as she was forever dead to him, he would do well to marry again. Accordingly he took to himself another partner, the one who now accompanied him on the Underground Railroad. Owen was a born mechanic, and his master practically tested his skill in various ways, sometimes in the blacksmith shop, at other times as a wheelwright — again at making brushes and brooms. During his leisure times he would try his hand in all these crafts. This jack-of-all-trades was, of course, very valuable to his master. Indeed his place was hard to fill.

Henry Fiery, a farmer, "about 64 years of age, a stout, crusty old fellow", was the owner of Owen and his two brothers. Besides slaves, the old man had a wife, whose name was Martha, and seven children, who were pretty well grown up. One of the sons owned Owen's wife and two children. Owen declared that they had been worked hard, while few privileges had been given them. Clothing of the poorest texture was only grudgingly furnished. Nothing like Sunday clothing was ever given them; for these comforts they were forced to do "overwork" at night.

For a long time the idea of escape had been uppermost in the minds of this party. The first of January was the time "solemnly" fixed upon to "take out," but for some reason or other (not found in the record book), their calculating minds did not see the way altogether clear, and they deferred starting until Easter Sunday. On that memorable evening, the men boldly harnessed two of Mr. Fiery's horses and, placing their wives and children in the carriage, started off via Hagerstown, in a direct line for Chambersburg, Pennsylvania, at a rate that allowed no grass to grow under the feet of the horses. In this manner they made good time, reached Chambersburg safely, and ventured to a hotel where they put up their horses.

Here the group left their horses and "took out" for Harrisburg by another mode of travel, the railroad. On their arrival in Harrisburg, they found their way to the Vigilance Committee, who hurried them off to Philadelphia. The Vigilance Committee in Philadelphia was sent a dispatch apprising the Committee there of their approach. They had scarcely reached Philadelphia before the Fierys, who were in hot pursuit of them, had traced the fugitives as far as Harrisburg, if not farther.

As a result of this bold and successful escape, the community in which the Fierys lived was deeply agitated for days as were the communities along the entire route to Chambersburg. The horses were easily reclaimed at the hotel where they were left, but, of course, they were mute as to what had become of their drivers. The furious Fierys probably got wind of the fact that they had made their way to Harrisburg. At any rate they were very diligent in their search at this point. While there prosecuting his hunting expedition, Fiery managed to open communication with at least one member of the Harrisburg Vigilance Committee, to whom his grievances were made known, but derived little satisfaction.

After searching for a few weeks, the pursuers came to the conclusion that there was no likelihood of recovering the property through their demands for help or through the Fugitive Slave Law. In despair, therefore, they resorted to another approach. All at once they became "sort-o-friendly", indeed more than half inclined to free their slaves.

The following excerpt from the Committee's letter may throw some light on the subject:

First Letter

"Harrisburg, 28 April 1856 "Friend Still:

"Your last [letter] came to hand in due season, and I am happy to hear of the safe arrival of those gents.

"I have before me the power-of-attorney of Mr. John S. Fiery, son of Mr. Henry Fiery, of Washington County, Maryland, the owner of those three men, two women, and three children, who arrived in your town on the 24th or 25th of March. He graciously condescends to liberate the oldest in a year, and the remainder in proportional time, if they will come back; or to sell them their time for $1300. He is sick of the job, and is ready to make any conditions. Now, if you personally can get word to them and get them to send him a letter, in my charge, informing him of their whereabouts and prospects, I think it will be the best answer I can make him. He will return here in a week or two to know what can be done. He offers $500 to see them.

"Or if you can send me word where they are, I will endeavor to write to them for his special satisfaction; or if you cannot do either, send me your latest information, for I intend to make him spend a few more dollars, and if possible get a little sicker of this bad job. Do try and send him a few bitter pills for his weak nerves and disturbed mind.

"Yours in great haste, "*Jos. C. Bustill.*"

A subsequent letter from Mr. Bustill contains an item related to the feeling of disappointment experienced by Mr. Fiery on learning that his property was in Canada.

Second Letter

"Harrisburg, 26 May 1856 "Friend Still:

"I embrace the opportunity presented by the visit of our friend, F. Williams, to drop you a few lines in relation to our future operations.

"The Lightning Train was put on the Road on last Monday, and as the traveling season has commenced and this is the southern route for Niagara Falls, I have concluded not to send by way of Auburn, except in cases of great danger; but hereafter we will use Lightning Train, which leaves here at 1:30 and arrives in your city at 5:00 in the morning, and I will telegraph about 5:30 in the afternoon, so it may reach you before you close. These four are the only ones that have come since my last. The woman has been here some time waiting for her child and her beau, which she expects here about the first of June. If possible, please keep a knowledge of her whereabouts, to enable me to inform him if he comes ....

"I have nothing more to send you, except that John Fiery has visited us again and much to his chagrin received the information of their being in Canada.

"Yours as ever, "*Jos. C. Bustill.*"

While the Fierys were working energetically to re-enslave these brave fugitives, the latter were daily drinking in more and more of the spirit of freedom and were busy with schemes for the deliverance of other near kin left behind under the yoke of slavery.

Several very interesting letters were received from Otho Taylor, related to a raid he hoped to make to rescue his family. Two brief examples must suffice.

Third Letter

"15 April 1857 "Sir,

"We arrived here safely. Mr. Syrus and his lady are well situated. They have a place for the year round $15 per month. We are all well and hope that you are all the same. Now I wish to know whether you would please to send me some money to go after those people. Send it here if you please.

"Yours truly, "*Otho Taylor*"

Fourth Letter

"St. Catharines, 26 January 1857 "Mr. William Still:

"Dear Sir,

"I write at this time in behalf of Otho Taylor. He is very anxious to go and get his family at Clear Spring, Washington County, Maryland. He would like to know if the Society there would furnish him the means to go after them from Philadelphia; you will be running no risk in doing this. If the Society can do this, he would not be absent from Philadelphia more than three days.

"He is so anxious to get his family from slavery that he is willing to do almost anything to get them to Canada. You may possibly recollect him, he was at your place last August. I think he can be trusted. If you can do something for him, he has the means to take himself to your place.

"Please let me know immediately if you can do this. "Respectfully yours, "*M.A.H. Wilson.*"

Such appeals came very frequently from Canada, causing much sadness, because little encouragement could be held out to such projects. In the first place, the danger of such expeditions was fearful, and in the second place, our funds were inadequate for this kind of work. Thus, in most cases, such appeals had to be refused. Of course, there were those whose continual coming (those who continued to escape by other means) could not be denied.

CHAPTER 47

Woman Arrives in a Box, Speechless.

In the winter of 1857 a young woman, who had just reached adulthood, was boxed up in Baltimore by her companion, a young man, who had the box conveyed as freight to the depot in Baltimore for subsequent shipment to Philadelphia. Nearly all of one night it remained at the depot with the living agony in it, and after being turned upside down more than once, the next day about ten o'clock it reached Philadelphia.

Her companion came to Philadelphia in advance of the box. He arranged with a hackman, George Custus, to take the box from the depot to the home of a Mrs. Myers, at 412 S. 7th Street, where the resurrection was to take place.

Custus, without knowing exactly what the box contained, suspected from the apparent anxiety and instructions of the young man who engaged him to go after it, that it was of great importance. When he reached the depot, the freight car still remained on the street and had not been unloaded. Custus asked the freight agent for the box, not wanting to wait the usual time for the delivery of freight. At first the freight agent refused to unload just the box, but the hackman insisted. He reminded the freight agent: "You know me. I have been coming here for many years every day, and will be responsible for it."

Reluctantly, the freight master told him to "take it and go ahead with it." This was done immediately. It was placed in a one-horse wagon at the direction of Custus, and driven to Seventh and Minister Streets.

The secret had been shared with Mrs. Myers by the young companion of the woman. A feeling of horror came over the aged woman, who had been suddenly entrusted with such responsibility. A few doors from her lived an old friend of the same religious faith as herself, well-known as a brave woman, and a friend of the slave — Mrs. Ash, the undertaker or shrouder — whom everybody knew among the colored people. Mrs. Myers felt that it would not be wise to move in the matter of this resurrection without the presence of the undertaker. Accordingly, she called Mrs. Ash in.

Even her own family was excluded from witnessing the scene. The two aged women chose to be alone in that fearful moment, shuddering at the thought that a corpse might meet their gaze instead of a living person. However, they mustered courage and pried off the lid. A woman was discovered in the straw but she gave no sign of life. Their fears seemed fulfilled. "Surely she is dead," thought the witnesses.

"Get up, my child," spoke one of the women. With scarcely life enough to move the straw covering, she, nevertheless, showed that she had not died. She could not speak, but, with help, was removed from the box. She was immediately taken upstairs, but still had not spoken a word.

After a short while she said, "I feel so deadly weak." She was then asked if she would not have some water or nourishment, which she declined. Before long, however, she was convinced to take a cup of tea. She then went to bed, and there remained all day, speaking very little during that time.

The second day she gained strength and was able to talk much better, but not with ease. The third day she began to come to herself and talk quite freely. She tried to describe her sufferings and fears while in the box, but in vain. In the midst of her severest agonies her chief fear was that she would be discovered and carried back to slavery.

She had a pair of scissors with her, and in order to obtain some fresh air she had made a hole in the box, but it was very small. How she ever managed to breathe and maintain her existence, being in the condition of becoming a mother, it was hard to comprehend. In this instance the utmost endurance was put to the test.

She was obviously nearer death than Henry Box Brown, or any of the other box or chest cases that ever came under the notice of the Vigilance Committee of Philadelphia.

In Baltimore she belonged to a wealthy and fashionable family, and had been a seamstress and ladies' servant generally. On one occasion when sent on an errand for certain articles in order to complete arrangements for the Grand Opening Ball at the Academy of Music, she took occasion not to return, but was among the missing.

A great search was made for her, and a large reward offered, but all to no purpose. A free colored woman, who washed for the family, was suspected of knowing something about her escape. When they failed to learn anything from her, she was fired.

Soon after the arrival of this traveler, Mrs. Myers sent for the Vigilance Committee and the above facts were soon learned. After spending some three or four days in Mrs. Myers' family she remained in the writer's family about the same length of time, and was then forwarded to Canada.

Mrs. Myers was originally from Baltimore, and had frequently been in the habit of receiving Underground Railroad passengers. She had always found Thomas Shipley, the faithful philanthropist, a source of help in time of need.

George Custus, the hackman, was a black man. He was cool, sensible, and reliable in the performance of his duties.

CHAPTER 48

William and Ellen Craft Arrive from Georgia — She Dressed as a Man, He as the Man's Servant.

At one time, William and Ellen Craft were slaves in the state of Georgia. With them, as with thousands of others, the desire to be free was very strong. For this jewel they were willing to make any sacrifice, or to endure any amount of suffering. In this state of mind they began planning their escape. After thinking of various ways that might be tried, it occurred to William and Ellen that one might act the part of master and the other the part of servant.

Ellen, being fair enough to pass for white, would have to be transformed into a young planter for the time being. All that was needed, however, to make this important change was that she should be dressed elegantly in a fashionable men's suit, and have her hair cut in the style usually worn by young planters. Her abundance of dark hair offered a fine opportunity for the change.

So far, this plan looked very tempting. But it occurred to the two that Ellen was beardless. After some careful thought, they came to the conclusion that this difficulty could be overcome by muffling the face as though the young planter was suffering badly with a toothache. With this and several other difficulties resolved, the young planter and his faithful servant soon were found in the railroad cars heading for the City of Brotherly Love.

Scarcely had they arrived on free soil when the toothache was gone, the beardless face was unmuffled, and in the presence of a few astonished friends of the slave, the facts of this unparalleled Underground Railroad feat were fully explained.

The constant strain and pressure on Ellen's nerves, however, had tried her so severely that for days afterwards she was physically exhausted, although joy and gladness beamed from her eyes and the expression on her face.

Never can the writer forget the impression made by their arrival. Even now, after a lapse of many years, it is easy to picture them in a private room, surrounded by a few friends, Ellen in her fine black suit, with her cloak and high-heeled boots, looking, in every respect, like a young gentleman. And then, after discarding her male attire, reappearing, in every line and feature, her femininity fully restored.

Her husband, William, was thoroughly colored. He also was a man of marked natural abilities, good manners, great courage, and perceptive mind.

It was necessary, however, in those days, that they should seek a permanent residence where their freedom would be more secure than in Philadelphia; therefore they were advised to go directly to Boston. It was thought that they would be safe there, since it had then been about a generation since a fugitive had been taken back from Massachusetts. Also, through the incessant labors of William Lloyd Garrison, the great antislavery pioneer, and his faithful co-workers, it was conceded that another fugitive slave case could never be tolerated on the free soil of that state. So, they went to Boston.

On arriving, the warm hearts of abolitionists welcomed them heartily. They did not pretend to keep their coming a secret. The story of their escape was broadcast over the country, North and South, and indeed over the entire civilized world. For two years or more, not the slightest fear was entertained that they were not just as safe in Boston as if they had gone to Canada. But the day the Fugitive Slave Bill passed, even the bravest abolitionist began to fear that a fugitive slave was no longer safe anywhere under the stars and stripes, North or South, and that William and Ellen Craft were liable to be captured at any moment by Georgia slave hunters. However, instead of running to Canada, fugitives generally armed themselves and thus said, "Give me liberty or give me death."

William and Ellen Craft believed that it was their duty, as citizens of Massachusetts, to observe a more legal mode of marriage than had been permitted them in slavery. Since Theodore Parker had shown himself to be a very warm friend to them, they agreed to have their wedding over again according to the laws of a free state. After performing the ceremony, the renowned and fearless advocate of equal rights (Parker) presented William with a revolver and a dirk-knife, counseling him to use them in defense of his wife and himself, if ever an attempt should be made by his owners or anybody else to re-enslave them.

To the surprise of all Boston, the owners of William and Ellen actually had the audacity to attempt to recapture them under the Fugitive Slave Law. How it was done, and the results, were reported in the *Old Liberator* (William Lloyd Garrison's paper), as follows:

The Old Liberator's Account

"1 November 1850

"Slave hunters in Boston.

"Our city, for a week past, has been thrown into a state of intense excitement by the appearance of two prowling villains, named Hughes and Knight, from Macon, Georgia, for the purpose of seizing William and Ellen Craft, under the infernal Fugitive Slave Bill, and carrying them back to the hell of slavery. Since the day of 1776, there has not been such a popular demonstration on the side of human freedom in this region. The humane and patriotic contagion has infected all classes. Hardly any other subject has been talked about in the streets, or in the social circle.

"On Thursday of last week, warrants for the arrest of William and Ellen were issued by Judge Levi Woodbury, but no officer has yet been found ready or bold enough to serve them. In the meantime, the Vigilance Committee, appointed at the Faneuil Hall meeting, has not been idle. Their number has been increased to upwards of a hundred 'good men and true,' including some 30 or 40 members of the bar; and they have been in constant session, devising every legal method to baffle the pursuing bloodhounds, and relieve the city of their hateful presence.

"On Saturday placards were posted up in all directions, announcing the arrival of these slave hunters, and describing their persons. On the same day, Hughes and Knight were arrested on the charge of slander against William Craft, the **Chronotype** says, the damages being laid at $10,000; bail was demanded in the same sum, and was promptly furnished.

"The question is by whom? An immense crowd was assembled in front of the sheriff's office while the bail matter was being arranged. The reporters were not admitted. It was only known that Watson Freeman, Esq. who once declared his readiness to hang any number of negroes remarkably cheap, came in, saying that the arrest was a shame, all a 'humbug,' the trick of the 'damned' abolitionists, and proclaimed his readiness to stand bail. John H. Pearson was also sent for, and came — the same John H. Pearson, merchant and southern packet agent, who immortalized himself by sending back, on the 10th of September, 1846, in the bark executioner, to consign a fellow-being to a life of bondage, in obedience to the law of a slave state, and in violation of the law of his own. This same John H. Pearson, not contented with his previous infamy, was on hand. There is a story that the slave hunters have been his table guests also, and whether he bailed them or not, we don't know.

"What we know is that soon after Pearson came out from the back room, where he and Knight and the sheriff had been closeted, the sheriff said that Knight was bailed, he would not say by whom. Knight, being looked after, was not to be found. He had slipped out through a back door, and thus cheated the crowd of the pleasure of greeting him, possibly with that rough and ready affection which Barclay's brewers bestowed upon Haynau. The escape was very fortunate. Hughes and Knight have since been twice arrested and put under bonds of $10,000 (making $30,000 in all), charged with a conspiracy to kidnap and abduct William Craft, a peaceable citizen of Massachusetts, etc. Bail was entered by Hamilton Willis of Willis & Co., 25 State Street, and Patrick Riley, U.S. Deputy Marshal."

The following (says the ***Chronotype***) is a verbatim et literatim copy of the letter sent by Knight to Craft to entice him to the U.S. Hotel, in order to kidnap him:

"Boston, 22 October 1850, 11:00 P.M. "Wm. Craft:
"Sir,
"I have to leave so early in the morning that I could not call according to promise, so if you want me to carry a letter home with me, you must bring it to the United States Hotel tomorrow and leave it in Box 44, or come yourself tomorrow evening after tea and bring it. Let me know if you come yourself by sending a note to Box 44 [at the] U.S. Hotel so that I may know whether to wait after tea or not by the bearer. If your wife wants to see me you could bring her with you if you come yourself.
"*John Knight.*
"P.S. I shall leave for home early Thursday morning. "*J.K.*"

At a meeting of colored people, held in Belknap Street Church, on Friday evening, the following resolutions were unanimously adopted:

"Resolved, That God willed us free; man willed us slaves. We will as God wills; God's will be done.
"Resolved, that our oft repeated determination to resist oppression is the same now as ever, and we pledge ourselves, at all hazards, to resist unto death any attempt upon our liberties.
"Resolved, That as South Carolina seizes and imprisons colored seamen from the North, under the plea that it is to prevent insurrection and rebellion

among her colored population, the authorities of this state, and city in particular, be requested to lay hold of, and put in prison immediately, any and all fugitive slave hunters who may be found among us, upon the same ground, and for similar reasons."

Spirited speeches were made by Messrs. Remond, of Salem, Roberts, Nell, and Allen, of Boston, and Davis, of Plymouth. Individuals and highly respected committees of gentlemen have repeatedly waited for these Georgia villains, to persuade them to make a speedy departure from the city. After promising to do so, and repeatedly acting to the contrary, it is said that they left on Wednesday afternoon, in the express train for New York, and thus (says the ***Chronotype***), they have "gone off with their ears full of fleas, to fire the solemn word for the dissolution of the Union!"

Telegraphic information was received that President Fillmore announced his determination to sustain the Fugitive Slave Bill, at all hazards. The fugitives, as well as the colored people generally, seem determined to carry out the spirit of the resolutions to their fullest extent.

Ellen first received information that the slave hunters from Georgia were after her through Mrs. George S. Hilliard, of Boston, who had been a good friend to her from the day of her arrival from slavery. How Mrs. Hilliard obtained the information, the impression it made on Ellen, and where Ellen was hidden is found in the following extract of a letter written by Mrs. Hilliard:

"In regard to William and Ellen Craft, it is true that we received her at our house when the first warrant under the act of 1850 was issued.

"Dr. Bowditch called upon us to say that the warrant must be for William and Ellen, as they were the only fugitives here known to have come from Georgia, and the doctor asked what we could do. I went to the house of the Rev. F.T. Gray, on Mt. Vernon Street, where Ellen was working with Miss Dean, an upholsterer, a friend of ours, who had told us she would teach Ellen her trade. I proposed to Ellen to come and do some work for me, intending not to alarm her. My manner, which I supposed to be indifferent and calm, betrayed me, and she threw herself into my arms, sobbing and weeping. She, however, recovered her composure as soon as we reached the street, and was very firm ever after.

"My husband wished her, by all means, to be brought to our house, and to remain under his protection, saying: 'I am perfectly willing to meet the penalty, should she be found here, but will never give her up.' The penalty, you remember, was six months' imprisonment and a thousand dollars fine. William Craft went, after a time, to Lewis Hayden. He was at first, as Dr. Bowditch told us, 'barricaded in his shop on Cambridge Street.' I saw him there, and he said, 'Ellen must not be left at your house.'

"'Why? William,' I said, 'do you think we would give her up?'

"'Never,' said he, 'but Mr. Hilliard is not only our friend, he is a U.S. commissioner, and should Ellen be found in his house, he must resign his office, as well as incur the penalty of the law, and I will not subject a friend to such a punishment for the sake of our safety.' Was not this noble, when you think how small was the penalty that anyone could receive for aiding slaves to escape, compared to the fate which threatened them in case they were captured? William C. made the same objection to having his wife taken to Mr. Ellis Gray Loring's, he also being a friend and a commissioner."

This deed of humanity and Christian charity is worthy to be commemorated and classed with the act of the good Samaritan, as the same spirit is shown in both cases. Mrs. Hilliard's house often was an asylum for fugitive slaves.

After the hunters had left the city in dismay, and the storm of excitement had partially subsided, the friends of William and Ellen concluded that they had better seek a country where they would not be in daily fear of slave catchers, backed by the government of the United States. They were, therefore, advised to go to Great Britain. Outfits were liberally provided for them, passages obtained, and they took their departure to live in a foreign land.

Much might be told concerning the warm reception they met with from the friends of humanity on every hand, during a stay in England of nearly 20 years, but we thought that the extract of a letter from William Farmer, Esq., of London to William Lloyd Garrison, written 26 June 1851, would suffice:

Excerpt from Farmer's Letter

"Fortunately, we have, at the present moment, in the British Metropolis, some specimens of what were once American 'chattels personal' in the persons of William and Ellen Craft, and William W. Brown, and their friends resolved that they should be exhibited under the world's huge glass case, in order that the world might form its opinion of the alleged mental inferiority of the African race, and their fitness or unfitness for freedom. A small party of antislavery friends was accordingly formed to accompany the fugitives through the [Crystal Palace] Exhibition. Mr. and Mrs. Estlin, of Bristol, and a lady friend, Mr. and Mrs. Richard Webb, of Dublin, and a son and daughter, Mr. McDonnell (a most influential member of the Executive Committee of the National Reform Association), these ladies and gentlemen, together with myself, at Mr. Thompson's house, and, in company with Mrs. Thompson, and Miss Amelia Thompson, the Crafts and Brown, proceeded there to the Exhibition. Saturday was selected, as a day upon which the largest number of the aristocracy and wealthy classes attend the Crystal Palace, and the company was, on this occasion, the most distinguished that had been gathered together within its walls since its opening day. Some 15,000, mostly of the upper classes, were there congregated, including the Queen, Prince Albert, and the royal children, the antislavery Duchess of Sutherland (by whom the fugitives were evidently favorably regarded), the Duke of Wellington, the Bishops of Winchester and St. Asaph, a large number of peers, peeresses, members of Parliament, merchants and bankers, and distinguished men from almost all parts of the world, surpassing, in variety of tongue, character, and costume, the description of the population of Jerusalem on the day of Pentecost, a season of which it is hoped the Great Exhibition will prove a type, in the copious outpouring of the holy spirit of brotherly union, and the consequent diffusion, throughout the world, of the antislavery gospel of good will to all men.

"In addition to the American exhibitors, it so happened that the American visitors were particularly numerous, among whom the experienced eyes of Brown and the Crafts enabled them to detect slaveholders by dozens. Mr. McDonnell escorted Mrs. Craft and Mrs. Thompson; Miss Thompson, at her own request, took the arm of William Wells Brown, whose companion she elected to be for the day; William Craft walked with Miss Amelia Thompson and myself. This arrangement was purposely made in order that there might be no appearance of patronizing the fugitives, but that it might be shown that we regarded them as our equals, and honored them for their heroic escape from slavery.

"Quite contrary to the feeling of ordinary visitors, the American department was our chief attraction. Upon arriving at Powers' 'Greek Slave,' our glorious antislavery friend, Punch's 'Virginia Slave' was produced. I hope you have seen this production of our great humorous moralist. It is an admirably drawn figure of a female slave in chains, with the inscription beneath, 'The Virginia Slave, a companion for Powers' Greek Slave.' The comparison of the two soon drew a small crowd, including several Americans, around and near us. Although they refrained from any audible expression of feeling, the object of the comparison was evidently understood and keenly felt. It would not have been prudent in us to have challenged, in words, an antislavery discussion in the World's Convention; but everything that we could with propriety do was done to induce them to break silence upon the subject. We had no intention, verbally, of taking the initiative in such a discussion; we confined ourselves to speaking at them, in order that they might be led to speak to us; but our efforts were of no avail.

"The gauntlet, which was unmistakably thrown down by our party, the Americans were too wary to take up. We spoke among each other of the wrongs of slavery; it was in vain. We discoursed freely upon the iniquity of a professedly Christian Republic holding three millions of its population in cruel and degrading bondage; you might as well have preached to the winds. Wm. Wells Brown took 'Punch's Virginia Slave' and deposited it within the enclosure by the 'Greek Slave,' saying audibly, 'As an American fugitive slave, I place this 'Virginia Slave' by the side of the 'Greek Slave,' as its most fitting companion.' Not a word, or reply, or word of protest from Yankee or Southerner. We had not, however, proceeded many steps from the place before the 'Virginia Slave' was removed. We returned to the statue, and stood near the American by whom it had been taken up to give him an opportunity of making any remarks he chose upon the matter. Whatever were his feelings, his policy was to keep his lips closed. If he had felt that the act was wrongful, would he not have appealed to the sense of justice of the British bystanders, who are always ready to resist an insult offered to a foreigner in this country? If it was an insult, why not resent it, as became high-spirited Americans? But no; the chivalry of the South tamely allowed itself to be plucked by the beard; the [talkativeness] of the North permitted itself to be silenced by three fugitive slaves ....

"We promenaded the Exhibition between six and seven hours, and visited nearly every portion of the vast edifice. Among the thousands whom we met in our tour, who dreamed of any impropriety in a gentleman of character and standing, like Mr. McDonnell, walking arm-in-arm with a colored woman; or an elegant and accomplished young lady, like Miss Thompson (daughter of the Hon. George Thompson, M.C.), becoming the promenading companion of a colored man? Did the English peers or peeresses? Not the most aristocratic among them. Did the representatives of any other country have their notions of propriety shocked by the matter? None but Americans. But even the New York Broadway bullies would not have dared to utter a word of insult, much less lift a finger against Wm. Wells Brown, when walking with his fair companion in the World's Exhibition.

"It was a circumstance not to be forgotten by these southern bloodhounds. Probably, for the first time in their lives, they felt themselves thoroughly muzzled; they dared not even to bark, much less bite. Like the meanest curs, they had to sneak through the Crystal Palace, unnoticed and uncared for; while the victims who had been rescued from their jaws were warmly greeted by visitors from all parts of the country.

"Brown and the Crafts have paid several other visits to the Great Exhibition, in one of which, Wm. Craft succeeded in getting some southerners 'out' upon the Fugitive Slave Bill, respecting which a discussion was held between them in the American department. Finding themselves worsted at every point, they were compelled to have recourse to lying, and unblushingly denied that the bill contained the provisions which Craft alleged it did. Craft took care to inform them who and what he was. He told them that there had been too much information upon that measure diffused in England for lying to conceal them. He has subsequently met the same parties, who, with contemptible hypocrisy, treated him with great respect."

In England the Crafts were highly respected. While under her British Majesty's protection, Ellen became the mother of several children (having had none under the stars and stripes). These they spared no pains in educating for usefulness in the world. Some two years after William and Ellen returned with two of their children to the United States, and after visiting Boston and other places, William concluded to visit Georgia, his old home, with a view of seeing what inducement war had opened up to enterprise, as he had felt a desire to remove his family there, if encouraged. Indeed he was prepared to purchase a plantation, if he found matters satisfactory. This visit evidently furnished the needed encouragement, judging from the fact that he did purchase a plantation somewhere in the neighborhood of Savannah, and subsequently moved his family there.

Obviously the Fugitive Slave Law in its crusade against William and Ellen Craft reaped no advantages, but on the contrary, liberty gained a great deal.

CHAPTER 49

Lewis Cobb and Nancy Brister
Arrive from Richmond, Virginia, by Boat.

No other southern city furnished a larger number of brave, intelligent, and fine–looking Underground Railroad passengers than the city of

Richmond. Lewis and Nancy were good examples of the class of travelers coming from that city. Lewis was described as a light yellow man, medium size, good-looking, and intelligent. In referring to bondage, he spoke with great earnestness, and in language very easily understood, especially when speaking of Samuel Myers, from whom he escaped, he did not hesitate to give him the character of being a very hard man who was never satisfied, no matter how hard the slaves might try to please him.

Myers was engaged in the commission and forwarding business, and was a man of some standing in Richmond. From him Lewis had received very severe floggings, the memory of which he would not only carry with him to Canada, but to the grave. It was owing to abuse of this kind that he became determined to look for a home under the protection of the British Lion. For eight months he longed to get away, and had no rest until he found himself on the Underground Railroad. His master was a member of the Century Methodist Church, as was also his wife and family; but Lewis thought that they were strangers to practical Christianity, judging from the manner that the slaves were treated by both master and mistress. Lewis was a Baptist, and belonged to the second church. Twelve hundred dollars had been offered for him. He left his father (Judville) and his brother, John Harris, both slaves. In looking forward to life in Canada, Lewis' thoughts overflowed with anticipation of freedom, and the Philadelphia Vigilance Committee felt great satisfaction in assisting him.

Nancy was also from Richmond, and came in the same boat with Lewis. She represented the most "likely-looking female bond servants." Indeed her appearance recommended her at once. She was neat, modest, and well-behaved, with a good figure and the picture of health, with a face beaming with joy and gladness, notwithstanding the recent struggles and sufferings through which she had passed.

Young as Nancy was, she had seen much of slavery, and had, doubtless, learned a great deal as a result. In all events, it was through cruel treatment, having been frequently beaten after she had passed her 18th year, that she was prompted to seek freedom. It was so common for her mistress to give way to unbridled passions that Nancy never felt safe. Under the severest infliction of punishment she was not allowed to complain. Neither from mistress nor master had she any reason to expect mercy or leniency, indeed she saw no way of escape but by the Underground Railroad.

It was true that the master, Mr. William Bears, was a Yankee from Connecticut, and his wife a member of the Episcopal Church, but Nancy's yoke seemed none the lighter for all that. Fully persuaded that she would never find her condition any better while remaining in their hands, she accepted the advice and aid of a young man to whom she was engaged; he was shrewd enough to find an agent in Richmond with whom he entered into an agreement to have Nancy brought away. With a cheerful heart, the journey was undertaken, and she safely reached the Committee. She left her mother, one brother, and a sister in Richmond. Her master lost "property" worth one thousand dollars when Nancy left.

Having been accommodated and aided by the Committee, they were forwarded to Canada. Lewis wrote back repeatedly and expressed his gratitude for favors received, as will be seen by the following letter:

―――――

"Toronto, 25 April 1857 "To Mr. Wm. Still, "Dear Sir:

"I take this opportunity of addressing these few lines to inform you that I am well and hope that they may find you and your family enjoying the same good health. Please give my love to you and your family. I had a very pleasant trip from your house that morning. Dear sir, you would oblige me much, if you have not sent that box to Mr. Robinson, to open it and take out the little yellow box that I tied up in the large one and send it on by express to me in Toronto. Lift up a few of the things and you will find it near the top. All the clothes that I have are in that box and I stand in need of them. You would oblige me much by so doing.

"I stopped at Mr. Jones' in Elmira, and was very well treated by him while there. I am now in Toronto and doing very well at present. I am very thankful to you and your family for the attention you paid to me while at your house. I wish you would see Mr. Ormsted and ask him if he has not some things for Mr. Anthony Loney, and if he has, please send them on with my things, as we are both living together at this time.

"Give my love to Mr. Anthony, also to Mr. Ormsted and family. Dear sir, we both would be very glad for you to attend to this, as we both do stand very much in need of them at this time. Dear sir, you will oblige me by giving my love to Miss Frances Watkins, and as she said she hoped to be out in the summer, I should like to see her. I have met with a gentleman here by the name of Mr. Truehart, and he sends his best love to you and your family. Mr. Truehart desires to know whether you received the letter he sent to you, and if so, answer it as soon as possible. Please answer this letter as soon as possible.

"I must now come to a close by saying that I remain your beloved friend, "Lewis Cobb.

"The young man who was there that morning, Mr. Robinson, got married to that young lady."

CHAPTER 50

Old Jane Davis Arrives from Maryland to Flee the Auction Block.

The following letter from Thomas Garrett will serve to introduce one of the most remarkable cases that it was our privilege to assist:

"Wilmington, 6 mo. [June], 9th, 1857 "Esteemed Friend,
"William Still:
"We have here in this place, at Comegys Munson's, an old colored woman, the mother of 12 children, one half of which has been sold south. She has been so ill-used, that she was compelled to leave husband and children behind, and is desirous of getting to a brother who lives at Buffalo. She was nearly naked. She called at my house on 7th day [Saturday] night, but being [away] from home, I did not see her until last evening. I ... obtained for her two undergarments, one new; two skirts, one new; a good frock with cape;

one of my wife's bonnets and stockings; and gave her five dollars in gold, which, if properly used, will put her pretty well on the way. I also gave her a letter to you. Since I gave them to her she has concluded to stay where she is until 7th day night, when Comegys Munson says he can leave his work and will go with her to thy house. I write this so that thee may be prepared for them; they ought to arrive between 11 and 12 o'clock. Perhaps thee may find some fugitive that will be willing to accompany her.

"With desire for thy welfare and the cause of the oppressed, I remain thy friend, *"Thomas Garrett."*

Jane did not know how old she was. She was probably 60 or 70. She fled to keep from being sold. She had been "whipped right smart," poorly fed, and poorly clothed by a certain Roger McZant, of the New Market District, Eastern Shore of Maryland. His wife was a "bad woman, too." Just before escaping, Jane "got a whisper" that her master was about to sell her; on asking him if the rumor was true, he was silent. He had been asking $100 for her.

Remembering that four of her children had been snatched away from her and sold south, and she herself was threatened with the same fate, she was willing to suffer hunger and sleep in the woods for nights and days while wandering towards Canada, rather than trust herself any longer under the protection of her "kind" owner. Before reaching a place of rest, she was in the woods and almost entirely without nourishment.

Jane, doubtless, represented thousands of old slave mothers, who after having been worn out under the yoke, were frequently either offered for sale for a trifle, turned out to die, or compelled to eke out their existence on the smallest allowance.

CHAPTER 51

Oscar D. Ball and Montgomery Graham Arrive from Alexandria, Virginia in 1857.

"Four Hundred Dollars Reward.

"Ran away from the owner in Alexandria, Virginia on the night of the 13th, two young negro men, from 20 to 25 years of age. Montgomery is [racially mixed], very bright, about five feet, six inches in height, of polite manners, and smiles much when speaking or spoken to. Oscar is of a tawny complexion, about six feet high, sluggish in his appearance and movements, and of awkward manners. Hundred dollars each will be paid for the delivery of the above slaves if taken in a slave state, or two hundred dollars each if taken in a free state. One or more slaves belonging to other owners, it is supposed, went in their company.

"Address: John T. Gordon. "Alexandria."

Although the name of John T. Gordon appears signed to the above advertisement, he was not the owner of Montgomery and Oscar. According to their own testimony they belonged to a maiden lady by the name of Miss Elizabeth Gordon, who probably thought that the business of advertising for runaway slaves was rather beneath her.

While both these passengers showed great satisfaction in leaving their mistress, they did not give her a bad name. On the contrary, they spoke rather well of her, as follows: "Mistress was a spare woman, tolerably tall, and very kind, except when sick, she would not pay much attention then. She was a member of the Southern Methodist Church, and was strict in her religion."

Having a good degree of faith in his mistress, Oscar boldly asked her one day how much she would take for him. She agreed to take $800. Oscar, wishing to drive a pretty shrewd bargain, offered her $700, hoping that she would view the matter in a religious light, and would come down $100. After reflection, instead of making a reduction, she raised the amount to $1000, which Oscar concluded was too much for himself. It was not, however, as much as he was worth according to his mistress' estimate, for she declared that she had often been offered $1500 for him.

Miss Gordon raised Oscar from a child and had treated him as a "pet." When he was a little "shaver" seven or eight years of age, she made it a practice to have him sleep in her room, to show that she had no prejudice.

In speaking of his mistress, Montgomery was not quite as complimentary as Oscar. With regard to giving "passes," he considered her narrow, to say the least. But he was in such good humor with everybody, owing to the fact that he had succeeded in getting his neck out of the yoke, that he evidently had no desire to say hard things about her.

Judging from his story, he had desired his freedom for a long time. He had tried to make connection with the Underground Railroad, but had encountered many obstacles that complicated his escape. Arriving in Philadelphia, finding himself breathing free air, and receiving aid and encouragement in a manner that he had never known before, he was an exceedingly happy person.

Oscar left his wife and one child, one brother, and two sisters. Montgomery left one sister, but no other near relatives.

Instead of going to Canada, Oscar and his friend chose to go to Oswego, New York, where they changed their names. Instead of returning themselves to their kind mistress, they were "wicked" enough to plot the escape of their friends via the Underground Railroad, as may be seen from the following letter from Oscar:

"Oswego, 25 October 1857 "Dear Sir:

"I take this opportunity of writing you these few lines to inform you that I am well and hope these few lines will find you the same and your family. You must excuse me for not writing to you before. I would have written to you before this but I put away the card you gave me and could not find it until a few days ago. I did not go to Canada for I got work in Oswego, but times are very dull here at present. I have been out of a job for about five weeks. I would like to go to Australia. Do you know of any gentleman that is going there or any other place, except south, that wants a servant to go there with him to wait on him or do any other work? I have a brother that wants to come north. I received a letter from him a few days ago. Can you tell me of any plan that I can fix to get him ... give my respects to Mrs. Still and all of your family. Please let me know if you hear of any berth of that kind. Nothing more at present.

"I remain your obedient servant.

"But my name is now John Delaney. Direct your letter to John Delaney, Oswego, New York care of R. Oliphant."

CHAPTER 52

James Conner Arrives from New Orleans, 1857.

James stated to the Vigilance Committee of Philadelphia that he was about 43 years old, that he was born a slave in Nelson County, Kentucky, and that he was first owned by a widow lady by the name of Ruth Head. "She (mistress) was like a mother to me," said Jim. "I was about 16 years old when she died; the estate was settled and I was sold south to a man named Vincent Turner, a planter, and about the worst man, I expect, that ever the sun shined on. His slaves he fairly murdered; 200 lashes were merely a promise for him. He owned about 300 slaves. I lived with Turner until he died. After his death I still lived on the plantation with his widow, Mrs. Virginia Turner." About 12 years ago (prior to Jim's escape) she was married to a Mr. Charles Parlange, "a poor man, though a very smart man, bad-hearted, and very barbarous."

Before her second marriage, cotton had always been cultivated, but a few years later sugar had taken the place of cotton, and had become the principal thing raised in that part of the country. Under the change, sugar was raised and the slaves were made to experience harder times than ever. They were allowed only from three to three and a half pounds of pork a week, with a peck of corn meal; nothing else was allowed. They began to work in the morning, just when they could barely see; they quit work in the evening when they could not see to work any longer.

The mistress was a large, portly woman, good-looking, and pretty well liked by her slaves. The place where the plantation was located was at Point Copee, on Falls River, about 150 miles from New Orleans. She also owned property and about 20 slaves in the city of New Orleans.

"I lived there and hired my time for awhile. I saw some hard times on the plantation. Many a time I have seen slaves whipped almost to death, well, I tell you I have seen them whipped to death. A slave named Sam was whipped to death tied to the ground. Joe, another slave, was whipped to death by the overseer: running away was their crime.

"Four times I was shot. Once [I tried to escape, and] all hands, young and old on the plantation, were on the chase after me. I was strongly armed with an axe, tomahawk, and butcher knife. I expected to be killed on the spot, but I got to the woods and stayed two days. At night I went back to the plantation and got something to eat. While going back to the woods I was shot in the thigh, legs, back, and head, was badly wounded, my mind was to die rather than be taken. I ran a half mile after I was shot, but was taken. I have shot in me now. Feel here on my head, feel my back, feel buck shot in my thigh. I shall carry shot in me to my grave. I have been shot four different times. I was shot twice by a fellow servant; it was my master's orders. Another time by the overseer. Shooting was no uncommon thing in Louisiana.

"At one time I was allowed to raise hogs. I had 25 taken from me without being allowed the first copper. My mistress promised me at another time $40 for gathering honey, but when I went to her, she said, by and by, but the by and by never came.

"In 1853 my freedom was promised; for five years before this time I had been overseer; during four years of this time a visit was made to France by my owners, but on their return my freedom was not given me. My mistress thought I had made enough money to buy myself. They asked $1150 for me. I told them that I hadn't the money. Then they said if I would go with them to Virginia after a number of slaves they wished to purchase, and would be a good boy, they would give me my freedom on the return of the trip. We started on the 8th of June 1857. I made fair promises, wishing to travel, and they placed all confidence in me. I was to carry the slaves back from Virginia.

"They came as far as Baltimore, and they began to talk of coming farther north, to Philadelphia. They talked very good to me, and told me that if they brought me with them to a free state that I must not leave them; talked a good deal about giving me my freedom, as had been promised before starting, etc. I let on to them that I had no wish to go north; that Baltimore was as far north as I wished to see, and that I had rather be going home than going north. I told them that I was tired of this country. In speaking of coming north, they made mention of the Allegheny Mountains. I told them that I would like to see that, but nothing more. They hated the north, and I made believe that I did, too. Mistress said that if I behaved myself I could go with them to France, when they went again, after they returned home, as they intended to go again.

"So they decided to take me with them to Philadelphia for a short visit before going into Virginia to buy up their drove of slaves for Louisiana. My heart leaped for joy when I found we were going to a free state; but I did not let my owners know my feelings.

"We reached Philadelphia and went to the Girard Hotel, and there I made up my mind that they should go back without me. I saw a colored man who talked with me, and told me about the [Vigilance] Committee. He brought me to the Anti-Slavery Office ...."

The Committee told Jim that he could go free immediately, without saying a word to anybody, as the simple fact of his masters bringing him into the state was sufficient to establish his freedom before the courts. At the same time the Committee assured him if he was willing to have his master arrested and brought before one of the judges of the city to show cause why he held a slave in Pennsylvania, contrary to the laws of the state, that he should lack neither friends nor money to aid him in the matter; and, moreover, his freedom would be publicly proclaimed.

Jim thought carefully about these options, but preferred not to meet his "kindhearted" master and mistress in court, as he was not quite sure that he would have the courage to face them and stand by his charges.

This was not strange. Indeed, not only slaves cowed before the eye of slaveholders. Did not even northern men, superior in education and wealth, fear to say their souls were their own in the same presence?

Jim, therefore, concluded to throw himself upon the protection of the Committee and take an Underground Railroad ticket, and thereby spare himself and his master and mistress the disagreeableness of meeting again. The Committee arranged matters for him, and gave him a passport for her British Majesty's possession, Canada.

The unvarnished facts, as they were then recorded, as told by Jim, and as they are reproduced here, comprise only a very meager part of his sad but interesting story. At the time Jim left his master and mistress in Philadelphia, some excitement existed at the attempt of his master to recover him through the Philadelphia police force, under the charge that he (Jim) had been stealing, as may be seen from the following letter which appeared in the ***National Anti-Slavery Standard***:

"Another Slave Hunt in Philadelphia "Philadelphia, Monday, 27 July 1857

"Yesterday afternoon a rumor was afloat that a negro man named Jim, who had accompanied his master (Mr. Charles Parlange), from New Orleans to this city, had left his master for the purpose of tasting the sweets of freedom. It was alleged by Mr. Parlange that the said 'Jim' had taken with him two tin boxes, one of which contained money. Mr. Parlange went on his way to New York, via the Camden and Amboy Railroad, and upon his arrival at the Walnut Street wharf, with two ladies, 'Jim' was missing. Mr. Parlange immediately made application to a Mr. Wallace, who is a police officer stationed at the Walnut Street depot. Mr. Wallace got into a carriage with Mr. Parlange and the two ladies, and, as Mr. Wallace stated, drove back to the Girard House, where 'Jim' had not been heard of since he had left for the Walnut Street wharf.

"A story was then set afloat to the effect that a negro of certain, but very 'particular' description (such as would be given by a Louisiana slave owner), had stolen two boxes as stated above. A notice signed 'Clarke' was received at the Police Telegraph Office by the operator (David Wunderly) containing a full description of Jim, also offering a reward of $100 for his capture. This notice was telegraphed to all the wards in every section.

"This morning Mr. Wunderly found fault with the reporters using the information, and, in presence of some four or five persons, said the notice signed 'Clarke' was a private paper, and no reporter had a right to look at it; at the same time asserting that if he knew where the [negro] was, he would give him up, as $100 did not come along every day. The policeman, Wallace, expressed the utmost fear that the name of Mr. Parlange would be discovered and stated that he was an intimate friend of his. It does not seem that the matter was communicated to the wards by any official authority whatever, and who the 'Clarke' is, whose name was signed to the notice, has not yet [been discovered]. Some of the papers noticed it briefly this morning, which has set several of the officers on their tips.

"There is little doubt that 'Jim' has merely exercised his own judgment about remaining with his master any longer, and took this opportunity to take himself to freedom. It is assumed that he was to precede his master to Walnut Street wharf with the baggage; but, singular enough to say, no complaint has been made about the baggage being missed, simply the two tin boxes, and particularly the one containing money. This is, doubtless, a ruse to engage the services of the Philadelphia police in the interesting game of [slave] hunting. Mr. Parlange, if he is staying in your city, will doubtless be glad to learn that the matter of his man 'Jim' and the two tin boxes has received ample publicity.

"*W.H.*"

Rev. Hiram Wilson, the Underground Railroad agent at St. Catharines, C.W., duly announced Jim's safe arrival as follows:

"Buffalo, 12 August 1857 "My Dear Friend,
"Wm. Still:

"I take the liberty to inform you that I had the pleasure of seeing a man of sable brand at my house in St. C. yesterday, by name of James Connor, lately from New Orleans, more recently from the City of Brotherly Love, where he took leave of his French master. He desired me to inform you of his safe arrival in the glorious land of freedom, and to send his kind regards to you and to Mr. Williamson; also to another person (the name [of whom] I have forgotten). Poor Malinda Smith, with her two little girls and young babe, is with us doing well.

"Affectionately yours, *"Hiram Wilson."*

CHAPTER 53

Harrison Cary Arrives from Washington, D.C.

The passenger bearing this name who applied to the Philadelphia Vigilance Committee for assistance was racially mixed and of medium size, with a pleasant countenance, and an intelligent mind. With only a moderate education he might have raised himself to the "top rung of the ladder," as a representative of the downtrodden slave. Seeking, as usual, to learn his background, the following questions and answers were exchanged during an interview with him:

"How old are you?"

"Twenty-eight years of age this coming March." "To whom did you belong?"

"Mrs. Jane E. Ashley."

"What kind of a woman was she?"

"She was a very clever woman; never said anything out of the way." "How many servants had she?"

"She had no other servants." "Did you live with her?"

"No. I hired my time for $22 a month." "How could you make so much money?"

"I was a bricklayer by trade, and ranked among the first in the city."

As Harrison talked so intelligently, the member of the Committee who was examining him was anxious to know how he came to be so knowledgeable — the fact that he could read being very evident.

Harrison went on to tell how he came to acquire the ability to both read and write. He explained that slaves caught out at night without passes from their master or mistress were invariably arrested. If they were unable to raise money to buy themselves off, they were taken and locked up in a place known as the "cage." In the morning the owner was notified, and after paying the fine, the unfortunate prisoner had to go to meet his fate at the hands of his owner.

Often the slave found himself or herself sentenced to take 39 or more lashes before atonement could be made for the violated law and the fine sustained by the enraged owner.

Harrison, having strong dislike for these "wholesome regulations" of the peculiar institution, saw the [only way for him to avoid paying these penalties] was to learn to write his own passes. To obtain this ability, he knew that the law against slaves being taught would have to be broken. Nevertheless, he was so anxious to learn that he was determined to run the risk. He subsequently developed the ability with very little difficulty or assistance. Valuing his prize highly, he improved more and more until he could write his own passes satisfactorily. The "cage" he denounced as a perfect "hog hole," and added, "it was more than I could bear."

He also spoke with equal dislike against the pass system. "The idea of working hard all day and then being obliged to have a pass" was one law he was willing to help others break. But he said nothing disrespectful against the individual to whom he had belonged. Once he had been sold, but the price was not noted on the records of the Vigilance Committee.

His mother had been sold several times. His brother, William Henry Cary, escaped from Washington, D.C. when still a youth. What became of him, Harrison did not know, but assumed that he had made his way to a free state, or Canada; and he hoped to find him. He had no knowledge of any other relatives.

In further conversation with him, he was asked why he had remained a single man. In response, he said that he had resolved not to entangle himself with a family until he had obtained his freedom.

He had found it pretty hard to meet his monthly hire, and consequently he was on the lookout to better his condition (seek his freedom) as soon as a favorable opportunity might offer. Harrison's mistress had a son named John James Ashley, who was then a minor. On becoming an adult, according to the will of this lad's father, he was to have possession of Harrison as his portion of his father's estate. Harrison had no plans to support the son. He thought that if John could not take care of himself when he grew up to be a man, there was a place for him in the poorhouse.

Harrison was also moved by another consideration. His mistress' sister had been trying to influence the mistress to sell him. Thus considering himself in danger, he made up his mind that the time had come for him to change his place of residence. So he resolved to try his fortune on the Underground Railroad.

CHAPTER 54

Harry Grimes Arrives from North Carolina after Having His Feet Slit and Being Flogged and Stabbed.

The coming of this passenger (Harry Grimes) was announced in the following letter from Thomas Garrett:

"Wilmington, 11th Mo. [November] 25th, 1857 "Respected Friend, William Steel (sic):

"I write to inform thee that Captain Fountain has arrived this evening from the South with three men, one of [whom] is nearly naked, and very lousy. He has been in the swamps of Carolina for 18 months past. One of the others has been some time out. I would send them on tonight, but will have to provide two of them with some clothes before they can be sent by railroad. I have forgotten the number of thy house. As most likely all are more or less lousy, having been compelled to sleep together, I thought best to write thee so that thee may get a suitable place to take them to, and meet them at Broad and Prime Streets on the arrival of the cars, about 11 o'clock tomorrow evening. I have engaged one of our men to take them to his house, and go to Philadelphia with them tomorrow evening. Johnson, who will accompany them, is a man in whom we can confide. Please send me the number of the house when thee writes.

"*Thomas Garrett.*"

This letter from the old friend of the fugitive, Thomas Garrett, excited unusual interest. Preparation was immediately made to give the fugitive a kind reception, and at the same time to destroy their fleas without mercy.

They arrived on schedule. The cleansing process was thoroughly carried out, and no vermin were left to tell the tale of the suffering they had caused. Immediately, the passengers were more comfortable in every way, and the spirit of freedom seemed to be brimming like "fire shut up in the bones."

In appearance, these men displayed "manhood" and wonderful natural ability. Members of the Philadelphia Vigilance Committee wanted to hear their story without a moment's delay.

Since Harry, who had suffered the most, was the hero of this party and was an intelligent man, he was first asked to make his statement and explain "how times had been with him in the prison house." He was about 46 years old, according to his guess, stood six feet tall, was muscular and rugged, and in his expression showed evident marks of firmness.

He said that he was born a slave in North Carolina, and had been sold three times. He was first sold when a child three years of age, and the second time when he was 13 years old. Finally, he was sold to Jesse Moore, from whom he fled. Prior to his coming into the hands of Moore he had not experienced any "very hard usage," at least nothing more severe than fell to the common lot of slave boys.

"How did Moore come by you?" was one of the questions directed his way. "Moore bought me," said Harry, "from a man by the name of Taylor, nine or ten years ago. Moore was as bad as he could be, couldn't be any worse to be alive. He was about 50 years of age when I left him, a right red-looking man, big-bellied old fellow, weighs about 240 pounds. He drinks hard, he is just like a rattlesnake, just as cross and crabbed when he speaks, seems like he could go through you. He flogged Richmond for not plowing the corn good, that was what he pretended to whip him for. Richmond ran away, was away four months, as near as I can guess, then they caught him, struck him a hundred lashes, and then they split both feet to the bone, and split both his insteps, and then master took his knife and stuck it into him in many places. After he done him that way, he put him into the barn to shuck corn. For a long time he was not able to work; when he did partly recover, he was set to work again."

We stopped recording anything further about Richmond. The account was too sickening and the desire to hear Harry's account about himself was too great to permit further delay; so Harry confined himself to the sufferings and adventures which had marked his own life.

Briefly he gave the following facts: "I have been treated bad. One day we were grubbing and master said we didn't do work enough. 'How come there was no more work done that day?' said master to me. I told him I did work. In a more stormy manner he repeated the question. I then spoke up and said: 'Massa, I don't know what to say.'

"At once massa plunged his knife into my neck causing me to stagger. Massa was drunk. He then drove me down to the black folks' houses (cabins of the slaves). He then got his gun, called the overseer, and told him to get some ropes. While he was gone I said, 'Massa, now you are going to tie me up and cut me all to pieces for nothing. I would just as [soon] leave you [and have you] take your gun and shoot me down as to tie me up and cut me all to pieces for nothing.'

"In a great rage he said 'Go.' I jumped, and he put up his gun and snapped both barrels at me. He then set his dogs on me, but as I had been in the habit of [being kind to] them, feeding them, etc., they would not follow me, and I kept on straight to the woods. My master and the overseer caught the horses and tried to run me down, but as the dogs would not follow me they couldn't make nothing of it. It was the last of August a year ago. The devil was into him, and he flogged and beat four of the slaves, one man and three of the women, and said if he could only get hold of me he wouldn't strike me 'nary-a-lick,' but would tie me to a tree and empty both barrels into me.

"In the woods I lived on nothing, you may say; but sometimes, too, I had bread and roasting ears and potatoes. I stayed in the hollow of a big poplar tree for seven months; the other part of the time I stayed in a cave. I suffered mighty bad with the cold and [hunger]. Once I got me some charcoal and made me a fire in my tree to warm me, and it liked to killed me, so I had to take the fire out. One time a snake come to the tree, poked its head in the hollow and was coming in, and I took my axe and chopped him in two. It was a poplar leaf moccasin, the most poisonous kind of a snake we have. While in the woods all my thoughts was how to get away to a free country."

Subsequently, in going back over his past history, he referred to the fact that he had once before sought the shelter of the woods and had stayed 27 months in a cave, before he surrendered himself, or was recaptured. His offense, on that occasion, was his desire to see his wife. He had "stole" away from his master's plantation and had gone five miles to where she lived to see her. For this grave crime his master threatened to give him a hundred lashes and to shoot him. The lapse of a dozen years and the severity of recent struggles for survival made him think lightly of his former troubles. He probably would have failed to recall his earlier conflicts if the Committee had not asked him about those years.

He was then asked, "Did you have a wife and family?"

"Yes, sir," he answered, "I had a wife and eight children, belonged to the widow Slade."

Harry gave the names of his wife and children as follows: Wife, Susan, and children, Oliver, Sabey, Washington, Daniel, Jonas, Harriet, Moses, and Rosetta, the last of whom he had never seen. "Between my master and my mistress there was not much difference."

CHAPTER 55

William Carney and Andrew Allen Arrive from Norfolk, Virginia.

William Carney was about 51 years old, a man of unmixed blood. Physically he was a superior man, and his mental abilities were quite above average.

He belonged to the estate of the late Mrs. Sarah Twyne, who bore the reputation of being a lady of wealth, and owned 112 slaves. Most of her slave property was kept on her plantation, which was not far from Old Point Comfort. According to William's testimony, "at times Mrs. Twyne would meddle too freely with the cup, and when under its influence she was very desperate, and acted as though she wanted to kill some of the slaves."

After the evil spirit left her and she had regained her composure she would pretend that she loved her "negroes," and would make a great fuss over them. Not infrequently she would have very serious difficulty with her overseers. Having license to do as they pleased, they would of course carry their cruelties to the most extreme verge of punishment. If a slave was maimed or killed under their correction, it was no loss of theirs. "One of the overseers by the name of Bill Anderson once shot a slave man called Luke and wounded him so seriously that he was not expected to live."

"At another time, one of the overseers beat and kicked a slave to death." This barbarity caused the mistress to be very "stirred up" and she declared that she would not have any more overseers, she condemned them for everything, and decided to change her plans in the future and to appoint her overseers from her own slaves, setting property to watch the property. This system was organized and times got somewhat better.

William had been hired out almost his entire life. For the last 2 of his 15 years he had been accustomed to hire his time for $130 per year. In order to meet this demand he commonly resorted to oystering. By the hardest toil he managed to maintain himself and his family in a humble way.

For the last 20 years prior to his escape, the slaves had been encouraged by their mistress' promises to believe that at her death they would be free and transported to Liberia, where they would enjoy liberty and be happy the remainder of their days.

With full faith in her promises year-by-year the slaves awaited her death with as much patience as possible, and often prayed that her time might be shortened for the general good of the oppressed. Fortunately, she had no children or near relatives to deprive them of their promised rights.

In November, the year before William's escape, her long looked-for departure took place. Every bondman who was old enough to realize the importance of the change felt a great anxiety to learn if the will of old mistress said whether she had actually freed them or not. Alas! the secret was disclosed and it was discovered that not a fetter was broken or a bond unloosed, and that no provision whatsoever had been made toward freedom. In this sad case, the slaves could imagine no other fate than soon to be torn apart and scattered. The fact was soon known that the high sheriff had administered liens on the estate of their late mistress. It was therefore obvious enough to William and the more intelligent slaves that the auction block was near at hand.

The trader, the slave pen, the auction block, the coffle gang, the rice swamp, the cotton plantation, bloodhounds, and cruel overseers loomed up before him — as they had never done before. Without stopping to consider the danger, he immediately made up his mind that he would make an effort to escape, cost what it might. He knew of no other way to escape except via the Underground Railroad. He was shrewd enough to find an agent. On examination, the agent found William to be sincere and reliable. A mutual understanding was entered into between William and one of the accommodating captains running on the Richmond and Philadelphia Line. William would have a first class Underground Railroad berth, so perfectly private that no law officer would ever find him.

The first ties to be severed were those that bound him to his wife and children, and next to the Baptist Church, to which he belonged. His family members were all slaves, and bore the following names: his wife, Nancy; and children, Simon Henry, William, Sarah, Mary Ann, Elizabeth, Louis, and Cornelius. It was no light matter to bid them farewell forever. The separation from them was a trial such as rarely falls to human beings; but he "nerved himself for the undertaking," and when the hour arrived his strength was sufficient for the occasion.

Thus in company with Andrew they embarked for an unknown shore, their entire interests entrusted to a stranger who was to bring them through difficulties and dangers, both seen and unseen.

Andrew Allen was about 24 years of age, very tall, quite black, and bore himself manfully. He too was of the same estate that William belonged to. He had served on the farm as a common farm laborer. He had had it "sometimes rough and sometimes smooth," to use his own language. The fear of what awaited the slaves prompted Andrew to escape. He too had a wife and one child, with whom he parted as a loved one parts with a companion when death separates them. Catharine was the name of Andrew's wife, and Anna Clarissa was the name of his child, both of whom were left in chains.

CHAPTER 56

Alfred S. Thornton Arrives from Virginia.

Alfred was a young man about 22 years of age, of dark color, and highly intelligent. Alfred found no fault with the ordinary treatment received at the hands of his master; he had evidently been on unusually good terms with him. Nor was any fault found with his mistress, so far as her treatment of him was concerned. Thus, compared to most slaves, he was "happy and contented," little dreaming of trader or a change of owners. One day, to his utter surprise, he saw a trader with a constable approaching him. As they drew nearer and nearer he began to grow nervous. What happened next will be told in Alfred's own words:

"William Noland (a constable) and the trader were making right up to me almost on my heels, and grabbed at me, they were so near. I flew, I took off my hat and run, took off my jacket and run harder, took off my vest and doubled my pace, the constable and the trader both on the chase hot foot. The trader fired two barrels of his revolver after me, and cried out as loud as he could call, but I never stopped running, but run for my master.

"Coming up to him, I cried out, 'Lord, master, have you sold me?' 'Yes,' was his answer.

"'To the trader?' I asked. "'Yes,' he answered.

"'Why couldn't you [have] sold me to some of the neighbors?' I pleaded. "'I don't know,' he said, in a dry way.

"With my arms around my master's neck, I begged and prayed him to tell me why he had sold me. The trader and constable was again pretty near. I let go [of] my master and took to my heels to save me. I run about a mile off and ... into a mill dam up to my head in water. I kept my head just above and hid the rest of my body for more than two hours. I had not made up my mind to escape until I had got into the water. I run only to have [a] little more time to breathe before going to Georgia or New Orleans; but I pretty soon made up my mind in the water to try and get to a free state, and go to Canada and make the trial anyhow but I didn't know which way to travel."

Great changes had occurred in Alfred's life in a very short time. As he hid in the pond, he began to imagine the fearful fate of being sent to the far South — a prospect he envisioned as more horrid than death. Suddenly, he decided to escape to the North. But the North Star, as it were, hid its face from Alfred. For a week, he tried to reach free soil, but the rain scarcely ceased for an hour. The entire journey was extremely hard, bleak, and discouraging; he took wrong directions and had to reverse his course; and he was hungry and tired. But he kept his faith and finally reached the safety of the Vigilance Committee in Philadelphia.

He left his father and mother, both slaves, living near Middleburg, Virginia, not far from the home of his master, who went by the name of C.E. Shinn. His master and mistress were said to be members of the South Baptist Church, and both had borne good characters until within a year or so prior to Alfred's departure. Since then a very serious disagreement had taken place between them, resulting in their separation, a heavy lawsuit, and consequently large outlays. It was this domestic trouble, in Alfred's opinion, that rendered his sale indispensable. Of the grave charges made by his master against his mistress, Alfred claimed to have formed no opinion. Alfred knew, however, that his master blamed a schoolmaster by the name of Conway for the sad state of things in his household.

Alfred derived great joy from the fact that his "heels" had saved him from a southern market. And the Vigilance Committee equally marveled and rejoiced at his wonderful and narrow escape.

CHAPTER 57

Nancy Grantham Arrives from Virginia.

Nancy Grantham fled from near Richmond, and was fortunate in that she escaped from the prison house at the age of 19. She possessed a mild appearance, was good-looking and interesting, and although born a slave, her father had been a white man, for she was fully half white.

She was determined to escape simply to shun her master's evil designs; his brutal purposes had only been frustrated in the past by the utmost resolution. This gentleman was a husband, the father of nine children, and the owner of 300 slaves. He belonged to a family bearing the name of Christian, and was said to be a medical doctor. "He was an old man, but very cruel to all his slaves."

Nancy said that her sister also was the object of his lust, but she too had resisted, and, as a result, was sold to New Orleans. The auction block was not the only punishment she was called upon to endure for resisting her master, but before being sold she was cruelly punished.

Nancy's sorrows first began in Alabama. Five years prior to her escape she was brought from a cotton plantation in Alabama, where she had been accustomed to toil in the cotton fields. In comparing and contrasting the usages of slaveholders in the two states in which she had served, she said she had "seen more flogging under old Christian" than she had been accustomed to see in Alabama; yet she concluded that she could hardly tell which state was the worst; her cup had been full and very bitter in both states.

Nancy said, "The very day before I escaped, I was required to go to his (her master's) bedchamber to keep the flies off of him as he lay sick, or pretended to be so. Notwithstanding, in talking with me, he said that he was coming to my pallet that night, and with an oath he declared if I made a noise he would cut my throat. I told him I would not be there. Accordingly he did go to my room, but I had gone for shelter to another room. At this his wrath was terrible. Next morning I was called to account for getting out of his way, and I was beaten awfully."

This outrage moved Nancy to seek her freedom, even at the risk of death. She succeeded by dressing herself in male attire.

After her harrowing story was told with so much earnestness and intelligence, she was asked about the treatment she had received from Mrs. Christian (her mistress). In relation to her, Nancy said, "Mrs. Christian was afraid of him (master); if it hadn't been for that I think she would have been clever; but I was often threatened by her, and once she undertook to beat me, but I could not stand it. I had to resist, and she got the worst of it that time."

The number of young slave girls shamefully exposed to the base lusts of their masters, as Nancy was, truly was very great. Nancy was one of the few who were able to successfully resist and escape their advances.

She was brought away hidden on a boat, but the record is silent as to which one of the two or three Underground Railroad captains (who at that time occasionally brought passengers) helped her to escape.

CHAPTER 58

George Laws and Comrade Arrive from Delaware.

George represented the ordinary young slave men of Delaware. He was of unmixed blood, medium size, and of humble appearance. He had no knowledge of spelling and reading. Slavery had stamped him unmistakably for life. Although he was scantily fed and clothed, and compelled to work without hire, George submitted without murmuring. Indeed, he knew that his so-called master, whose name was Denny, would not listen to complaints from a slave. He therefore dragged his chain and yielded to his daily task.

One day, while hauling dirt with a stubborn horse, the animal displayed an unwillingness to perform his duty satisfactorily. At this point, the master charged George with provoking the beast "to do wickedly," and in a rage he collared George and ordered him to accompany him to the upstairs of the soap house. Not daring to resist, George went along with him. Rope was tied around both of his wrists, the block and tackle was fastened to them. George soon found himself hoisted on tiptoe with his feet almost clear of the floor.

The "kindhearted master" then tore George's old shirt off his back, and said: "I will give you [what you deserve for] pouting around me; stay there till I go uptown for my cowhide."

George begged piteously, but in vain. The commotion caused some excitement among those who overheard him. It so happened that a circus was in town, which, as was usual in the country, attracted a great many people from a distance. When the master returned with his cowhide, to his surprise, he found that a large number of curiosity seekers had been attracted to the soap house to see Mr. Denny perform with his cowhide on George's back. Many had evidently made up their minds that it would be more amusing to see the cowhiding of George than the circus.

The spectators numbered about 300. This was a larger number than Mr. Denny had been accustomed to perform before and he was seized with embarrassment. Looking confused he left the soap house and went to his office to wait for the crowd to disperse.

The throng finally dispersed, leaving George hanging in mortal agony. George struggled desperately and was able to loosen the cords which bound his wrists. He unbound himself, and struck out for his freedom.

George fled from Kent, accompanied by a friend, and finally made his way to the Vigilance Committee in Philadelphia.

CHAPTER 59

William Thomas Cope, John Boice Grey, Henry Boice and Isaac White Cross the Bay in a Skiff.

These young bondmen, while writhing under the tortures heaped upon them, resolved, at the cost of their lives, to make a desperate effort to reach free land. The land route seemed less promising to them than a water route; but they knew very little about either of these options.

After much anxious reflection, they finally decided to make their Underground Railroad exit by water. Having lived all their lives not far from the Delaware Bay, they had some knowledge of small boats, skiffs in particular, but, of course, they did not possess one. Feeling that there was no time to lose, they concluded to borrow a skiff, though they would never return it.

One Saturday evening, toward the end of January, the four young slaves stood on the beach near Lewes, Delaware, and cast their longing eyes in the direction of the New Jersey shore. A fierce storm was blowing, and the waves were running fearfully high. Undaunted, they unanimously resolved to take their lives in their hands and embark on their bold adventure.

With simple faith they entered the skiff; and two of them took the oars. They remained steadfast, even when they were on the verge of being overwhelmed with the waves. At every new stage of danger they summoned courage by remembering that they were escaping for their lives.

Late on Sunday afternoon, the following day, they reached their much-desired haven — the Jersey shore. The relief and joy were unspeakably great, yet they were strangers in a strange land. They did not know which way to steer. True, they knew that New Jersey bore the name of being a free state; but they had reason to fear that they were in danger. In this dilemma they were discovered by the captain of an oyster boat whose sense of humanity was so strongly appealed to by their appearance that he agreed to pilot them to Philadelphia. The following account of them was recorded by the Vigilance Committee:

William Thomas was a yellow man, 24 years of age, and a lively person. He accused Shepherd P. Houston of having kept him as his slave, and testified that Houston was a very bad man. His vocation was that of a small farmer; and as a slaveholder he was numbered with the "small fry." Both master and mistress were members of the Methodist Church. According to William Thomas' testimony, his mistress was also very hard on the slaves in various ways, especially in the matter of food and clothing. It would require a great deal of hard preaching to convince him that their Christianity was genuine.

John Boice Grey stated that David Henry Houston, a farmer, took it upon himself to exercise authority over him. Said John, "If you didn't do the work right, he got [ornery] and wouldn't give you anything to eat for a whole day at a time; he said a '[negro] and a mule hadn't any feeling.'"

He described Houston as follows: "Houston is a very small man; for some time his affairs had been in a bad way; he had been broke; some say he had bad luck for killing my brother. My brother was sick, but master said he wasn't sick, and he took a chunk [of wood] and beat on him, and he died a few days after."

John firmly believed that his brother had been the victim of a monstrous outrage, and that he too was liable to receive the same treatment.

John was only 19 years of age, slightly built, of a chestnut color, and had considerable courage.

Henry Boice was what might be termed a very smart young man, considering that he had been deprived of the knowledge of reading. He was a brother of John, and said that he also had been wrongfully enslaved by David Houston. He fully corroborated the statement of his brother, and declared, moreover, that his sister had recently been sold south, and that he had heard enough to fully convince him that he and his brother were to be put up for sale. Of their mistress, John said that she was a "pretty easy kind of a woman, only she didn't ... allow enough to eat, and wouldn't mend any clothes for us."

Isaac White was 22, quite dark, and belonged to the "rising" young slaves of Delaware. He stated that he had been owned by a "blacksmith, a very hard man, by the name of Thomas Carper." Isaac was disgusted with his master's ignorance, and criticized him, in his crude way, to a considerable extent. Isaac had learned blacksmithing under Carper.

Both master and mistress were Methodists. Isaac said that he "could not recommend his mistress, as she was given to bad practices" so much so that he could hardly endure her. He also charged the blacksmith with being addicted to bad habits. Sometimes Isaac would be called upon to receive correction from his master, which would generally be dealt out with a "chunk of wood" over his "no feeling" head. Recently, when Isaac was being chunked beyond measure, he resisted, but the persistent blacksmith did not yield until he had so badly disabled Isaac that he was rendered helpless for the next two weeks. While in this state he pledged himself to freedom and Canada, and resolved to win the prize by crossing the Delaware Bay.

While these young passengers possessed considerable brains and bravery, at the same time they brought with them an unusual amount of Delaware soil; they and their old worn-out clothing were full of it. A room with hot water and soap were provided them. This process over, they were given clean and comfortable clothing. The change in their appearance was so marked that they might have passed as strangers, which is exactly how members of the Vigilance Committee wanted them to appear to slave catchers and former masters.

Raised in the country and on farms, their masters and mistresses had never encouraged them to conform to any habits of cleanliness; washing their persons and changing their garments were not common occurrences. The coarse clothing, once put on, might never be taken off as long as it would hold together. The filthy cabins provided for their shelter were in themselves incentives to personal uncleanliness. In some districts this was more apparent than in others. From some portions of Maryland and Delaware, in particular, passengers brought deplorable evidence of the absence of knowledge and improvement in the area of sanitation, cleanliness, and personal hygiene. But the master, not the slave, was the cause of this. The master usually provided one set of clothing for working (and sometimes none for Sunday). Consequently if Tom was set to ditching one day and became muddy and dirty, and the next day he was required to haul manure, the muddy clothing from the day before was still worn; and if the next day he was called into the harvest field, he continued to wear the muddy clothing he wore while hauling manure, and so on to the end.

Frequently such passengers were thoroughly washed for the first time in their lives at the Philadelphia station. Some needed practical lessons in hygiene before they understood the reason for bathing. Also, having never been used to bathing, many feared they might catch a cold in the process, etc., and these fears had to be gently explained away.

It was customary to say to them: "We want to give you some clean clothing, but you need washing before putting them on. It will make you feel like a new person to have the dirt of slavery all washed off. Nothing that could be done for you would make you feel better after the fatigue of travel than a thorough bath. Probably you have not been allowed the opportunity of taking a good bath, and so have not enjoyed one since your mother bathed you. Don't be afraid of the water or soap, the harder you rub yourself the better you will feel. If you need help, we will wash your back and neck for you. We want you to look good while traveling on the Underground Railroad, and not forget from this time forth to try to take care of yourself," etc.

By this course the reluctance, where it existed, would be overcome and the proposal would be readily agreed to, if the water was not too cool. On the other hand, if cool, a slight shudder might be visible, sufficient to raise a hearty laugh. Yet, when the bath was finished, the fugitive always expressed a hearty sense of satisfaction, and was truly thankful for this attention.

CHAPTER 60

Jenny Buchanan Arrives from Virginia.

Jenny was about 45 years of age, racially mixed, of medium stature, with modest and graceful manners; she had served only in high society and thus had acquired a great deal of interesting information.

Jenny stated that she was born a slave, under John Bower, of Rockbridge, Virginia, and that he was the owner of a large plantation with a great number of slaves. He was considered to be a good man to his servants, and was generally loved by them. Suddenly, however, he was taken ill with paralysis, which confined him to his bed. During this illness one of the sons, a young gentleman, offered an insult to Jenny, for which she felt justified in giving him a good scolding. For this grave offense she was condemned to be sold to a trader by the name of William Watts, who owned a place in Mississippi. The conditions of sale were that she was to be taken out of the state and never be allowed to return.

It so happened, however, before Jenny was sent south by Watts, his business failed. Governor McDowell of Virginia was one of those to whom Watts was largely indebted, for a number of slaves which he, the governor, had placed in Watts' hands for disposal some time before. Therefore, as the governor was anxious to recover his loss as much as possible, he seized Jenny. It was through this interference that the condition related to her being sent out of the state was broken. "The governor," said Jenny, "was a very fine gentleman, as good as I could expect of Virginia. He allowed his slaves to raise chickens and hogs, with many privileges of one kind and another; besides he kept them all together; but he took sick and died. There was a great change shortly after that. The slaves were soon scattered like the wind. The governor had nine sons and daughters."

After his death, Mrs. McDowell, alias Mrs. Sally Thomas, took possession, and employed an overseer by the name of Henry Morgan. He appeared to be a very good man, but he would get drunk and sell his employer's property to get whiskey. Mrs. McDowell would let him do just as he pleased. For the slightest complaint the overseer might see fit to make against any of the slaves, she would tell him to sell them, "Sell, Mr. Morgan."

"He would treat them worse than he would any dog; would beat them over the head with great hickory sticks, the same as he would beat an ox. He would pasture cows and horses on the plantation, and keep the money. We slaves all knew it, and we told her; but our words would not go in court against a white man, and until she was told by Mr. White, and her cousin, Dr. Taylor, and Mr. Barclay, she would not believe how shamefully this overseer was cheating her. But at last she was convinced, and discharged him, and hired another by the name of John Moore. The new one, if anything, was worse than the old one, for he could do the most unblushing acts of cruelty with pleasure. He was a demon."

Finally the estate had to be settled, and the property divided. At this time it was in the hands of the oldest daughter, Sally, who had been married to Frank Thomas, the governor of Maryland. But the governor had discarded her for some reason or other, and according to his published account of her it might seem that he had good reason for doing so. It was understood that he gave her a divorce, so she was considered single. It was also understood that she was to be allowed to buy the homestead at a moderate price, with as many slaves as she might desire.

Jenny said, "I was sold at this settlement sale, and bought in by the 'grass widow' for $400. The place and a number of slaves were bought in on terms equally as low. After this the widow became smitten with a reverend gentleman, by the name of John Miller, who had formerly lived in the North; he had been a popular preacher. After a courtship, which did not last very long, they were married. This took place three years ago. After the marriage, Rev. Mr. Miller moved to the old homestead and entered upon his duties as a slaveholder in good earnest."

"How did you like him?" asked a member of the Vigilance Committee of Philadelphia.

"I despised him," was Jenny's prompt answer. "Why did you despise him?"

"Because he had such mean ways with him," said Jenny.

She then went on to remark as follows: "Coming there, taking so much authority over other people's servants. He was so mean that he broke up all the privileges the servants had before he came. He stopped all hands from raising chickens, pigs, etc. He don't like to see them hold up their heads above their shoulders."

"Didn't he preach?" she was asked.

"Yes, but I never heard him preach; I have heard him pray though. On Thursday nights, when he would not want the servants to go into town to a meeting, he would keep up until it would be too late for them to go. He is now carrying on the farm, and follows butchering. He has not yet sold any of the slaves, but has threatened to sell all hands to the trader."

Jenny once had a husband, but he went to Canada, and that was all she could tell about him, as she had never had a letter or any direct information from him since he left. That she was childless, she regarded as a matter of great satisfaction, considering all the circumstances.

CHAPTER 61

Thomas Sipple; His Wife, Mary Ann; Henry Burkett; His Wife, Elizabeth; John Purnell; and Hale Burton Cross the Delaware Bay in a Batteau.

This group of slaves lived near Kunkletown, in Worcester County, Maryland, and had become restless in their bondage. Although they did not know a letter of the alphabet, they were fully persuaded that they were entitled to their freedom. In considering what means of escape would be safest, they concluded that the water would be less dangerous than any other route.

Since freedom had been on their minds for a long time, they had frequently considered the cost, and had been saving the trifling amounts of money they had gotten from time-to-time. Together, they had about $30. As they could not go by water without a boat, one of their number purchased an old batteau [flat-bottom boat] for the small sum of $6.

The Delaware Bay lay between them and the Jersey shore, which they desired to reach. Undaunted by the perils they might encounter, the party went to the bay, and at 10:00 P.M. embarked directly for the other shore.

Near Kate's Hammock, on the Delaware shore, they were attacked by five white men in a small boat. One of them seized the chain of the fugitives' boat, and claimed it.

"This is not your boat, we bought this boat and paid for it," spoke one of the brave fugitives.

"I am an officer and must have it," said the white man, holding on to the chain. Being armed, the white men threatened to shoot. Bravely the black men stood up for their rights, and declared that they did not mean to give up their boat alive. The confrontation quickly became physical. One of the white men dealt a heavy blow with his oar upon the head of one of the black men, which knocked him down, and broke the oar at the same time. The blow was immediately returned by Thomas Sipple, and one of the white men was laid flat on the bottom of the boat.

The white men were instantly seized with panic and retreated. After getting some yards off they shot their handguns several times at the fugitives, and one load of small buckshot was fired into them. John received two shot in the forehead, but was not dangerously hurt. George received some in the arms, Hale Burton got one in his temple, and Thomas got a few in one of his arms; but the shot being light, none of the fugitives were seriously injured. But some of the shot will remain in them as long as life lasts.

The conflict lasted for several minutes, but the fugitives felt even more satisfaction in their escape, seeing the foe retreat. They rowed with renewed energy and landed on a small island. They had no idea where they were or what to do next. One whole night they passed in this sad spot. Their spirits were greatly cast down; but the next morning they set out to see what they could find on the island. The young women were very sick, and men were exhausted.

However, after walking for some time they came across a captain of an oyster boat. They noticed that he spoke in a friendly way, and they at once asked directions to Philadelphia. He gave them the desired information, and even offered to take them to the city if they could pay him for his services. They had about $25 left. This they willingly gave him, and he transported them to Philadelphia according to agreement. (When they found the captain, they were not far from Cape May lighthouse.)

Taking into account that it was night when they started, that their little boat was old and weak, and that they knew nothing about navigation or handling a boat, any intelligent man would have been justified in predicting for them a watery grave, long before the bay was half crossed. But they crossed it safely.

When they reached Philadelphia, they greatly needed food, clothing, rest, and money, which they were freely given. Shortly thereafter, they were forwarded to John W. Jones, Underground Railroad agent, at Elmira, New York. The following letter gives an account of their arrival:

———

"Elmira, 6 June 1860 "Friend Wm. Still:

"All six came safe to this place. The two men came last night, about 12:00; the man and woman stopped at the depot, and went east on the next train, about 18 miles, and did not get back until tonight, so that the two men went this morning, and the four went this evening.

"O, old master don't cry for me,

"For I am going to Canada where colored men are free.

"P.S. What is the news in the city? Will you tell me how many you have sent over to Canada? I would like to know. They all send their love to you. I have nothing new to tell you. We are all in good health. I see there is a law passed in Maryland not to set any slaves free. They had better get the consent of the Underground Railroad before they pass such a thing.

"Good night from your friend, "John W. Jones (for them)."

CHAPTER 62

On Her Last 'Trip' to Maryland, Harriet Tubman Brings Back Stephen Ennets and His Family of Five from Dorcester County.

The following letter from Thomas Garrett throws light upon this arrival:

"Wilmington, 12th mo. [December], 1st, 1860

"Respected Friend: "William Still:

"I write to let thee know that Harriet Tubman is again in these parts. She arrived last evening from one of her trips of mercy to God's poor, bringing two men with her as far as New Castle. I agreed to pay a man last evening to pilot them on their way to Chester County; the wife of one of the men, with two or three children, was left some 30 miles below, and I gave Harriet $10 to hire a man with carriage to take them to Chester County. She said a man had offered for that sum to bring them on. I shall be very uneasy about them till I hear they are safe. "There is now much more risk on the road — till they arrive here — than there has been for several months past, as we find that some poor, worthless wretches are constantly on the lookout on two roads that they cannot avoid traveling. They are certainly going to suspect a carriage; yet, as it is Harriet who seems to have had a special angel to guard her on her journey of mercy, I have hope. "Thy Friend,

"*Thomas Garrett.*

"N.B. We hope all will be in Chester County tomorrow."

These slaves from Maryland were the last that Harriet Tubman piloted out of the prison house of bondage, and these "came through great tribulation."

Stephen, the husband, had been a slave of John Kaiger, who would not allow him to live with his wife. She lived eight miles away, hired her time, maintained herself, and took care of her children (until they became of service to their owner), and paid $10 a year for her hire. She was owned by Algier Pearcy. Both mother and father desired to deliver their children from his grasp.

Harriet Tubman, being well acquainted in their neighborhood and knowing of their situation, had confidence that they would be worthy passengers on the Underground Railroad. She thus brought them within reach of Wilmington, to Thomas Garrett's place. Thus the father and mother, with their children and a young man named John, found aid and comfort on their way, with Harriet as their "Moses." A poor woman escaping from Baltimore, who was in a "delicate state," happened to meet Harriet's party at the station, and was forwarded on with them. They were provided clothing, food, and material aid, and sped on to Canada.

Notes taken at that time were very brief; it was not wise to keep more complete reports as had been the desire of the Vigilance Committee prior to 1859. The capture of John Brown's papers and letters, with full names and plans, warned us that such papers and correspondence as had been preserved concerning the Underground Railroad might be captured by a pro-slavery mob. For a year or more after the Harper's Ferry battle, the pro-slavery mob spirit was very violent in all the principal northern cities, as well as southern ("to save the Union") ones. Even in Boston, abolition meetings were fiercely assaulted by mobs. During this period, the writer omitted some of the most important details concerning escapes and the narratives of fugitives. Books and papers were sent away and hidden for a long time; and during this time, local records were kept simply on loose slips of paper.

Ennets, Stephen.

CHAPTER 63

A Member of the Vigilance Committee Impersonates Slave Hunter George F. Alberti.

One afternoon, the quiet of the Anti-Slavery Office was suddenly broken by the contents of a letter, privately placed in the hands of J. Miller McKim by one of the clerks of the Philadelphia Ledger Office. The letter apparently had been dropped into the box of the office, instead of the U.S. postal box (one of which was also in the office of the ledger), by mistake. And seeing that the letter bore the name of a well-known slave catcher, George F. Alberti, the clerk had a great desire to know its content. Whether it was or was not sealed, the writer cannot say, but it certainly was not sealed when it reached the Anti-Slavery Office.

The letter stated that a lady from Maryland was then in Philadelphia, staying at a boardinghouse on Arch Street, and that she wanted to see the above mentioned Alberti in order to enlist his services to help catch an Underground Railroad traveler, whom she claimed was her property. Whether she wrote the letter could not be proven, but that it was sent by her consent, of that there was no doubt.

In order to save the traveler from his impending doom, it seemed that a bold maneuver was in order. Mr. McKim proposed to find someone who would be willing to play the role of Alberti. Cyrus Whitson, a member of the Philadelphia Vigilance Committee, in Mr. McKim's judgment, could manage the matter successfully. At that time, C. Whitson was engaged in the Free Labor store at the corner of Fifth and Cherry Streets, which was near the Anti-Slavery Office.

On being sent for, Whitson immediately answered the summons, and Mr. McKim at once told him of the plan. The plan was to save a fellow man from being dragged back to bondage by visiting the slave owner, learning from her the whereabouts of the fugitives, the names of the witnesses, and all related details. Nothing could have delighted the shrewd Whitson more; he saw just how he could accomplish the objective without the slightest chance of failure. So off he started for the boardinghouse.

Arriving, he rang the bell, and when the servant appeared, he asked if Miss Wilson, from Maryland, was staying there.

"She is," was the answer.

"I wish to see her." "Walk in the parlor, sir."

In went Mr. W., with his big whiskers. Soon Miss Wilson entered the parlor, a tall, and rather fine-looking, well-dressed lady. Mr. Whitson bowing, politely addressed her:

"I have come to see you instead of Mr. George F. Alberti, to whom you addressed a note this morning. Circumstances, over which Mr. A. had no control, prevented his coming, so I have come, madam, to look after your business in his place. Now, madam, I wish it to be distinctly understood in the outset that whatever transpires between us, so far as this business is concerned, must be kept strictly confidential; by no means must this matter be allowed to leak out; if it does, the darned abolitionists (excuse me) may ruin me; at any rate we should not be able to succeed in getting your slave. I am particular on this point, remember." "You are perfectly right, Sir; indeed I am very glad that your plan is to conduct this matter in this manner, for I do not want my name mixed up with it in any way either."

"Very well, madam, I think we understand each other pretty well; now please give me the name of the fugitive, his age, size, and color, and where he may be found, how long he has been away, and the witness who can be relied on to identify him after he is arrested."

Miss Wilson carefully communicated these important details, while Mr. Whitson faithfully penciled down every word. At the close of their meeting, Whitson told her that the matter would be attended to immediately, and that he thought there would be no difficulty in securing the fugitive. "You shall hear from me soon, madam, good afternoon."

In five minutes after this interview Whitson was back to the Anti-Slavery Office with all Miss Wilson's secrets. The first thing to do was to send a messenger to the place where the fugitive was working, in order to hide him securely. The man was found, and, frightened almost out of his wits, he dropped what he was doing and followed the messenger, who bore him the warning. In the meantime, Mr. McKim was quickly preparing the following document for the enlightenment and warning of all.

"To Whom It May Concern: "Beware of Slave catchers.

"Miss Wilson, of Georgetown Cross Roads, Kent County, Maryland is now in the city in pursuit of her alleged slave man, Butler. J.M. Cummings and John Wilson of the same place are understood to be here on [a] similar errand. This is to caution Butler and his friends to be on their guard. Let them keep clear of the above-named individuals. Also, let them have an eye on all persons known to be friends of Dr. High, of Georgetown Cross Roads, and Mr. D.B. Cummings, who is not of Georgetown Cross Roads.

"It is requested that all parties to whom a copy of this may be sent will post it in a public place, and that the friends of freedom and humanity will have [these] facts ... openly read in their respective churches.

"'Hide the outcast; betray not him that wandereth.' Isaiah xvi. 3.

"'Thou shalt not deliver unto his master the servant that has escaped from his master unto thee.' Deut. xxiii. 15."

This document was printed as a large poster about three feet square, and was displayed in large numbers over the city. It attracted much attention and comment, which facts were quickly conveyed to Miss Wilson, at her boardinghouse. At first, she was greatly shocked to find herself the object of everyone's conversation. She unhesitatingly took her baggage and left for "My Maryland." Thus ended one of the most pleasant interviews that ever took place between a slave hunter and the Vigilance Committee of Philadelphia.

CHAPTER 64

Henry Langhord, alias William Scott, Arrives from Richmond, Virginia.

This "chattel" from Richmond, Virginia was of a yellow complexion, with some knowledge of reading and writing; he was about 23 years of age and considered himself in great danger of being subjected to the auction block by one Charles L. Hobson. Hobson and Henry had grown up from boyhood together; for years they had even occupied the same room, Henry as a servant-boy and protector of his prospective young master. Under these relations a strong friendship grew between them, and Henry succeeded in gaining a knowledge of the alphabet with an occasional lesson in spelling.

Both reached adulthood. William was hired out at the American Hotel, and being a "smart, likely-looking boy," commanded good wages for his young master's benefit, who had commenced business as a tobacco merchant, with about seven head of slaves in his possession. A year or two's experiment proved that the young master was not succeeding as a merchant, and before the expiration of three years he had sold all his slaves except Henry. From such indications, Henry was fully persuaded that his time was close at hand, and great was his anxiety as he contemplated the auction block.

In Henry's heart he resolved time and again that he would never be sold. He at first resolved to buy himself, but in counting the cost he found that he would by no means be able to accumulate as much money as his master would be likely to demand for him. He, therefore, abandoned this idea and turned his attention to the Underground Railroad, by which means he had often heard of slaves escaping. He felt the need for money. He tried to make and save an extra quarter whenever he could, and soon learned to be very careful with his money. Being exceedingly accommodating in waiting upon gentlemen at the hotel and at the springs, he found his little "pile" increasing weekly. His object was to have enough to pay for a private berth on one of the Richmond steamers and also to have a little left to fall back on after landing in a strange land and among strangers. He saved about $200 in cash.

He was now ready to make his move, and he arranged all his plans with an agent in Richmond to leave by one of the steamers during the Christmas holidays. "You must come down to the steamer about dark," said the agent "and if all is right you will see the Underground Railroad agent come out with some ashes as a signal, and by this you may know that all is ready."

"I will be there," said Henry. In the past he had been granted Christmas week as a holiday, and he was confident the time would be granted as usual. A few days before Christmas, he went to his master and asked permission to spend the holiday with his mother in Cumberland County, adding that he would need some spending money — enough at least to pay his fare, etc. The young master freely granted his request, wrote him a pass, and gave him enough money to pay his fare there, but concluded that Henry could pay his way back out of his extra change. Henry expressed his appreciation and returned to the American Hotel.

The evening before his Underground Railroad voyage, he had several reasons for wanting to speak to the Underground Railroad agent. He asked the hotel clerk to give him a pass. However, this favor was refused. Henry, "not willing to give it up so easily," sat down and wrote a pass for himself. This proved to be all that he needed, and he was thus able to accomplish his business satisfactorily.

The next day his Christmas holiday began, but instead of enjoying the sight of his mother, he was saddened by the thought he may have seen her for the last time. It was a very depressing time for him. That evening at dark, he was at the wharf, according to promise. The man with the ashes immediately appeared and signaled him. In his three suits of clothing (he was wearing them all), he walked on the boat, and was conducted to the coal covering, where total darkness prevailed.

The scheduled hour for the departure of the steamer was 10:00 the following morning. By the aid of prayer, he endured the suffering that night. No sooner had the steamer gotten under way, than a heavy gale was encountered. For between three and four days the gale and fog combined and threatened the steamer with total destruction. All the freight on deck, consisting of tobacco and cotton, had to be thrown overboard in order to save the passengers.

Henry, in his state of darkness, saw nothing, nor could he know the imminent peril that his life was in. Fortunately he was not seasick, but slept well and long on the voyage. It took five days for the steamer to make the trip to Philadelphia. On landing, Henry could barely see or walk. However, the spirit of freedom was burning brightly in the hidden man, and a few hours of fresh air and free soil soon enabled him to overcome these difficulties. Soon, he was one of the most joyful mortals living.

After spending two days with his friends in Philadelphia, Henry hastened on to Boston. After being in Boston two months, he was passing through the market one day, when, to his surprise, he saw his young master, Charles L. Hobson! Henry was sure, however, that he was not recognized, but suspected that he was being hunted. Instantly, Henry pulled up his coat collar, and drew his hat over his face to disguise himself as much as possible, but he could not completely recover from the shock he had just received.

He turned away from the market and soon met a friend, also formerly from Richmond, who had been a slave in the tobacco factory owned by his master. Henry tried to prevail on him to spot Hobson in the market, to see if he could possibly be mistaken. But his friend would not take a step in that direction. He had been away for several years, but still he was a fugitive, and didn't like the idea of renewing his acquaintance with old or new friends with white skin from Virginia. Henry, however, would not be content until he had taken another good look — to make sure it was Mr. Hobson. Disguising himself he again took a stroll through the market, looking on the right and left as he passed along. Presently he saw Hobson seated at a butcher's stall. Henry examined him to his satisfaction, and then went speedily to the headquarters of the Anti-Slavery Office. He told of his discovery, and stated that he believed his master had no other errand in Boston than to capture him.

Measures were at once taken to determine if a man by the name of Charles L. Hobson was booked at any of the hotels in Boston. On finding that this was really a fact, Henry was offered and accepted private quarters with the well-known philanthropist and friend of the fugitive, Francis Jackson. His house as well as his funds were always open to the slave.

While Henry was safely hidden at the home of Mr. Jackson, Hobson advertised for him, described him very accurately, and offered a reward of

$250 for him. In response, Henry's friends thought that they would return the compliment to Mr. Hobson by publishing a detailed description of him in the Boston papers — if not as high a reward for him. Their advertisement read: "Charles L. Hobson, 22 years of age, six feet high, with a slouched hat on, mixed coat, black pants, with a goatee, is stopping at the Tremont Hotel," and on and on. This came as a bombshell to Mr. Hobson, and he immediately took the hint, steering his trunks and himself for the sunny South.

A day or two later, Henry felt it advisable to visit Canada. After arriving there he wrote back to his young master, to let him know where he was, and why he left, and what he was doing.

For five years, Henry lived in Boston and worked on a boat trading with eastern Canada. He saved up his money and took good care of himself. He was soon prepared to go into some business that would pay him better than working on the boat. Two of his young friends agreed with him that they could do better in Philadelphia than in Boston, so they came to the City of Brotherly Love and opened a first-class dining saloon near Third and Chestnut Streets. For a time they successfully carried on the business, but one of the partners became disgusted with the prejudices of the city concerning seating on the passenger railway cars, and felt that he could no longer live here.

Henry, known after leaving slavery only by the name of William Scott, left the restaurant business and found employment as a messenger under Thomas Scott, Esq., Vice President of the Pennsylvania Central Railroad. He worked there for many years.

Henry was an industrious, sober, steady, upright, and intelligent young man, and took care of his wife and child in a comfortable three-story brick house, which he owned.

CHAPTER 65

Miles Robinson Arrives from Richmond, Virginia.

Miles Robinson was the slave of Mrs. Roberts, a widow lady living in York County, Virginia. He did not live with her, however, but was hired out in the city of Richmond. He had been fortunate to fall into hands that had not treated him harshly.

He was not contented, however. Much of his leisure he devoted to the banjo. As a player on this instrument he had become quite gifted, but music in Richmond was not liberty. The latter he craved, and his thoughts were often far beyond the Mason-Dixon line, enjoying that which was denied him in Virginia.

Although only 22 years old, Miles was manly, good-looking, determined, and intelligent. Hearing that he was to be sold, he did not discuss plans with his mother, brothers, or sisters (who were living as slaves in Richmond), but secretly resolved to escape by the first means that presented itself.

Turning his attention to the Underground Railroad, he found an agent who conveyed his wishes to a black woman who was working as cook or chambermaid on one of the Philadelphia and Richmond steamers. She took charge of him, and found him a safe berth in one of the closets where the pots and other cooking utensils were stored.

It was a rather tight and uncomfortable spot, but Miles felt that for liberty he must pass through the ordeal without murmuring, which he did. Success was achieved and he found himself in Philadelphia.

Miles wanted to go to Boston, and after recuperating a short while in Philadelphia, he made his way there. Finding liberty there as sweet as he had fondly imagined it, he applied himself unceasingly to industrial pursuits, economy, self-education, and the elevation of other blacks. For four years he lived and worked there, under the shadow of Bunker Hill. At the end of that time he invested the earnings, which he had saved, in a business with two young friends in Philadelphia. All being first-class waiters and understanding catering, they decided to open a large dining saloon. Miles was one of the two friends mentioned in the narrative of Henry Langhord (William Scott). Since their success and consequent fortunes were described in that narrative, it will not be repeated here.

However, Miles subsequently was involved in two contests that sought to drive colored people from the street cars of that city.

At the corner of Fourth and Walnut Streets, Miles, in company with two other young men, Wallace and Marshall, one evening in a most orderly manner entered a car and took his seat. The conductor ordered them to the front platform; they did not budge. He stopped the car and ordered them out; this did no good. He read rules, and was not a little embarrassed by these polite and well-dressed young men. Finally the conductor called for the police, who arrested all three. Miles did not yield his seat without a struggle. In being pulled out his resistance was such that several window lights were broken in the car. The police being in strong force, however, succeeded in marching their prisoners to the mayor's police station at the corner of Fifth and Chestnut Streets where they were locked up to wait further investigation. The prisoners thought they were back in "old Virginny" again. Miles gritted his teeth and felt very indignant, but what could he do?

The infamous prejudice against which they had borne testimony was the practice on all the lines of city passenger railways in Philadelphia. While Miles and his friends were willing to suffer for a principle, the dirt, filth, cold, and disagreeableness of the quarters that they most likely would be forced to occupy all night and the following day (Sunday) forbade submission. Added to this, Miles felt that his young wife would hardly be able to contain her worry while he was locked up. They sent for the writer [William Still] to negotiate for them.

At a late hour of the night, William Still went looking for the alderman who could help him. Still was sent from the alderman's boardinghouse to a fire engine house and other places, where it was supposed that he might be found. However, on returning a third time to the alderman's hotel, a little before midnight, he was discovered to be in bed, and it was then learned that he had not been out all that evening, as the night was very stormy.

William Still could not tell whether or not the fruitless chase on which we had been sent in search of the alderman was in keeping with the spirit that had locked the men up, and was designed to mislead him. However, the alderman at last agreed to see Still, and accepted Still's offer to bail all of them out, and finally issued a discharge. This was quickly delivered to the station, and the prisoners were released.

But Miles was not satisfied. He had breathed free air in Massachusetts for four years, and being a man of high spirit he felt that he must further test the prejudices of the Philadelphia passenger cars. Consequently one very cold night, when a deep snow covered the pavements, he went out with his wife. Since his wife was very fair and could pass for white, Miles put her on the car at the corner of Third and Pine Streets. He walked to the corner of Fourth and Pine Streets, where he stepped into the car and took his seat.

The conductor straightway ordered him out on account of his color. God had shaded him a little too much. "How is this, my wife is in this car," spoke Miles. All eyes gazed around to see who his wife was. By this time the car had been stopped, and the wrath of the conductor had grown appreciably. He did not, however, lay violent hands upon Miles. A late decision in court had taught the police that they had no right to interfere, except in cases where the peace was actually being broken.

To get rid of this troublesome customer, the conductor ran the car off the track. The shivering passengers all left it, as though flying from a plague, with the exception of Miles, his wife, and another black man who got on with Miles. The conductor then hoisted all the windows, took out the cushions, and unhitched the horses. But Miles and his party stood the cold and discomfort bravely.

All the time, Miles was burning with indignation at this exhibition of prejudice in the City of Brotherly Love. Miles felt that this prejudice was nearly the same as slavery, and gave to slavery its chief support.

The occupants of the now-horseless car, which was being aired so thoroughly, remained in it for some time, until they had sufficiently made their point.

Prior to this event, by his industry and hard-earned savings, Miles had become the owner of a comfortable brick house. At first he had made up his mind to remain a citizen of Philadelphia, but the spirit which prompted this treatment on the passenger cars reminded him too much of his days under slavery. Before long he offered his property for sale, including his business, and resolved to return to Boston. He received an offer for his property, accepted it, and again hopefully turned his face toward Boston.

The ambitious Miles started a business in Chelsea, near Boston, where he purchased a comfortable home. From that time on, he was successfully engaged in the sale of kerosene oil. Instead of seeking pleasure in the banjo, as he had done while in Virginia, he subsequently found delight in the Reverend Grimes' Baptist Church, of which he was a prominent member, and in other useful pursuits that helped better the condition of society in general.

CHAPTER 66

John William Dungy Arrives from Richmond, Virginia, on a Pass from Ex-Governor Gregory.

"He ought to be put in a cage and kept for a show," said Anna Brown, daughter of John Brown, at the house of the writer [William Still], where she happened to meet the above-named Underground Railroad passenger. He had then just returned from Canada, after being a refugee for four years. In the meantime through the war and the Emancipation Proclamation, the fetters had been torn from the limbs of the slave, and the way to Richmond was open to all.

On this occasion, John William was on his way to Richmond to see how his brethren and their old oppressors looked facing each other as freemen. Miss Anna Brown was en route to Norfolk, where she planned to establish a school for the former slaves. The return of the refugee was as unexpected as it was gratifying. Scarcely had the cordial greetings of the writer and his family ended — and the daughter of John Brown been introduced — before John William was bombarded with many questions concerning his journey to and his stay in Canada, etc.

"How have you been getting along in Canada? Do you like the country?"
"First-rate," said John William.
"You look as though you have neither been starved nor frozen. Have you had plenty of work, made some money, and taken care of yourself?"
"Yes."
"When you were on the Underground Railroad on your way to Canada you promised that you were going to keep from all bad habits; how about alcohol? Do you take a little sometimes?"
"No, I have not drank a drop since I left the South," replied John William with emphasis.
"Good! Do you still smoke and chew at any rate?" "No, neither. I never think of such a thing."
"Now don't you keep late hours at night and swear occasionally?"
"No, Sir. All the leisure that I have of evenings is spent over my books as a general thing; I have not fallen into the fashionable customs of young men."
Miss Brown, who had been an attentive listener, remarked: "He ought to be put in a cage ... "

He was 27 years of age when he first landed in Philadelphia in February 1860, on the steamer Pennsylvania, in which he had been stowed away in a storeroom containing rubbish and furniture. In this way he reached City Point. Here a family of Irish emigrants, who were very dirty, were taken on board, and orders were given that accommodations should be made for them in the room occupied by J.W. A possible crisis was at hand, but only for a moment. Those into whose charge he had been placed on the boat knew that the kettle and pot closet had often been used for hiding Underground Railroad passengers; and he was safely conducted to quarters among the pots. The room was exceedingly cramped; but he stood it bravely.

On landing he was not able to stand. It required not only his personal efforts but the help of friends to get him off the boat. No sooner had he reached the shore, however, than he began to cry aloud for joy. "Thank God!" rang out sonorously from his overflowing soul. Alarmed at this indication of gratitude, his friends immediately told him that that would never do; that all hands would be betrayed; and that he was far from being safe in Philadelphia. He suppressed his emotions.

After being delivered safely into the hands of the Vigilance Committee, where he was in more private quarters, he fully expressed his joy on reaching this city. He said that he had been trying for five years to obtain his freedom. For this special purpose he had saved up $68.15, all of which, except the 15 cents, he had willingly paid for his passage on the boat. Fifteen cents, the balance of his entire capital, was all that he had when he landed in Philadelphia.

Before leaving the South he was hired in the family of ex-Governor Gregory. Of the governor and his wife he spoke very highly, he said that they were kind to him and would readily grant his request whenever he asked them for a favor. He stated that after making his arrangements to start north, in order that he might get away several days before being missed, he told Mrs. Gregory that he wanted to spend a week with his mother, who lived some distance away in the country. As he was not feeling very well she kindly granted his request, and told him to ask the governor for a pass and some money. The governor was busy writing, but he at once granted the prayer, wrote him a pass, gave John five dollars, adding that he was sorry that he did not have more in his pocket, etc.

John bowed and thanked the governor, and soon got ready for his visit; but his route lay in a far different direction than that contemplated by the governor and his lady. He was aiming for the Underground Railroad.

John William was not owned by the governor, but by the Ferrell heirs, five children who had moved from Virginia to Alabama years back. "Every Ferrell that lives is down on slaves; they are very severe," said John.

Since John William had been a dining room servant, he had not suffered as many others had who belonged to them. At one time the Ferrells had owned large numbers of slaves, but lately they had been selling them off. The Ferrells had notified John, as well as the governor, that in a short while he was to be taken to Alabama, contrary to John's wishes. This persuaded John to act with great promptness in leaving at the time that he did.

After passing several years in Canada, as has already been noted, John William returned to Richmond and paid a visit to his old home. He found that the governor and his wife had both died, but two of their daughters (young ladies by that time) were still alive. They were both glad to see him; the younger especially; she told him that she was glad that he escaped, and that she had "prayed for him." The elder remarked that she had always thought that he was "too good a Christian to run away." Another thing which she referred to, apparently with much feeling, was this: On his way to Canada, he wrote to the governor from Rochester, New York, "that he [the governor] need put himself to no trouble in hunting him up, as he had made up his mind to visit Canada." She thought that John was rather "naughty" to write in such a manner to her "papa;" nevertheless, she was willing to forgive him after she had frankly spoken her mind.

John found Richmond, which so long had held him in chains, fully humbled, and its slave power utterly crushed. His wondering eyes gazed until he was perfectly satisfied that it was the Lord's doings, and it was marvelous in his eyes. He was more than ever resolved to get an education, and to go back to Virginia, to help teach his brethren who had been denied the privilege for so long. It was not long before he was at Oberlin College, a faithful student, commanding the highest respect from all the faculty for his bright mind and studious habits.

After advancing rapidly at Oberlin, he was offered an opportunity to pursue his studies with less expense at a college in one of the eastern states. He accepted the favors of friends who offered him assistance. It was his friends' intention to help prepare him for a mission among the freedmen, believing that he possessed the skills needed to be a successful worker, preacher, organizer, and teacher. Since these friends also planned to start a college at Harper's Ferry specifically for the benefit of the freedmen, they hoped his future work would also benefit the college. Before he graduated, his services were badly needed in the South. He was asked to be an agent for the Storer College, and to enter upon a mission under the patronage of the Free-Will Baptists in Martinsburg, Virginia. For three or four years he labored in this field with considerable devotion, gathering young and old in day and Sunday schools, and also organizing churches.

But, as a result of his constant labors, his health declined. Receiving a call from a church in Providence, Rhode Island, he accepted, but not before he knew that his mission was to be left in faithful hands, to carry on the good work.

There was still need of efficient laborers in the Shenandoah Valley, according to the testimony of Mr. Dungy. There still were scores of places where the children had no school; and where many, both old and young alike, had never had the opportunity to enter a meetinghouse or church since the end of the Civil War. According to him, the spirit of the white Christians in these regions was greatly embittered against the colored people, owing to the abolition of slavery; and the whites would not invite them to either church or school.

At different times, Mr. Dungy eloquently described the condition of the black churches of the South and in the city of Philadelphia. As a speaker, Mr. Dungy was capable and interesting, remarkably graceful in his manners, and possessed a great deal of useful information.

The following excerpt from an official circular, which was issued by the Board of Instruction of Storer College, provides further information about that institution:

"Storer College, Harper's Ferry, West Virginia

"This Institution, deriving its name from John Storer, Esq., late of Sanford, Maine, who gave $10,000 to aid in its establishment, is located at Harper's Ferry, West Virginia, and has been chartered with full powers by a special act of the Legislature. The Corporation has been regularly organized, about $30,000 in money has been obtained, a large tract of land has been purchased, ample buildings have been secured, and a Normal School has been in successful operation during the last 18 months. The U.S. authorities have repeatedly expressed their confidence in and sympathy with this undertaking, by liberal grants of money and buildings, and the agent for the distribution of the Peabody Fund, has pledged financial aid to the best of the pupils in attendance, who may be in need of such assistance.

"*Rev. J. Calder, D.D., Pres.,*

"*Rev. N.C. Brackett, Act. Sec'y.*, "Harrisburg, Pennsylvania

"Harper's Ferry, West Virginia, 1 March 1869"

CHAPTER 67

Aunt Hannah Moore Arrives from Missouri.

In 1854, in company with her so-called mistress and owner (Mary Moore), Aunt Hannah arrived in Philadelphia from Missouri. The mistress had relatives in this city and stayed a short time. Aunt Hannah's owner undoubtedly believed that she had sufficient control over her to keep her from contact with either abolitionists or those of her own color, and that she would have no difficulty taking her back to Missouri.

But Mary Moore was greatly mistaken. For although Aunt Hannah had always been deprived of book learning, she nevertheless was a thoughtful woman with considerable natural ability. While she wisely concealed her thoughts from her mistress, she took care to make her wishes known to an abolitionist. She had passed many years under the yoke with different owners, and now seeing a ray of hope she grasped the opportunity to secure her freedom.

Hannah had occasion to go to a store in the neighborhood where she was staying. To her unspeakable joy she found that the proprietor was an abolitionist and a friend, who asked about her condition and offered her assistance. The storekeeper quickly alerted the Anti-Slavery Office, and very soon J.M. McKim and Charles Wise, both abolitionists and members of the Vigilance Committee, showed up at the stopping place of the mistress and her slave. They demanded in the name of humanity and the laws of Pennsylvania that Aunt Hannah should be no longer held in bondage, but that she should be immediately proclaimed free. In the eyes of the mistress this procedure was so extraordinary that she became very excited and for a moment threatened them with the "broomstick." But her raving had no effect on McKim and Wise, who did not leave until Aunt Hannah was safely in their hands.

Hannah had lived as a slave in Moore's family in the state of Missouri for about ten years and said she was treated well, had plenty to eat, plenty to wear, and plenty of work. It was prior to her coming into the possession of Moore that Aunt Hannah had been made to feel the bitter oppression of slavery. From this point, some of the incidents of her life are described in her words:

———

"Moore bought me from a man named McCaully, who owned me about a year. I fared dreadfully bad under McCaully. One day in a rage he undertook to beat me with the limb of a cherry tree; he began at me and tried in the first place to snatch my clothes off, but he did not succeed. After that he beat the cherry tree limb all to pieces over me. The first blow struck me on the back of my neck and knocked me down; his wife was looking on, sitting on the side of the bed crying for him to lay [it on me]. After the limb was worn out he then went out to the yard and got a lath (a flat strip of wood), and he come at me again and beat me with that until he broke it all to pieces. He was not satisfied then; he next went to the fence and tore off a paling, and with that he took both hands, 'cursing' me all the time as hard as he could. With an oath he would say, 'Now don't you love me?' 'Oh master, I will pray for you,' I would cry; then he would cuss harder than ever. He beat me until he was tired and quit. I crept out of doors and threw up blood; for some days I was hardly able to move. From this beating I was laid up several weeks.

"Another time Mistress McCaully got very angry. One day she beat me as bad as he did. She was a woman who would get very mad in a minute. One day she began scolding and said the kitchen wasn't kept clean. I told her the kitchen was kept as clean as any kitchen in the place; she spoke very angry, and said she didn't go by other folks, but she had rules of her own. She soon ordered me to come in to her. I went in as she ordered me; she met me with a mule rope, and ordered me to cross my hands. I crossed my hands and she tied me to the bedstead.

Here her husband said, 'My dear, now let me do the fighting.' In her mad fit she said he shouldn't do it, and told him to stand back and keep out of the way or 'I will give you the cowhide,' she said to him. He then 'sot' down in a 'cheer' and looked like a man condemned to be hung; then she whipped me with the cowhide until I sunk to the floor. He then begged her to quit. He said to his wife, 'She has begged and begged and you have whipped her enough.' She only raged...turned the butt end of the cowhide and struck me five or six blows over my head as hard as she could; she then threw the cowhide down and told a little girl to untie me. The little girl was not able to do it; Mr. McCaully then untied me himself. Both times that I was beat the blood run down from my head to my feet.

"They wouldn't give you anything to eat hardly. McCaully [was in the habit] of coming by free colored children without buying them, and selling them afterwards. One boy on the place always said that he was free but had been kidnapped from Arkansas. He could tell all about how he was kidnapped, but could not find anybody to do anything for him, so he had to content himself.

"McCaully bought me from a man by the name of Landers. While in Landers' hands I had the rheumatism and was not able to work. He was afraid I was going to die, or he would lose me, and I would not be of any service to him, so he took and traded me off for a wagon. I was something better [in health] when he traded me off; well enough to be about. My health remained bad for about four years, and I never got my health until Moore bought me. Moore took me for a debt.

McCaully owed Moore for wagons. I was not born in Missouri but was born in Virginia. From my earliest memory I was owned by Conrad Hackler; he lived in Grason County. He was a very poor man, and had no other slave but me. He bought me before I was quite four years old, for $100. Hackler bought me from a man named William Scott.

"I must go back by good rights to the beginning and tell all: Scott bought me first from a young man he met one day in the road, with a bundle in his arms. Scott, wishing to know what the young man had in his bundle, was told that he had a baby. 'What are you going to do with it?' said Scott. The young man said that he was going to take it to his sister; that its mother was dead, and it had nobody to take care of it. Scott offered the young man a horse for it, and the young man took him up [on it]. This is the way I was told that Scott came by me. I never knew anything about my mother or father, but I have always believed that my mother was a white woman, and that I was put away to save her character; I have always thought this. Under

Hackler I was treated more like an animal than a human being. I was fed like the dogs; had a trough dug out of a piece of wood for a plate.

"After I [reached the age of 10] they made me sleep out in an old house standing off some distance from the main house where my master and mistress lived. A bed of straw and old rags was made for me in a big trough called the tan trough (a trough having been used for tanning purposes). The cats about the place came and slept with me, and was all the company I had. I had to work with the hoe in the field and help do everything indoors and out in all weathers. The place was so poor that some seasons he would not raise 20 bushels of corn and hardly 3 bushels of wheat. As for shoes I never knew what it was to have a pair of shoes until I had grown up.

"After I grew up to be a woman my master thought nothing of taking my clothes off, and would whip me until the blood would run down to the ground. After I was 25 years old they did not treat me so bad; they both professed to get religion about that time; and my master said he would never lay the weight of his finger on me again. Once after that mistress wanted him to whip me, but he didn't do it, nor [did he ever do it again].

"After awhile my master died; if they had gone according to law I would have been hired out or sold, but my mistress wanted to keep me to carry on the place for her support. So I was kept for seven or eight years after his death. It was understood between my mistress, and her children, and her friends, who all met after master died, that I was to take care of mistress, and after mistress died I should not serve anybody else. I done my best to keep my mistress from suffering. After a few years they all became dissatisfied and moved to Missouri. They scattered, and took up government land. Without means they lived as poor people commonly live, on small farms in the woods. I still lived with my mistress. Some of the heirs got dissatisfied, and sued for their rights or a settlement; then I was sold with my child, a boy."

Thus Aunt Hannah reviewed her slave life, showing that she had been in the hands of six different owners, and had seen great hardship under each of them, except the last; that she had never known a mother's or a father's care;

that slavery had given her one child, but no husband as a protector or a father. The half of what she passed through in the way of suffering has scarcely been hinted at in this sketch. Fifty-seven years were passed in bondage before she reached Philadelphia. Under the good fortune through which she came in possession of her freedom, she found a kind home with a family of abolitionists (Mrs. Gillingham's), whose hearts had been in deep sympathy with the slave for many years. In this situation Aunt Hannah remained several years, honest, faithful, and obliging, taking care of her earnings, which were invested to earn interest for her by her friends. Her mind was deeply imbued with religious feeling, and she held unshaken confidence and trust in God. She connected herself with the A.M.E. Bethel Church of Philadelphia, where she worshiped and served for many years. There may never have been a member of that large congregation whose simple faith and whose walk and conversation were more sincere than Aunt Hannah's.

Although she passed through so many hardships she was a woman of good judgment and more than average intelligence. In freedom, she enjoyed good health, vigor, and peace of mind in her old days, with a small income just sufficient to meet her humble needs without having to work for others.

After living in Philadelphia for several years, she was married to a man about her own age, who possessed all her good qualities. He had served a lifetime in a highly respected Quaker family of that city, and had so won the respect of his kind employer that at his death the employer left him a comfortable house for life, so that he no longer needed to serve another. The name of the recipient of the Quaker employer's bounty, who became Aunt Hannah's husband, was Thomas Todd. After only a few years of marriage, Aunt Hannah was left alone again in the world by the death of her husband. His death was mourned by many friends, both black and white, who knew and respected him.

CHAPTER 68

The Kidnapping of Rachel and Elizabeth Parker, and the Murder of Joseph C. Miller.

Those who were interested in the antislavery cause and kept posted with reference to the frequent cases of kidnapping occurring in different free states, especially in Pennsylvania, during the 20 years prior to emancipation could not fail to remember the kidnapping of Rachel and Elizabeth Parker, and the murder of Joseph C. Miller. At the time of these events, the latter part of 1851 and the beginning of 1852, they were living in West Nottingham Township, Chester County, Pennsylvania.

Both the kidnapping and the murder shocked and excited the better-thinking and humane classes, not only in Pennsylvania, but to a considerable extent over all the northern states. It may be said, without contradiction, that Chester County, at least, was never more aroused by any one single outrage that had taken place within her borders, than by these occurrences. For a long time afterwards, interest was kept alive, and even as late as 1870, the case caused concern among the citizens of Chester County.

Judge Benjamin I. Passmore, in defense of truth in an exhaustive article published in the *Village Record*, West Chester, on 12 October 1870, gives a reliable version of the matter, as follows:

"Tom McCreary "Friend Evans:

"I noticed in the *Village Record*, a short time ago, an article taken from the Delaware *Transcript*, an obituary notice of the death of the noted character whose name heads this article, in which false statements were made, relative to the outrage he committed in kidnapping Rachel and Elizabeth Parker, two colored girls who were then, in 1851, residing in the southern portion of Chester County.

In your paper of the 13th October, I also read an answer to the charges and insinuations made by the destroyed and other citizens of Chester County.

Since the occurrence took place in my immediate neighborhood, and I was familiar with all the facts and circumstances, I propose to give a truthful history of that vile and wicked transaction.

"In the winter of 1851, McCreary in some unexplained way, took Elizabeth Parker, one of the colored girls, from the house of one Donally (not McDonald), in the township of East Nottingham, where she was living; but little was said about it by Donally, or anyone else. Soon after McCreary with two or three others of [similar inclinations] called at the house of Joseph C. Miller, in West Nottingham, where Rachel was living, and seized her, gagged her, and placed her in a carriage and drove off. The screams of Mrs. Miller and her children soon brought the husband and father to the rescue; he pursued them on foot, and at a short distance overtook them in a narrow private road, disputing with James Pollock, the owner of the land, whose wagon prevented them from passing. They turned and took another road, and came out at Stubb's Mill, making for the Maryland line with all possible speed; they arrived at Perryville before the train for Baltimore.

"Eli Haines and a young man named Wiley, who lived near Rising Sun, Maryland, about two miles from Joseph C. Miller's, arrived at the same place soon after, intending to go to Philadelphia. Mr. Haines knew Rachel, and seeing McCreary there, and her so overwhelmed in sorrow, at once guessed the situation of affairs, and he and Wiley changed their intentions of going to Philadelphia, and went in the same car with McCreary and his victim to Baltimore, and quietly watched what disposition would be made of her, as they felt certain pursuit would be made.

"As soon as possible, after McCreary had escaped from West Nottingham, Joseph C. Miller, William Morris, Abner Richardson, Jesse B. Kirk, and H.G. Coates started in pursuit on horseback; when they arrived at Perryville, the train had gone, with the kidnapper and the girl; they followed in the next train. Soon after they arrived in Baltimore, they were met by Haines and Wiley, who had been on the lookout for a pursuing party, and they gave the information that Rachel was deposited in Campbell's slave pen. They were directed by an acquaintance of one of the party to Francis S. Cochran, a prominent member of the Society of Friends.

"Francis informed them he was well acquainted with Campbell, and he at once accompanied them. Campbell assured Friend Cochran that while he approved of slavery and catching runaway slaves, he despised kidnapping and kidnappers; and on the arrival of McCreary, he ordered him to remove Rachel forthwith, which he proceeded to do. Friend Cochran insisted on going with them, and saw the girl deposited in jail to await a legal investigation.

"By this time it was evening, and the Chester County men all went home with Cochran, where they had their suppers; the excitement being great, Friend Cochran did not consider it safe for them to go to the depot direct; he procured their tickets and had them driven by a circuitous route to the depot, charging them to keep together and take their seats in the cars at once.

"Soon after they were seated and before the cars started, Miller stepped out on the platform to smoke, against the expostulations of his friends. Jesse B. Kirk, his brother-in-law, and Abner Richardson followed immediately, and although they were right at his heels, he was gone; they called him by name, and stepped down into the crowd, but soon became alarmed for their own safety, and returned to their seats. A consultation was held, and it was agreed that Wiley, who was least known, and not directly identified with the affair, should pass through the train when it started, and see if Miller had not mistakenly got into another car.

"At Stemen's Run station, Wiley returned to the party with the sad tidings that Joseph C. Miller was not on that train. [After] consultation, it was agreed that Jesse B. Kirk and Abner Richardson should return from Perryville in the next train, and prosecute further search for Miller. They did so return, and McCreary also returned to Baltimore in the same car, he having left Baltimore in the car in the evening with the Chester County men; they arrived late in the night, and locked themselves up in a room in the first hotel they came to.

"Their search was fruitless, and they were forced to return home with the sad tidings that Miller could not be found. This intelligence concerned the whole neighborhood; public meetings were held to consult about what was best to be done. The writer presided at one of those meeting, which was largely attended, and it was with difficulty that the people could be restrained from organizing an armed force to kidnap and lynch McCreary.

Better counsels, however, finally prevailed and it was resolved to send a party to Baltimore to prosecute further the search for Miller.

"About 20 men volunteered for the service; I went to the house of Joseph C. Miller, the morning they were to start, but they had met at Lewis Mellrath's, a brother-in-law of Miller. I was there endeavoring to console the aged mother and distracted wife and children of Joseph C. Miller, when word came that he had been found hanging to a limb in the bushes near Stemen's Run station, and such a scene of distress I hope may never again be my lot to witness; it was heartrending in the extreme.

"The party went to Baltimore, and such was the excitement that it was considered unsafe for the party to go out in a body in daytime. Levi Brown, who then resided in Baltimore, went with them by moonlight, and they disinterred the body, which they found about two feet underground, in a rough box, with a narrow lid that freely admitted the dirt to surround his body in the box. No undertaker in Baltimore could be found that would allow the body left at his place of business while a coffin was prepared, and it was deposited in a vault; a coffin was finally procured and William Morris and Abner Richardson started with it for his home. "When they arrived at Perryville no one would render them any assistance, and they were compelled to leave the corpse in an old saw mill, and walk up to Port Deposit, a distance of five miles, in the night, the weather being extremely cold, and a deep snow on the ground. There they procured horses and a sled and started with the body, but when within a short distance of the Pennsylvania line they were overtaken by a messenger with a requisition from the governor of Maryland to return the body to Baltimore County, in order that an inquisition and post-mortem examination might be held in legal form.

"With sorrowful hearts they turned back (one of these young men told me that at no place south of Port Deposit could they get anyone to assist them in handling the corpse). By this time the affair had created a great excitement, both in Chester County and the city of Baltimore. Rev. John M. Dickey, Hon. Henry S. Evans, then a member of the Senate, Brinton Darlington, then sheriff of Chester County, and very many of the leading men took a deep interest in the matter; we all did our part. The Society of Friends in Baltimore took the matter in hand, and many other worthy citizens belonging to the Presbyterian Church and others lent their aid and influence. Hon. Henry S. Evans, who was then in the Senate of Pennsylvania, brought the matter before the Legislature, and the result, was that the governor appointed Judges Campbell and Bell, the latter of our county to defend these two poor colored girls thus foully kidnapped.

"The body of Miller underwent a post-mortem examination in Baltimore County, at which a great number of rowdies attended, who occupied their time drinking whiskey and cursing the Pennsylvania abolitionists; the body finally reached its distressed home for burial. Drs. Hutchinson and Dickey were called upon to make an examination, at which I was present, and all were clearly of opinion that he had been foully murdered. His wrists and ankles bore the unmistakable marks of manacles; across the abdomen was a black mark as if made by a rope or cord; the end of his nose bore marks as if held by some instrument of torture. His funeral took place, and his remains were followed to the grave by an immense concourse of sympathizing friends and neighbors.

"Such, however, was the excitement that the public demanded a further examination; he was disinterred again, and the same two eminent physicians made a thorough post-mortem examination, and one of them told the writer that there were not two ounces of contents in his stomach and bowels, and that there was abundant evidence of the presence of arsenic. His remains were again interred and, this time, remained undisturbed.

"The theory of his friends was that he had been suddenly snatched from the platform of the car in the Baltimore Depot, gagged, stripped, and lashed down by the ankles and wrists, and a rope across his abdomen, that his nose had been held by some instrument, and that he was in this situation drenched with arsenic, and puked and purged to death, and that McCreary, or someone for him, had heard Wiley repeat at Stemen's Run station that he was not on the train, and conceived the idea of taking his body there and hanging it to a tree to convey the idea that he had committed suicide at that place, and such was the statement published by some of the Maryland newspapers. His companions said he ate a very hearty supper that evening at Francis S. Cochran's, which with the other facts that his clothing were not soiled, and his stomach and bowels were empty, goes strongly to substantiate the theory that he had been stripped and foully murdered, as above indicated.

"Never was there a more false assertion than that the 'broad-brimmed Quakers in Pennsylvania were accomplices of McCreary,' as it is well known that opposition to slavery has been a cardinal principle of the Society of Friends for a century. And that Joseph C. Miller committed suicide because of his being implicated in the kidnapping is a base fabrication. I knew Joseph C. Miller from boyhood intimately, and I here take pleasure in saying that he was an honest, unassuming man, of good moral character and stern integrity, and would have spurned the idea of any complication, directly or indirectly, with slavery or kidnapping.

"It appears his foul murder was not sufficient to satisfy the friends of slavery and kidnapping, but an attempt is now made, after the victim has slumbered near 20 years in the grave, to blast his good name by insinuating that he was a party, or implicated in the vile transactions here narrated.

"Rachel remained in jail; Elizabeth, who had been sold to parties in New Orleans, was sent for by Campbell, ample security having been given that she should be returned if proved to be a slave. Their trial finally came on, and after a long and tedious investigation they were both proven, by hosts of respectable witnesses, to be free. They returned to their mother, in Chester County, who was still living.

"The Grand Jury of Chester County found a true bill against McCreary for kidnapping, a requisition was obtained, and B. Darlington, Esq., then high sheriff, proceeded with it to Annapolis; but the governor of Maryland refused to allow McCreary to be arrested in that state.

"Thus terminated this terrible affair, which cost the state of Pennsylvania nearly $3000, as well as a heavy expense to many citizens of Baltimore, and those of this county who took an active part, and while it is to be hoped that the principal actor in this sad transaction fully atoned for his evil deeds while living, and his friends may have had a right to eulogize him after death, they should not have gone out of their way to traduce other parties, dead and alive, whose reputations were known by living witnesses, to be beyond reproach.

"Justice."

CHAPTER 69

Mary Millburn, alias Louisa F. Jones, Arrives from Norfolk, Virginia, Dressed in Male Attire.

Neither in personal appearance, manners, nor language were any traces of the "peculiar institution" visible in Mary Millburn. On the contrary, she passed as a young lady with a respectable education and very refined manners and appearance. She had been a slave under Mrs. Chapman, who had been singularly kind to her, taking special pains with her in regards to the company she should keep, and so on. Mary had a happy disposition, was obliging and competent, and recognized that her life was pretty good. But despite all this, she was not satisfied; slavery, in its most dreaded aspect, was all around her, continually causing the heart to bleed and eyes of both young and old to weep. The auction block and slave pen were constantly in view. Young girls as promising as herself, she well knew, had been exposed, examined, and sold to the vilest slaveholders living.

With her knowledge of the practical wickedness of the system, how could she be satisfied? She determined to escape. She could be accommodated on the Underground Railroad, but it would not be an easy berth. No flowery beds of ease could be provided in her case, any more than in the case of others. Mary took the Underground Railroad enterprise into consideration. The opportunity of a passage on a steamer was extended to her, which she could accept or refuse. The spirit of freedom dictated that she should accept the offer and leave by the first boat.

Told that she could reach the boat and also travel more safely in male attire she at once said, "Any way so I succeed." When the hour arrived for the boat to depart, Mary was nicely hidden in a box (place), where she was not discovered when the police officers made their usual search.

On arriving in Philadelphia, she mingled her rejoicing with those of the Vigilance Committee of Philadelphia. And she spoke about the importance of the Underground Railroad, and to the carefulness of its agents in guarding against accidents.

After remaining a short time in Philadelphia, she chose to make Boston her future residence. With a letter of introduction to William Lloyd Garrison, she proceeded there. How she was received, and what she thought of the place and people, may be learned from the following letter (written by herself):

"Boston, 15 May 1858 "Dear Friend:

"I have selected this opportunity to write you a few lines, hoping that they may find you and yours enjoying health and happiness. I arrived here on Thursday last, and had a letter of introduction ... to Mr. Garrison in Boston; I found him and his lady both to be very clever. I stopped with them the first day of my arrival here, since that time I have been living with Mrs. Hilliard. I have met with so many of my acquaintances here that I almost imagine myself to be in the old country. I have not been to Canada yet, as you expected. I had the pleasure of seeing the letter that you wrote to them on the subject. I suffered much on the road with a headache but since that time I have no reason to complain. Please do not forget to send the daguerreotypes in the Shaimpain basket with Dr. Lundys; Mr. Lesley said he will send them by express. Tell Julia Kelly, that through mistake, I took one of her pocket handkerchiefs, that was laying on the table, but I shall keep it in remembrance of the owner. I must bring my letter to a close as I have nothing more to say, and believe me to be your faithful friend.

"*Louisa F. Jones.*

"P.S. Remember me to each and every member of your family and all inquiring friends."

Being industrious, she found work immediately. From that day on, she gained respect for her excellent character and her skills as a fashionable dressmaker.

CHAPTER 70

Fifteen from Norfolk, Virginia Arrive on a Schooner.

About 4 July 1856 a message reached the secretary that a schooner containing 15 Underground Railroad passengers, from Norfolk, Virginia would be landed near League Island, directly at the foot of Broad Street, that evening at a late hour, and a request accompanied the message asking the Philadelphia Vigilance Committee to be on hand to receive them. Accordingly the secretary arranged for three carriages with trustworthy drivers, and between ten and eleven o'clock at night arrived on the banks of the Schuylkill, where all was quiet as a "country graveyard."

The moon was shining and soon the mast of a schooner was discovered. No sign of any other vessel was then in sight. On approaching the bank, in the direction of the discovered mast, the schooner itself was seen. The hearts of those on board were swelling with unutterable joy; yet even at that hour of night, far from any sign of foes, no one felt at liberty to rejoice, except in a whisper.

The name of the captain and schooner were at once recognized, and the first impulse was to jump down on the deck to welcome them. But, on second view, it was seen that the descent to the deck was too great. In a moment, it was concluded that the passengers could be pulled up the embankment from the deck below by grabbing hold of their hands as they stood on tiptoe.

One after another was pulled up, and warmly greeted, until it came the turn of a large woman, weighing about 260 pounds, fully large enough to make two ordinary women. The captain, who had experienced much inconvenience with her on the voyage, owing to the space she required, chuckled over the fact that the Committee would have its hands full for once.

Poor Mrs. Walker, however, stretched out her large arms, and members of the Committee seized her hands vigorously. The captain laughed heartily as did the other passengers at the tug of war that now commenced. Committee members pulled with all their might, but Mrs. Walker remained on the deck. The strength of a horse was needed. The pullers caught their breath, and again took hold, this time calling upon the captain to lend a helping hand. The captain prepared to do so, and as Mrs. Walker was being raised, he placed himself in a position for pushing to the full extent of his powers. Thus she was safely landed. Everyone was then placed in the carriages, and they were driven to the station where they were made comfortable.

On the voyage they had encountered more than the usual dangers. Indeed troubles set in before they had set sail from Norfolk. The first indication of danger appeared as they stood on the bank of the river awaiting the arrival of a small boat that would take them to the waiting schooner. Although they had sought a safe place some distance from the areas usually patrolled by the police, still, in the darkness, they imagined they heard watchmen coming.

Just on the edge of the river, opposite where they were waiting, a boat was under repairs in the stocks. In order to evade the advancing watchmen, they all scrambled into the river, the water being shallow at that point, and hid behind the vessel. There they remained for an hour and a half. They were thoroughly soaked, if nothing more. However, about ten o'clock a small oyster boat came to their relief, and all were soon placed aboard the schooner, which was loaded with corn. All, with the exception of the large woman and one other female, were required to enter a hole apparently leading through the bottom of the boat, but in reality only to a compartment that had been expressly constructed for the Underground Railroad business, at the expense of the captain, and in accordance with his own plan.

The entrance was not sufficiently large to admit Mrs. Walker, so she and another female who was thought "too large" to endure the close confinement, were hidden behind corn in back of the cabin, a place so secluded that none save well-experienced searchers would be likely to find them. In this way the captain put out to sea. After some 15 hours he felt it was safe to bring his passengers up on deck where they could inhale pure air, which was greatly needed, as they had been next to suffocation and death. The change of air had such an effect on one of the passengers (Scott) that, in his excitement, he refused to conform to the orders of the captain. For reasons of safety, the captain threatened to throw him overboard, whereupon Scott lowered his voice.

Before reaching the lock, the captain became concerned that they might be in danger from contact with boats, etc., and again called upon them "to go into their hole" under the deck. Not even the big woman was excused now. She pleaded that she could not get through; her fellow sufferers said that she must get through, or they all might have great danger to face. The big woman again tried to make an entrance, but in vain.

One of the more resolute sisters then said, "She must take off her clothes then, it will never do to have her staying up on deck to betray all the rest." This resolute stand being unanimous, the poor woman had to comply, and, except a single garment, was ready to make another attempt. With the help of passengers below, she was squeezed through, but not without bruising and breaking the skin in many places.

All were now beneath the deck, the well-fitting oil cloth was put over the hole covering the cabin floor snugly, and a heavy table was set over the hole. They were within sight of the lock, but no human beings were visible about the schooner except for the captain, the mate, and a small boy, the son of the captain. At the lock not unexpectedly three officers came on board of the boat and stopped it.

The captain was told that they had received a telegraph dispatch from Norfolk to the effect that his boat was suspected of having slaves hidden on board. They talked with the captain and mate separately for a considerable while, and questioned the boy even more intently, but gained no information except that "the yellow fever had been raging very bad in Norfolk." At this fever news the officers were considerably alarmed, and they now lost no time in attending to their official errand.

They searched the cabin where the two large women were hidden initially and other parts of the boat pretty thoroughly. They then began to take up the hatchways, but the place seemed so filled with foul air that the men started back and declared that nobody could live in such a place, and swore that it smelled like the yellow fever. The captain laughed at them, and signified that they were perfectly welcome to search to their hearts' content.

The officers concluded that there were no slaves on that boat, that nobody could live there, etc., etc., and discharged the captain.

The children had been put under the influence of liquor to keep them still, so they made no noise; the others endured their hour of agony patiently until the lock was safely passed, and the river reached. Fresh air was then allowed them, and the great danger was considered overcome. The captain, however, far from believing it advisable to land his live cargo at the wharves of Philadelphia, delivered them at League Island. The passengers testified that Captain B. was very kind as well as smart.

CHAPTER 71

Euphemia Williams, Part 1 —
Arrested as a Fugitive Slave Under the Fugitive Slave Law after Having Lived in Pennsylvania for More than 20 Years.

Scarcely had the infamous statute been in existence six months before the worst predictions of the friends of the slave were fulfilled in different northern states. It is hardly too much to say that Pennsylvania was considered wholly unsafe to nine-tenths of her black population. The kidnapper's work was fully illustrated in another case — that of Rachel and Elizabeth Parker — as he appeared on the soil of Pennsylvania, doing his vile work in the dead of night, entering the homes of unprotected females and children, and so on. But that was just one of many cases, including the following:

The case of Euphemia Williams illustrates the milder form of kidnapping, in open daylight and in the name of the law.

On 6 February 1851, Euphemia Williams, the mother of six children, the youngest at the breast, was arrested in the upper part of the city (Philadelphia), and hurried before Edward D. Ingraham, a United States Commissioner, upon the charge of being a fugitive from labor. She was claimed by William T.J. Purnell, of Worcester County, Maryland, who admitted that she had been away from him for 22 years, or since 1829.

Her children were born on the soil of Pennsylvania, and the eldest daughter was 17 years of age. Euphemia was about 40 years old.

Euphemia was living in her own house, and had been a member of church, in good and regular standing, for about 17 years. When the arrest was made, Euphemia had just risen from her bed. She was only partly dressed, when a little after daylight, several persons entered her room and arrested her.

"Murder! Murder!" was cried loudly, and awakened everyone in the house.

Her children screamed in terror, and her eldest daughter cried, "They've got my mother! They've got my mother!"

"For God's sake, save me," cried Euphemia, to a woman in the second story, who was an eyewitness to this monstrous outrage. But despite the piteous appeals of the mother and children, the poor woman was hastened into a horse-drawn cab, and taken to the marshal's office.

Through the vigilance of J.M. McKim and Passmore Williamson, a writ of habeas corpus returnable forthwith was obtained at about one o'clock. When her children were brought into the room where she was detained, great drops of sweat standing on her face plainly indicated her agony.

CHAPTER 72

Euphemia Williams, Part 2 — The Prosecution at Her Trial.

By mutual arrangement between the claimants of Euphemia Williams and her counsel, a hearing was fixed for 7 February 1851, at the hour of three o'clock. According to the arrangement, at three o'clock Euphemia was brought face-to-face with her claimant, William T.J. Purnell. The news had already gone out that the trial would come off at the time fixed; hence many persons were on hand to witness the proceedings in the case. The sympathy of antislavery ladies was excited, and many were present in the courtroom to show their feelings in behalf of the stricken woman.

The eloquent David Paul Brown (the terror of slave hunters) and William S. Pierce, Esqrs., appeared for Euphemia; R.C. McMurtrie, Esq., for the claimant.

Mr. McMurtrie rose and said that it was with extreme regret that he saw an attempt to influence the decision of this case by tumult and agitation. The sympathy shown by so many friendly ladies was not a favorable sign for the slaveholder. Notwithstanding, Mr. McMurtrie said that he would "prove that Mahala, sometimes called Mahala Purnell, was born and bred a slave of Dr. George W. Purnell, of Worcester County, Maryland, who was in the habit of hiring her to the neighbors, and while under a contract of hiring, she escaped with a boy, with whom she had taken up, belonging to the person who hired her." The present claimant claimed her as the administrator of Dr. George W. Purnell.

The Examination of Robert F. Bowen

In order to sustain this claim many witnesses and much positive sworn testimony were called forth. Robert F. Bowen, the first witness, swore that he knew both Mahala and her master perfectly well, that he had worked as a carpenter in helping to build a house for the latter, and also had hired the former directly from her owner.

Definite time and circumstances were all harmoniously fixed by this leading witness. One of the important circumstances that made it possible for him to be so positive was, as he testified on cross-examination, that he was from home at a camp meeting (when she ran away).

"Our camp meetings," said the witness, "are held in the last of August or the first of September ... the year I fix by founding it upon knowledge ... the year before she ran away, I professed religion ... I have something at home to fix the year ... she was with me a part of a year ... I hired her for the year 1848 as a house servant ... I hired her directly from Dr. George W. Purnell.

"When she ran away I proceeded after her. I advertised in Delaware in written advertisements, in Georgetown, Milford, and Millsborough, and described her and the boy; her [by her] general features. I no longer have the advertisement and can't tell how she was described ... Dr. George Purnell united with me in the advertisement ... I followed her to Delaware City ... that's all I have done since, about inquiring after them — until now.

"I came, after 22 years' absence, to seek my own rights, and as an evidence for my friend. I have not seen her more than once since she ran away, until she was arrested ... I saw her two or three times in court. I saw her first in a wretched-looking room, at Fifth and Germantown Road ... it was yesterday morning ... it was the evening before at Congress Hall ... I arrived here last Tuesday a week ... a man told me where she was."

"I beg the court," Mr. McMurtrie made an objection to his mentioning the person. The court, however, said the question could be asked.

Witness: "I was pledged not to tell the name ... the person signed her name Louisa Truit ... the information was got by letter ... the reason I did not tell, because I thought she might be murdered ... I have not the letters, and can't tell the contents ... the letter that I received required a pledge that I would not tell ... I was directed to send my letter to the post office without any definite place ... the representative of Louisa Truit was a man ... I saw him in Market Street between Third and Fourth, at Taylor and Paulding's store, in the course of last week ... I was brought into contact with the representative of Louisa by appointment in the letter, to get the information ... I never heard him tell his name ... he was neither colored nor white ... we call them with us mixed blood ... I suppose he lives somewhere up there ... I saw him at my room the next morning ... I did not learn from him who wrote the letter ... he did not describe the person of the woman in the letter written to me, only her general appearance ... I subsequently burnt the letter."

Mr. Brown demanded the letter, or the proof of its destruction.

"I never wrote myself, but my friend, Mr. Henry did ... he said so ... I never received a letter ... it was written to Robert J. Henry ... part of the letter was written to me, but not directed to me ... the Louisa Truit who wrote stated that for the information she wanted $100 for one of the fugitives ... he was referred to the store of Taylor & Paulding, and Mr. Henry would meet him there ... when I got to the store, some of the concerned let Mr. Henry know that a man wanted to see him... I heard at the store the man was there ... he was a mulatto man, middle-aged, and middling tall ... he is not here, that I know of ... can't tell when I last saw him... his name I understood to be Gloucester."

Under the severe cross-examination that Robert Bowen had been subjected to under D.P. Brown, he became very faint, and called for water. Large drops of sweat stood upon his forehead, and he was forced to sit down, or risk falling down. "Take a seat," said Mr. Brown tauntingly, "and enjoy yourself, while I proceed with my interrogations."

But the witness was completely used up, and was allowed to withdraw to another room, where fresh air was more plentiful. The cause of the poor slave woman was greatly strengthened by this failure.

Another witness, named Zachariah Bowen, for the claimants, swore positively that he knew the prisoner well; that she had been hired to his brother for three years by Dr. Purnell, whose slave she was; also he swore that he knew her parents, who were slaves to the said Doctor Purnell; that he last saw her in 1827, etc.

On cross-examination he swore: "I last saw her in 1827 ... she was about 16 or 17 ... she was about an ordinary size, not the smallest size, nor the largest ... she was neither thick nor thin ... there was nothing remarkable in her more than is common ... nothing in her speech ... she was about the same color as the woman here ... I never saw a great deal of change in a [negro], from 16 to 35 or 40, sometimes they grow fatter, and sometimes leaner."

As to recognizing her in Philadelphia, he had not the slightest difficulty. He went on to swear that he first saw her in a cab in the city.

"I knew her yesterday, if you could see the rest of the family you could pick her out yourself in 30 ... I knew her by her general favor, and have no particular mark ... I would not attempt to describe features; her appearance is familiar to me ... I never saw any marks upon her."

Here Mr. Brown said he would not examine this witness further until he had concluded the examination of the witness who had become sick. The court then adjourned until nine o'clock the next morning.

The avenues to the court were filled with anxious persons, and in the front and rear of the statehouse the crowd was very great.

The next morning, at an early hour, the courtroom, and all the avenues to it were densely crowded by people interested in behalf of the woman whose case was under trial. A large number of respectable ladies formed a part of the large gathering.

Robert F. Bowen, the witness who had become sick, was recalled.

Witness: "I saw the colored person, who gave the information, the next evening ... after I saw him in Market Street, at Congress Hall, in our room .... The gentleman who keeps the hotel we did not wish to place under any responsibility, as he might be accused of carrying on the business."

"Of kidnapping," suggested Mr. Brown.

"No," said the witness, "that is what you call it ... the woman would have run away [if she had gotten word of our intent]. [The person who informed on her]

... heard his name was Gloucester, that gave the information ... I saw him three times ... once on the street ... I have never been in his house ... I have been to a house where I heard he lived ... gave a pledge not to disclose the matter ... I made a personal pledge to Gloucester in our room last week at Congress Hall ... he said he was afraid of being abused by the population of his own color for telling that this girl run away from Dr. Purnell ... I understood that Louisa Truit was Gloucester's wife.

Under searching cross-examination, Mr. Brown compelled him not only to tell all and more than he knew about his friend, the claimant, but wrung from him the secrets that he pledged never to disclose.

Witness: "I know no marks ... she was in the condition of a married woman when she left me ... it was the particular [similarity to] her father and mother that made me recognize her ... nothing else ... she was pretty well built for her size."

While this witness remembered everything so accurately occurring in relation to the life and escape of the girl of 16, and was prepared to swear to her identity simply "by her favor," as he termed it, he was found sadly deficient in memory of the owner, whom he had known much longer, and more intimately than he had the girl, as will be seen from the following facts in this witness' testimony:

Witness: "I don't know when Dr. P. died ... I can't tell the year; I should suppose about 14 years ago ... I was at the funeral, and helped to make his coffin... it was in the fall, I think ... it was after the camp meeting I spoke of

... at that time I went regularly, but not of late ... I have no certain recollection of the year he died ... I kept a record of the event of my conversion, and have referred to it often. It has been a reference every year, and perhaps a thousand times a year ... it was in the Bible, and I was in the habit of looking into it ... I was in the habit of turning over the leaves of this precious book ... I think it was 18 years ago ... can't say I'm certain ... can't say it was more than 12 years ... Dr. P. left six children ... two remain in our county, and one in Louisiana, and the one, who is here, making four ... I have no interest in the fugitive ... I made no contract in regard to this case ... there was an offer ... are you waiting for an answer? The offer was this, that I was to come on after my fugitive, and if I did not get him they were to pay my expenses ... I hesitated about coming ... it was a long time before I made up my mind ... they said they would pay my expenses if I didn't succeed in getting mine out of 'prison.'"

Examination of Zachariah Bowen, Overseer

Zachariah Bowen recalled: "I didn't come here on any terms ... I hardly understand what you mean by terms ... I made no contract ... I came upon my own hook ... there was no contract ... I have no expectations ... I don't know that Dr.P. ever [freed] any female slaves ... I never knew that she was in the family way when she ran away ... I heard of it about that time ... she ran off in the fall of 1828... Dr. P. told me so ... in the fall of 1828 .... In 1825, '26, '27, she lived with my brother ... in 1825 I lived there ... in 1827 and '28 I lived with Dr. P. I moved there and was overseer for him ... I was overseer for 15 years for him ... two years at his house ... I ceased to be his overseer in 1841, I think ... he was living in 1841 ... I am certain of that year, I think ... Dr. Purnell died in 1844, I feel certain ... I said to Mr. Purnell that I did not know what ailed the other Mr. Bowen, for the doctor died in 1844 ... he died in the latter part of the spring of 1844 ... Mr. Bowen made a mistake in saying it was 18 years ago ... if you recall him he will rectify the mistake, I think ... several slaves escaped from Dr. Purnell ... a boy, that lived with my brother, ran away in 1827 ... the others were not hired to my brother ... I don't know that I could tell the exact time, nor the year ... the doctor used to say to us, there is another of my [negroes] ran away ... the reason that I can tell when Mahala ran away, is because she took a husband and ran away ... I was married that year ... the reason I cannot tell about the others is because they went at different times in five years ... the first who ran away before Mahala, was named Grace ... she went in 1827 ... I don't know when the last went, or who it was.

"Gloucester said they had raised a mob on him, on account of this case, and he would have to leave the city ... the case of this woman or these proceedings was not spoken of there ... he stayed but a short time ... he said one of the witnesses had betrayed him in court, yesterday, and they attacked him last night ... I asked him how he escaped from so many ... he said very few were in the city who could outrun him ... I asked him where he was going, he replied he had a notion to [go to] Canada ... some of the gentlemen proposed his going to Baltimore ... he said that would not do, as the laws of Maryland would catch him ... he was going to get a boat and go to New Jersey, and then to New York ... Mr. Purnell gave him just $35 last night [but] he paused a while, and Mr. P. told him to hand it back ... he then took out his money and put some more to it, and said: 'Here is $50.' P. said that if he got the slave he would leave $50 more with a person in the city."

Question by the judge: "You have spoken of a conversation in which Mr. P. told you of certain letters of correspondence, and that they had reference to this alleged fugitive. I want you to give me, to the best of your recollection, everything he said the letters contained."

Witness: "Mr. P. told me when he first mentioned it to me, he said that he was going to mention something to me, that he did not want anything said, in regard to some negroes that had run away from his father; he said he wanted me to come on here, and he did not want me to tell any person before we left our county; that if the negroes heard of it, they could get information to the parties before he could get here. I told him I would not tell any person except my wife; he then said he had correspondence with a person here, for a month or two, and he had no doubt but that several of his negroes were here, from what he had heard from his correspondent; he asked me if I could recognize the favor of this Mahala? I told him I didn't know; he then said if anybody would know her, I would, as she had lived with my brother three years; he then said that he would want to start the next week, but he would see me again at that time; that was all he said at that time, only we turned into a hotel, and he said don't breathe this to anybody; on Saturday before we left home, he came to my house, and said, 'Well, I shall want you to start for Philadelphia on Monday morning; suppose you will go?' I told him I would rather not, if he could do without me; but as I told him before, I would go if he still requested it, I would go; that's all, sir, except that I said I would be along in the stage."

The Testimony of J. T. Hammond

J.T. Hammond was then called. He is a young man who admitted he had never seen the respondent until he came to the courthouse, but was ready to swear that he would have known her by her resemblance to Dr. Purnell's set of negroes.

"His whole set?" said Mr. Brown.

"Yes," came the answer. (Derisive laughter.)

Mr. McMurtrie offered to prove, by persons who had known the two witnesses who had testified in this case from their youth, that they were respectable and worthy men. D.P. Brown said that if the gentleman found it necessary to sustain the reputation of his witnesses, in consequence of the peculiar dilemma they had gotten into, he would object ... But he said that if Mr. McMurtrie supposed that he [Mr. Brown] was about to contradict them in some point in the defense, he [McMurtrie] certainly was right. But, since the case could not be concluded today, Brown asked to have the matter adjourned until the next Tuesday.

Mr. McMurtrie objected, saying that his client was anxious to have the matter disposed of as soon as possible, as he had been subjected to numerous insults since the matter had been before the court.

Judge Kane noted that no weight was to be attached to this consideration, as the full power of the court was at his disposal for the purpose of protecting his client from insult.

Mr. McMurtrie replied that he did not know whether words spoken came within the meaning of the act of Congress in such matters. The court took a recess until a quarter to three o'clock. The court met again at a quarter to three o'clock.

Mr. McMurtrie asked that the witnesses for the defense be excluded from the courtroom, except the one upon the stand. This was objected to by Mr. Brown, as the witnesses for the prosecution had not been required to do so. Subsequently Mr. Brown withdrew his objections, and notified Mr. McMurtrie that he would require any witnesses he might have to stay out of the courtroom while others were testifying, if McMurtrie would have his witness leave as well. But, Brown said he would object to any of them being heard if they remained.

CHAPTER 73

Euphemia Williams, Part 3 — The Defense, Judgment, and Aftermath of the Trial.

Mr. Pierce opened the case for the defendant by saying that the testimony for the defense would be clear and conclusive and that the witnesses for the prosecution were mistaken in the identity of the alleged fugitive. That at the time they alleged to have been in Maryland on the plantation of Dr. Purnell, she was in Chester County, and in the year Lafayette visited this country, she was in this city. He would confine the testimony exclusively to these two counties, and show that she is not the alleged slave.

Henry C. Cornish was sworn and testified: "I live in this city, and am a shoemaker ... I came here in the year 1830 ... before that I lived in Chester County, East Whiteland Township, with Wm. Latta ... my father lived with Mr. Latta six or eight years ... I lived there three years before that time, and was familiar with the place for more than six years before 1830 ... I saw the alleged fugitive some five years before 1830, at George Amos', in Uwchlan Township, some eight or ten miles from our house ... I fix the time from a meeting being held on the Valley Hill by a minister named Nathan D. Tierney that must have been in 1825 ... I am positive it was before the beginning of the year 1828 ... I have not the least doubt ... I joined church about that time ... it was the first of my uniting with the church ... it was in 1825 ... I joined the Methodist Episcopal Church ... before they built a church they held meetings alternately at people's houses ... I met her at Amos' house, I recollect my father going to dig the foundation of the church: I saw her there before the church was built ... I knew her before she was married ... and since I left there I have met her at the annual meetings of the church ... I have kept up the acquaintance ever since ... I knew that she had two children that were buried as long as 21 or 22 years ago ... if the boy had lived he would have been 23 or 24 years old ... he was the oldest ... she was not married when I first saw her in 1827 ... she did not appear to be anything but a girl, and was not married, and she of course could not be in the condition of a married woman ... I was not at her wedding ... if I had not continued to know her, I would not now know her ... she was then a small person ... age and flesh would change her a little ... her complexion has not changed ... I think she worked for Mrs. Amos; a church record is now kept very correct ... but when I first went into the church, colored men could not read and write ... I acted as the clerk of the church ... I united with the church after I first saw her; I have seen her very often since I left Chester ... 500 times to speak safely ... I worship downtown and she up in Brown Street ... to the best of my recollection they moved over Schuylkill about 12 years ago ... she has lived here about nine years ... she has six children, I have heard ... I have seen five ... the oldest is 18 or 19 ... the youngest a sucking babe ... I have visited her house since I have been here; I was not sent for by my uncle, who was employed by Joseph Smith & Co., next to the Girard Bank ... I was with Edward Biddle for four years, until he was elected President of the Morris Canal and Banking Company, and then I went to learn shoemaking under instructions, since which time I have been in business for myself ... my father burnt limestone for Mr. Latta ... he and his wife are dead ... I was there a day or two ago for witnesses to testify in this case."

Henry testified as follows under cross-examination: "I was born in 1814, and am 37 years of age ... when I first knew her I suppose she was 15-years old ... she was married about three years afterwards ... her husband's name is

Micajah Williams ... I heard he was in prison for stealing ... her name before marriage was Phamie Coates ... I didn't know her husband before they were married ... don't know whether they came from Maryland ... I never knew of Mahala Richardson before last evening in court ... the difference in her appearance is a natural one, that everybody is acquainted with ... I mean that a little boy is not a man, and a growing girl is not a woman ... age and flesh and size make a difference ... if I had not conversed with her during the 21 years, I would not have known her ... I never exchanged a word with her about the case, except to say I was sorry to see her here ... I knew her the moment I saw her ... her arrest could not have been in the newspapers of the morning as she was not arrested until seven o'clock that day ... I went to Chester to look for witnesses ... I came to the court because I am a vigilant man, and my principle is to save any person whose liberty is in danger ... I had heard that a woman was arrested ... her business is to get work wherever she can." Deborah Ann Boyer was sworn and testified as follows: "I was 33 last January ... I live within one mile of West Chester ... I am a married woman ... I have lived there since 1835. I went there with my mother ... I can read ... I have seen the alleged fugitive before this ... I first knew her at Downingtown, when she came to my mother's house ... that was before I had gone to West Chester with my mother ... you can tell how long it was, for it was in 1826 ... my brother was born in that year ... I was quite small then ... don't know how she came there ... she was with my mother during her confinement ... my brother is dead ... it is written down in our testament ... and I took an epitaph from it to put on the tombstone ... the last time I saw it was when the fellow killed the schoolmistress. I looked because about 1830, a man killed a woman, and was hung, and I wanted to see how long ago it was. I have seen her more or less ever since, until within two years ... I don't remember when she went from mother, but I saw her at Mr. Latta's afterwards. I have no doubt she is the woman ... she was then a slim, tall girl, larger than myself ... she is not darker now, but heavier set in every way."

Sarah Gayly affirmed this testimony: "I am between 47 and 48 years of age. I live in the city at this time. I was raised in Chester County, in 1824, and have been here about five years. I lived in Downingtown nine or ten years. I lived awhile in West Chester, and lived in Chester County until about five years ago. I know the alleged fugitive. I first saw her in the neighborhood of Downingtown, at a place they call Downing's old stage office ... she worked in the house with me ... it was somewhere near 1824, just before Lafayette came about ... she worked off and on days' work, to wash dishes ... she was a small girl then, very thin, and younger than me. I met with her, as near as I can tell you, down in the valley, at a place called the Valley Inn. I used to see her off and on at church, in 1826 I visited her at Mr. Latta's after she lived at the Valley Inn. I don't know when she left that county. I know the alleged fugitive is the same person ... she belonged to the same church, Ebenezer. I know the brothers Cornish, and have whipped them many a time. I lived with Latta myself, and the Cornish, who is now a minister, lived there ... he lived there before I did, and so did the alleged fugitive. I was then between 23 and 25 years old ... she was a strip of a girl ... she was not in the family way when she came there."

Under cross-examination, she added: "I have not seen her since 1826, until I saw her here in the courtroom ... I recognized her when I first saw her here without anybody pointing her out, and she recognized me ... I have reason to know her, because she has the same sort of a scar on her forehead that I have ... we used to make fun of each other about the marks ... she went by the name of Fanny Coates. I know nothing about her husband ... she did not do the work of a woman in 1826... she washed dishes, scrubbed .... I heard her say her father and mother were dead, and that they lived somewhere in that neighborhood ... she at that time made her home with a family named Amos."

The judge asked to see the scar on the witness's forehead and that on the forehead of the respondent. They were brought near the bench, and the marks inspected, which were plainly seen on both. During this time the infant of the respondent was entrusted to another colored woman. The child, who, up to this time, had been quiet, raised a piteous cry and would not be silenced. The whole scene excited a great sensation.

Mr. Brown then rose in reply to the plaintiff's counsel, and said: "If I consulted my own views, I should not say one syllable in answer to the arguments of the learned counsel upon the other side. And relying as I do upon the evidence, and out of respect to the convenience of your honor, I shall say very little as it is. The views of the counsel, it appears to me, are most extraordinary indeed. He seems to take it for granted that everything that is said on the part of the witnesses for the claimant is gospel, and that what is said on the part of the witnesses for the respondent is to be considered a matter of suspicion.

"Now I rate no man by his size, color, or position, but I appeal to you in looking at the testimony that has been produced here, on the different sides of the question, and judging it by its intrinsic worth, whether there is the slightest possible comparison between the witnesses on the part of the plaintiff, and those of the defendant, either in intelligence, memory, language, thought, or anything else. This is a fine commentary upon the disparagement of color! Looking at the men as they are, as you will, I say that the testimony exhibited on the part of the respondent would outweigh a whole theatre of such men as are exhibited on the part of the complainant. I say nothing here about their respectability. It would have been proper for the learned counsel on the part of the plaintiff, if he thought the witnesses on the part of the respondent unworthy of belief to have proved them so; but instead of that, he attempts to bolster up men, who, whether respectable or otherwise, from their inconsistency in regard to this case, produce no possible effect upon the judicial mind, except that which is unfavorable to themselves.

"Are they impartial men? How do they appear to you? They appear underhanded from first to last; stand upon their fight to resist inquiries legitimately presented to them; burn up letters since they have arrived — letters that would have shed light upon this subject; and before they come here, correspond with and derive information from a man, an evident kidnapper, who dares not sign his name but gets his wife to sign hers. This is the character these men exhibit here before you; clandestinely meeting together at the tavern, and that meeting was to corroborate their stories in order to identity a person about whom they know nothing. Can they refer to any marks by which to identify this person? Nothing at all of the kind. Do they, with the exception of the first witness examined, state even the time when she left? Have they produced the letter written by this kidnapper, showing how he described her? Why, let me ask, is not the full light allowed to shine on this case? But even with the light they have shed upon it, I would have been perfectly content to have rested my case, relying upon their testimony alone, for a just decision.

"Now what man among them claims to have seen this woman for 21 years? Not one. The learned gentleman attempts to sustain his case, because one of our witnesses, certainly not more than one, has not seen this woman for about the same length of time: but don't you perceive that in this case they all lived in the same state, if not in the same county, they had [conversation] with persons mutually acquainted with her, and three out of four of them met her for several months at the same church; and one witness, who had long been in her society, and in close association with her, knew she had a mark upon her forehead corresponding to the one she bore on her own. And by the force of all these matters, this long continued acquaintance only reviving the impressions received in early life, they had no doubt of the identity of the person. Was there ever a more perfect train of evidence exhibited to prove the identity of a person, than on the present occasion?

"We have called witnesses on this point alone, and have more than countered the evidence produced upon the opposite side. And we have not only made it manifest that she was a free woman, but we have confirmed her charter by separate proof. What does the gentleman say further? Do I understand him to say we have no right to determine this matter judicially? Now what is all this about? Why is it before you, taking your time day after day? According to this argument, you have nothing to do but to give the master the flesh he claims. But you are to be satisfied that you have sufficient reason to believe that these claims are well founded. And if you leave that matter in a state of doubt, it does not require a single witness to be called on the part of the respondent, to prove on the opposite side of the question. But we have come in with a weight of evidence demolishing the structure he has raised, restoring the woman to her original position in the estimation of the law.

"Well," says the gentleman, "it is like the case of a fugitive from justice." But it is not, and if it were, it would not benefit his case. The case of a fugitive from justice is one in which the prisoner is remanded to the custody of the law, handed over for legal purposes. The case of a fugitive from labor is a case in which the individual is handed over sometimes to a merciless master, and very rarely to a charitable one. Does the counsel mean to say that in the case of a fugitive from justice he is not bound to satisfy the judge before whom the question is heard? He should prove our witnesses unworthy of belief. As Judge Grier said, upon a former occasion, 'You can choose your own time; you have full and abundant opportunities on every side to prepare against any contingency.' Why don't they do so? He is not to come here and force on a case, and say, I suppose you take everything for granted. He is to come prepared to prove the justice of his claim before the tribunal who is to decide upon it. That he has not done successfully, and I would, therefore, ask your Honor, after the elaborate argument on the part of the plaintiff, to discharge this woman; for after such an abundance of testimony unbroken and incontestable as that we have exhibited here, it would be a monstrous perversion of reason to suppose that anything more could be required."

Mr. McMurtrie replied by reasserting his positions. It was a grave question for the court to consider what evidence was required. He thought that this decision might be the turning case to show whether the act of Congress would be carried out or whether we were to return in fact to the state affairs under the old laws.

Judge Kane said, in reference to the remarks at the close of Mr. McMurtrie's speech: "So long as I retain my seat on this bench, I shall endeavor to enforce this law without reference to my own sympathies, or the sympathies and opinions of others. I do not think, in the cases under this act of Congress, or a treaty, or constitutional, or legal provision for the extradition of fugitives from justice, that it is possible to imagine that conclusive proof of identity could be established by depositions. From the nature of the case and the facts to be proved, proof cannot be made in anticipation of the identity of the party. That being established, it is the office of the judge to determine whether a prima facie case indicates the identity of the party charged, with the party before him.

"On the other hand, the evidence of the claimant has been met, and regarding the bearing of the witnesses for the respondent, met by witnesses who testified, with apparent candor and great intelligence. If they are believed, then the witnesses for the claimant are mistaken. The question is, whether two witnesses for the claimant, who have not seen the respondent for twenty-three, one for twenty-four years, are to be believed in preference to four witnesses on the other side, three of whom have seen her frequently since 1826, and [have] known her as Euphemia Williams, and the fourth, who has not seen her for a quarter of a century, but testifies that when they were children, they used to jest each other about scars, which they still bear upon their persons; I am bound to say that the proof by the four witnesses has not been overthrown by the contrary evidence of the two who only recognized her when they called on her with the marshal. One says he called her Mahala Purnell as soon as he saw her. He might be mistaken. He inferred he would find her at the place to which he went. There were three persons in the room, one was Mahala Richardson, whom he knew as a young girl, and the prisoner. If she had been alone, his recognition would have been of no avail.

"The fact is obvious to this court that the respondent has no peculiar physical feature or gait. It has been shown she has no peculiarity of voice; I cannot but feel that the fact alleged by the claimant is very doubtful, when the witnesses, without mark or peculiarity, testify that they can readily recognize the girl of 15 in the woman of 40. The prisoner is therefore discharged."

Upon hearing the dismissal of the charges against Euphemia Williams, there was a slight attempt at applause in the courtroom, but it was promptly suppressed. Word about the discharge of the woman was quickly spread to those outside, who raised shouts of joy. The woman, with her children, was hurried into a carriage, which was driven first to the Anti-Slavery Office and then to the Philadelphia Institute on Lombard Street above Seventh. Here she was introduced to a large audience of black people, who hailed her appearance with lively joy, several excited speeches were made, and great enthusiasm was evident inside and outside the building and the adjacent streets. When Euphemia came out, the horses were taken out of the carriage, and a long rope was attached, which was taken by as many black persons as could get hold of it, and the woman and her children were thus taken to their home.

The procession was accompanied by several hundred men, women, and boys. They dragged the carriage past the residence of the counsel for the respondent, cheering them by huzzahs of the wildest kind, and then took the vehicle and its contents to the residence of the woman, Germantown Road near Fifth Street, paving the way with songs and shouts. The whole scene was one of wild, ungovernable excitement, produced by exuberance of joy.

The masterly management of abolitionists in connection with the counsel saved poor Euphemia from being dragged from her children into hopeless bondage. While the victory was a source of great momentary rejoicing on the part of the friends of the slave, it was nevertheless quite apparent that she was only saved by the "skin of her teeth," or, in this case, "a scar on her forehead."

Relative to this important mark, a few of Euphemia's friends enjoyed a very pleasing anecdote, which, at the time, could not be told to the public, but it is too good to be kept any longer.

For a time, Euphemia was kept in durance vile up in the dome of Independence Hall, partly in the custody of Lieutenant Gouldy of the Mayor's Police, who turned out to be the right man in the right place [as his] sympathies were secretly on the side of the slave. While his pitying eyes gazed on Euphemia's sad face, he observed a very large scar on her forehead, and was immediately struck by the thought that that old scar might be used with damaging effect by the witnesses and counsel against her. At once he decided that the scar must be concealed, at least, until after the examination of the claimant's witnesses.

Accordingly a large turban was obtained and placed on Euphemia's head in such a way as to hide the scar completely, and without exciting the least suspicion in the minds of any. So when the witnesses against her swore that she had no particular mark, David Paul Brown made them clinch this part of their testimony irrevocably. Now, when Sarah Gayly affirmed (on the part of the prisoner) that "I have reason to know her because she has the same sort of a scar on her forehead that I have, we used to make fun of each other about the marks ...." if it was not evident to all, it was to some, that she had "stolen their thunder," as the "chap-fallen" faces of the slaveholder's witnesses indicated in a moment. Despair was depicted on all faces sympathizing with the pursuers.

With heavy financial losses and sad damage of character and comfortless, the unhappy claimant and his witnesses were compelled to return to Maryland. The account of this interesting trial has been condensed from a very careful and elaborate report of it published in the *Pennsylvania Freeman* of 13 January 1857.

CHAPTER 74

Fugitive Slave Law Kidnappings in Pennsylvania — a Letter from James Miller McKim.

The vigilance of slave hunters was not deterred by the defeat of William T.J. Purnell at the trial of Euphemia Williams. If the records of the old Abolitionist Society could be published, as they should be, they would show that many hard-fought battles have taken place between freedom and slavery in Philadelphia and Pennsylvania.

The Fugitive Slave Law and arrests under it were constantly opposed by the Anti-Slavery Society, which did all it could to protect the free black as well as the fugitive from slavery. James Miller McKim, who was well known to stand in the front ranks of both the Anti-Slavery Society and the Underground Railroad cause through all the long and trying contest, during which the country was agitated by the question of immediate emancipation, shared the full confidence and respect of Abolitionists of all classes throughout the United States and Great Britain.

In 1851, McKim wrote the following letter to Hon. George Thompson, the distinguished abolitionist of England. The following excerpts speak for itself.

Letter from Mr. McKim to George Thompson, 1851

"The accompanying parcel of extracts will give you a full account of the different slave cases tried in this city under the new Fugitive Slave Law up to this time. Full and accurate as these reports are, they will afford you but a faint idea of the anguish and confusion that have been produced in this part of the country by this infamous statute. It has turned southeastern Pennsylvania into another Guinea Coast, and caused a large portion of the inhabitants to feel as insecure from the brutal violence and diabolical acts of the kidnapper, as are the unhappy creatures who people the shores of Africa. Ruffians from the other side of the slave line, aided by professional kidnappers on our own soil, a class of men whose 'occupation' until lately, had been 'gone' — are continually prowling through the community, and every now and then seizing and carrying away their prey. As a specimen of the boldness, though fortunately, not of the success always with which these wretches prosecute their evil trade, read the enclosed article, which I cut from the *Freeman*, of 2 January 1851, and bear in mind that in no respect are the facts here mentioned overstated."

From the *Freeman* of 2 January

"This affair occurred in Chester County, one of the most orderly and intelligent counties in the state, a county settled principally by Quakers. A week or two after this occurrence, and not far from the same place, a farmhouse was entered by a band of armed ruffians, in the evening, and at a time when all the able-bodied occupants, save one, were known to be absent. This was [the home of] a colored man, who was seated by the kitchen fire, and in the act of taking off his shoes. He was instantly knocked down and gagged, but, still resisting, he was beaten most unmercifully. There was a woman, and also a feeble old man, in the house, who were attracted to the spot by the scuffle, but they could neither render any assistance, nor (the light being put out) could they recognize the parties engaged in it. The unhappy victim, being fairly overcome, was dragged like a slain beast to a wagon, which was about a hundred yards distant, waiting to receive him. In this he was placed, and conveyed across the line, which was about 20 miles further south; and that was the last, so far as I know, that has ever been heard of him. The alarm was given, of course, as soon as possible, and the neighbors were quickly in pursuit; but the kidnappers had got the start of them. The next morning the trail between the house, and the place where the wagon stood, was distinctly visible, and deeply marked with blood."

Letter Continued

"About a fortnight since, a letter was brought to our office, from a well-known friend, the contents of which were in substance as follows: A case of kidnapping had occurred in the vicinity of West Caln Township, Chester County, at about half past one on Sunday morning, the 16th of March. A black man, by the name of Thomas Hall, an honest, sober, and industrious individual, living in the midst of a settlement of farmers, had been stolen by persons who knocked at his door, and told him that his nearest neighbor wanted him to come to his house, one of his children being sick. Hall did not immediately open his door to the strangers, and so it was burst in, and three men rushed into his house; Hall was felled by the bludgeons of the men. His wife received several severe blows, and on making for the door was told that if she attempted to go out or call out for help she would have her brains blown out. She, however, escaped through a back window, and gave the alarm; but before any person arrived upon the ground, they had fled with their victim. He was taken without any clothing, except his night clothes. A six-barreled revolver, heavily loaded, was dropped in the scuffle, and left; also a silk handkerchief, and some old advertisement of a bear bait, that was to take place in Emmittsburg, Maryland. In how many cases the persons stolen are legally liable to capture, it is impossible to state. The law, you know, authorizes arrests to be made, with or without [due] process, and nothing is easier under such circumstances than to kidnap persons who are free born.

"The very same day that I received the above mentioned letter, and while our hearts were still aching over its contents, another was brought us from Thomas Garrett, of Wilmington, Delaware, announcing the abduction, a night or two before, of a free colored man of that city. The outrage was committed by an ex-policeman, who, pretending to be acting under the commission which he had been known to hold, entered, near the hour of midnight, the house of the victim, and alleging against him some petty act of disorder, seized him, handcuffed him in the presence of his dismayed family, and carried him off to Maryland. The cheat that had been practiced was not discovered by the family until next evening; but it was too late, the man was gone.

"At the time Mr. Garrett's letter was handed to me, narrating the foregoing case of man stealing, I was listening to the sad tales of two colored women who had come to the office for advice and assistance. One of them was an elderly person, whose son had been pursued by the marshal's deputies, and who had just escaped with 'the skin of his teeth.' She did not come on her own account, however.... She came to accompany the young woman who was with her. This young woman was a remarkably intelligent, lady-like person, and her story made a strong appeal to my feelings.

"She is a resident of Washington, and her errand here was to obtain the liberation of a sister-in-law, who is confined in that city, under very peculiar circumstances. The sister-in-law had run away from her mistress about nine months since, and was hidden in the room of an acquaintance, who was cook in a distinguished slaveholding family in Washington; her intention being, there to wait until all search should be over, and an opportunity offer of escape to the North. But, as yet, no such opportunity had presented itself; at least none that was available, and for nine long months that poor girl had been confined in the narrow limits of the cook's chamber, watched over day and night by that faithful friend with a vigilance as sleepless as it was disinterested. The time had come, however, when something had to be done. The family in whose house she was hid was about to be broken up, and the house to be vacated, and the girl must either be rescued from her peril, or she, and all her accomplices must be exposed. What to do under these circumstances was the question which brought this woman to Philadelphia. I advised her to the best of my ability, and sent her away hopeful, if not rejoicing. "But in many of these cases we can render no aid whatever. All we can do is to commend them to the God of the oppressed, and labor on for the day of general deliverance. But, oh! the horrors of this hell-born system, and the havoc made by this, its last foul offspring, the Fugitive Slave Law. The anguish, the terror, the agony inflicted by this infamous statute, must be witnessed to be fully appreciated. "You must hear the tale of the broken-hearted mother, who has just received tidings that her son is in the hands of thieves. You must listen to the impassioned appeal of the wife, whose husband's retreat has been discovered, and whose footsteps are dogged by the bloodhounds of slavery. You must hear the husband, as I did, a few weeks ago, himself bound and helpless, beg you for God's sake to save his wife. You must see such a woman as Hannah Dellam, with her noble-looking boy at her side, pleading in vain before a pro-slavery judge, that she is of right free; that her son is entitled to his freedom; and above all, that her babe, about to be born, should be permitted to open its eyes upon the light of liberty. You must hear the judge's decision, remorselessly giving up the woman with her children born and unborn into the hands of their claimants — by them to be carried to the slave prison, and then to be sold to a returnless distance from the remaining but scattered fragments of her once-happy family. These things you must see and hear for yourself before you can form any adequate idea of the bitterness of this cup which the unhappy children of oppression along this southern border are called upon to drink.

"Displays like these have we been obliged either to witness ourselves, or hear the recital of from others, almost daily, for weeks together. Our aching hearts have known but little respite lately. A shadow has been cast over our home circles, and a check been given to the wonted cheerfulness of our families. One night, the night that the woman and the boy and the unborn babe received their doom, my wife, long after midnight literally wept herself to sleep. For the last fortnight we have had no cases; out even now, when I go home in the evening, if I happen to look more serious than usual, my wife notices it, and asks: 'Is there another slave case?' and my little girls look up anxiously for my reply."

CHAPTER 75

Fugitive Slave Law Kidnappings in Pennsylvania —
a Letter from Mary B. Thomas.

Daring outrage! burglary and kidnapping! The following letter tells its own startling and most painful story. Every courageous and generous heart must burn with indignation at the villainy it describes, and bleed with sympathy for the almost broken-hearted sufferers.

This letter was written by Mary Thomas. She was a highly respectable and intelligent lady, belonging to the Society of Friends, or Quakers, and a most devoted friend of the slave.

Letter

"Downington, 19th, 4th mo. [April], 1848 "My Dear Friend:

"This morning our family was aroused by the screams of a young colored girl, who has been living with us nearly a year past; but we were awakened only in time to see her borne off by three white men, ruffians indeed, to a carriage at our door, and in an instant she was on her way to the South. I feel so much excited by the attendant circumstances of this daring and atrocious deed, as scarcely to be able to give you a coherent account of it, but I know that it is a duty to make known, and, I therefore write this immediately.

"As soon as the house was opened in the morning, these men who were lurking without, having a carriage in waiting in the street, entered on their horrid errand. They encountered no one in their entrance, except a colored boy, who was making the fire; and who, being frightened at their approach, ran and hid himself; taking a lighted candle from the kitchen, and carrying it upstairs, they went directly to the chamber in which the poor girl lay in a sound sleep. They lifted her from her bed and carried her downstairs. In the entry of the second floor they met one of my sisters, who, hearing an unusual noise, had sprung from her bed. Her screams, and those of the poor girl, who was now thoroughly awakened to the dreadful truth, aroused my father, who hurried undressed from his chamber on the ground floor. My father's efforts were powerless against the three; they threw him off, and with frightful imprecations hurried the girl to the carriage.

"As quickly as possible my father started in pursuit, and reached West Chester only to learn that the carriage had driven through the borough at full speed, about half an hour before. They had two horses to their vehicle, and there were three men besides those in the house. These particulars we gather from the colored boy Ned, who, from his hiding place, was watching them in the road.

"Can anything be done for the rescue of this girl from the kidnappers? We are surprised and alarmed! This deliberate invasion of our house is a thing unimagined. There must be some informer, who is acquainted with our house and its arrangements, or they never would have come so boldly through. Truly, there is no need to preach about slavery in the abstract; this individual case combines every wickedness by which human nature can be degraded.

"Truly, thy friend, "*Mary B. Thomas.*"

In a subsequent letter, our friend says: "As to detail, the whole transaction was like a flash to those who saw the miserable ending. I was impelled to write without delay, by the thought that it would be in time for the ***Freeman***, and that any procrastination on my part, might jeopardize others of these suffering people, who are living, as was this poor girl, in fancied security. Our consternation was inexpressible; our sorrow and indignation deepen daily, as the thought returns of the awful announcement with which we were awakened: they have carried Martha to the South. To do what will be of most service to the cause, not their cause, ours, that of our race, is our burning desire."

Index

Location of Escape

Delaware, Kent	Ch. 58
Delaware, Lewes	Ch. 59
District of Columbia	Chs. 10, 23, 53
Washington, D.C.	See District of Columbia.
Georgia	Ch. 48
Georgia, Savannah	Ch. 35
Louisiana, Point Copee	Ch. 52
Maryland	Ch. 63
Maryland, Baltimore	Chs. 1, 25, 32, 39, 45, 47
Maryland, Benedict	Ch. 3
Maryland, Chester County, Indian Creek	Ch. 36
Maryland, Chestertown	Ch. 43
Maryland, Clear Springs	Ch. 46
Maryland, Dorcester	Ch. 62
Maryland, New Market	Ch. 50
Maryland, Worcester County	Ch. 71
Maryland, Worcester County, Kunkletown	Ch. 61
Mississippi, Harrison County	Ch. 16
Missouri	Ch. 67
North Carolina	Chs. 15, 54
North Carolina, Wilmington	Ch. 20
Pennsylvania, Philadelphia	Chs. 12, 67
South Carolina, Charleston	Ch. 34
Virginia	Chs. 60, 66
Virginia, Alexandria	Ch. 51
Virginia, Fauquier County	Ch. 14

Virginia, Harpers Ferry	Ch. 2
Virginia, King George County	Ch. 40
Virginia, Leesburg	Ch. 32
Virginia, Loudon County, Alder	Ch. 14
Virginia, Martinsburg	Ch. 13
Virginia, Middleburg	Ch. 56
Virginia, Norfolk	Chs. 6, 22, 27, 31, 33, 37, 38, 44, 55, 69, 70
Virginia, Old Point Comfort	Ch. 33
Virginia, Petersburg	Chs. 9, 21, 29
Virginia, Portsmouth	Chs. 5, 7, 42
Virginia, Richmond	Chs. 4, 8, 9, 11, 17, 18, 19, 21, 22, 24, 26, 28, 29, 30, 33, 49, 57, 64, 65, 66
Virginia, Temperanceville	Ch. 41

Method of Escape

Boat (Small)	Chs. 59, 61
Box	See Shipping container
Chest	See Shipping container
Crate	See Shipping container
Horse and carriage	Chs. 14, 32, 43, 46
Horseback	Chs. 2, 13, 14, 32
Disguise	See Impersonation
Impersonation	Chs. 5, 32, 33, 48, 57, 69
Legal document	See Official document
Official document	Chs. 19, 26, 53, 67
On foot	See Walking
"Pass"	See Official document
Ship stowaway	Chs. 4, 5, 6, 7, 9, 15, 16, 18, 20, 21, 22, 24, 27, 28, 29, 30, 31, 33, 35, 37,

	38, 42, 44, 49, 57, 64, 65, 66, 69, 70
Shipping container	Chs. 1, 11, 39, 47
Train	Chs. 32, 46
Walking	Chs. 2, 3, 10, 12, 13, 34, 40, 41, 45, 50, 51, 54, 56, 58, 62
Weapons	Chs. 2, 14

Freedom-Seeker Destinations

Canada	Chs. 1, 2, 3, 6, 8, 12, 14, 18, 19, 20, 22, 25, 32, 36, 40, 41, 43, 44, 45, 47, 61, 62, 64
Canada, St. Catharines	Chs. 9, 10, 24, 31, 42, 46, 52
Canada, Toronto	Chs. 26, 28, 29, 49
Delaware, Wilmington	Chs. 43, 62
England	Ch. 48
England, Liverpool	Ch. 16
Massachusetts, Boston	Chs. 7, 27, 30, 48, 64, 65, 68, 69
Massachusetts, New Bedford	Chs. 5, 15, 37, 38
Michigan, Detroit	Ch. 19
New Jersey	Ch. 59
New York State	Ch. 11
New York, Buffalo	Ch. 50
New York, Cayuga County, Sennett	Ch. 32
New York, Elmira	Chs. 39, 61
New York, Oswego	Ch. 51
New York, Syracuse	Chs. 22, 23
Pennsylvania, Harrisburg	Ch. 13
Pennsylvania, Philadelphia	Chs. 1-60, 62-71

Freedom-Seekers: By Name

Adams, William	Ch. 39	Carney, William	Ch. 55
Allen, Andrew	Ch. 55	Carr, Daniel	Ch. 27
Amos, Stephen	Ch. 25	Cary, Harrison	Ch. 53
Atkins, William Henry	Ch. 31	Chapman, Emeline	Ch. 23
Atkinson, John	Ch. 42	Christian, James Hambleton	Ch. 8
Banks, Henry	Ch. 40	Clayton, John	Ch. 4
Bayne, Thomas	Ch. 37	Cobb, Lewis	Ch. 49
Ball, Oscar D.	Ch. 51	Conner, James	Ch. 52
Bell, Susan	Ch. 23	Cook, Susan	Ch. 31
Bird, Charles	Ch. 32	Cope, William Thomas	Ch. 59
Blow, Anthony	Ch. 6	Craft, Ellen	Ch. 48
Boice, Henry	Ch. 59	Craft, William	Ch. 48
Bowlegs, Jim	Ch. 34	Davis, Clarissa	Ch. 5
Boyer, John	Ch. 14	Davis, Edward	Ch. 35
Brister, Nancy	Ch. 49	Davis, Jane	Ch. 50
Brooks, Susan	Ch. 31	Delaney, John	Ch. 51
Brown, Albert	Ch. 32	Donar, William	Ch. 38
Brown, Angeline	Ch. 32	Dorsey, George	Ch. 32
Brown, Charles	Ch. 32	Dorsey, Maria	Ch. 10
Brown, Emma	Ch. 9	Dungy, John William	Ch. 66
Brown, Henry Box	Ch. 11	Eden, Richard	Ch. 20
Brown, John	Ch. 27	Eglin, Harriet	Ch. 32
Brown, Robert	Ch. 13	Ennets, Stephen	Ch. 62
Brown, Thomas	Ch. 45	Epps, Mary	Ch. 9
Brown, William	Ch. 27	Fletcher, Benjamin R.	Ch. 10
Buchanan, Jenny	Ch. 60	Ford, Sheridan	Ch. 7
Burkett, Elizabeth	Ch. 61	Foster, Emily	Ch. 14
Burkett, Henry	Ch. 61	Foster, James	Ch. 27
Burton, Hale	Ch. 61	Frances, Elizabeth	Ch. 38

Freedman, Thomas	Ch. 27	Jones, Thomas	Ch. 13
Galloway, Abram	Ch. 20	Jones, William "Box" Peel	Ch. 1
Gardener, Nathaniel	Ch. 27	Jordon, William	Ch. 15
Gault, Phillis	Ch. 27	Kinnard, Wesley (the son)	Ch. 36
Gilbert, Charles	Ch. 33	Langhord, Henry	Ch. 64
Giles, Charlotte	Ch. 32	Laws, George	Ch. 58
Gilliam, William H.	Ch. 4	Levison, Harry	Ch. 6
Graham, Montgomery	Ch. 51	Little, Nancy	Ch. 27
Grant, Joseph	Ch. 16	Loney, Cordelia	Ch. 12
Grantham, Nancy	Ch. 57	Matthews, Pete	Ch. 41
Green, Lear	Ch. 39	McCoy, Eliza	Ch. 38
Green, Samuel (the father)	Ch. 36	McCoy, Robert	Ch. 38
Green, Samuel (the son)	Ch. 36	McKim, James Miller	Ch. 74
Grey, John Boice	Ch. 59	Mercer, James	Ch. 4
Griffin, James	Ch. 45	Milburn, Mary	Ch. 69
Grigby, Barnaby	Ch. 14	Miller, Joseph C.	Ch. 68
Grigby, Mary Elizabeth	Ch. 14	Moore, Hannah	Ch. 67
Grimes, Harry	Ch. 54	Moore, James	Ch. 44
Haines, Francis	Ch. 27	Neall, Daniel	Ch. 10
Hall, Romulus	Ch. 3	Nickless, Kit	Ch. 40
Hall, Thomas	Ch. 74	Nixon, Frederick	Ch. 27
Harris, Abram	Ch. 3	Nixon, Sam	Ch. 37
Harris, Wesley	Ch. 2	Nixon, Thomas	Ch. 27
Hill, Hezekiah	Ch. 29	Parker, Elizabeth	Ch. 68
Hill, James	Ch. 30	Parker, Rachel	Ch. 68
Hill, John Henry	Ch. 28	Peel, William	Ch. 1
Hilton, Elijah	Ch. 26	Pettifoot, John	Ch. 21
Jackson, Robert	Ch. 2	Petty, Peter	Ch. 27
Johnson, David	Ch. 27	Price, William	Ch. 15
Johnson, Samuel W.	Ch. 24	Purnell, John	Ch. 61
Jones, Alice	Ch. 27	Richards, John Henry	Ch. 32
Jones, Louisa F.	Ch. 69	Ringold, Charles H.	Ch. 32

Robinson, Joseph . . . . Ch. 9
Robinson, Miles . . . . Ch. 65
Robinson, Robert . . . . Ch. 9
Saunders, Ellen . . . . Ch. 38
Scott, Godfrey . . . . Ch. 27
Scott, Jane . . . . Ch. 32
Scott, Robert . . . . Ch. 14
Scott, William . . . . Ch. 64
Shephard, Harriet . . . . Ch. 43
Sipple, Mary Ann . . . . Ch. 61
Sipple, Thomas . . . . Ch. 61
Smith, Betsey . . . . Ch. 14
Smith, Jeremiah W. . . . . Ch. 18
Smith, John . . . . Ch. 27
Smith, Julia . . . . Ch. 18
Smith, Robert . . . . Ch. 32
Smith, Samuel A. . . . . Ch. 11
Smith, Vincent . . . . Ch. 14
Solomon, George . . . . Ch. 10
Somlor, Washington . . . . . . Ch. 44
Sparrows, Samuel . . . . Ch. 41
Speak, John . . . . Ch. 16
Stewart, Robert . . . . Ch. 14
Tatum, Alan . . . . Ch. 27
Taylor, Benjamin . . . . Ch. 46
Taylor, Mary Ann . . . . Ch. 46
Taylor, Otho . . . . Ch. 46
Taylor, Owen . . . . Ch. 46
Taylor, William N. . . . . Ch. 17
Thomas, Mary B. . . . . Ch. 75
Thompson, Charles . . . . Ch. 19
Thornton, Alfred S. . . . . Ch. 56

Vaughn, Michael . . . . Ch. 27
Walker, Mrs . . . . Ch. 70
Wanzer, Frank . . . . Ch. 14
Weems, Arrah . . . . Ch. 23
Weems, George . . . . Ch. 3
White, Emanuel T. . . . . Ch. 32
White, Isac . . . . Ch. 59
White, William B. . . . . Ch. 31
Williams, Euphemia . . Chs. 71, 72, 73
Williams, Isac . . . . Ch. 40
Wilson, Ned . . . . Ch. 27
Wilson, Willis . . . . Ch. 27
Wood, Ann . . . . Ch. 14

www.ingramcontent.com/pod-product-compliance
Lightning Source LLC
Chambersburg PA
CBHW071620170426
43195CB00038B/1495